Reading STREET

Grade **5**

Scott Foresman

On-Level
Take-Home Readers

ISBN: 0-328-20015-8
Copyright © Pearson Education, Inc.
All Rights Reserved. Printed in the United States of America. This publication,
or parts thereof, may be used with appropriate equipment to reproduce copies
for classroom use only.
1 2 3 4 5 6 7 8 9 10 V084 14 13 12 11 10 09 08 07 06 05

PEARSON
Scott
Foresman

Editorial Offices: Glenview, Illinois • Parsippany, New Jersey • New York, New York
Sales Offices: Needham, Massachusetts • Duluth, Georgia • Glenview, Illinois
Coppell, Texas • Sacramento, California • Mesa, Arizona

Contents

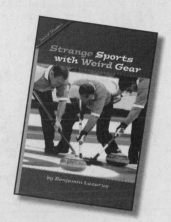
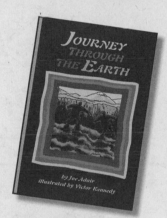

How to Use the Take-Home Leveled Readers

1. Tear out the pages for each Take-Home Leveled Reader. There are two pages back-to-back. Make a copy for each student.

2. Fold the pages in half to make a booklet.

3. Staple the pages on the left-hand side.

4. Have students read and discuss the Take-Home Leveled Readers with family members.

Suggested levels for Guided Reading, DRA™,
Lexile® and Reading Recovery™ are provided
in the Pearson Scott Foresman Leveling Guide.

Genre	Comprehension Skill and Strategy
Fiction	• Character and Plot • Prior Knowledge

Scott Foresman Reading Street 5.1.1

PEARSON

Scott
Foresman

scottforesman.com

ISBN 0-328-13503-8

90000

9 780328 135035

Learning from
Ms. Liang

by Juna Loch

illustrated by K. E. Lewis

Reader Response

1. How did the narrator change in a way that made her able to think about her classmates differently?

2. What did you learn about Emily Dickinson by reading this story? What more would you still like to learn about her? Make a chart like the one below and list what you learned about Emily Dickinson from this story and what more you want to know.

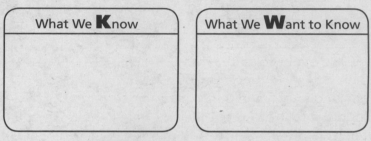

What We **K**now	What We **W**ant to Know

3. Four of the vocabulary words in this book—*acquainted, expanded, guaranteed*, and *worshipped*—are verbs that have been changed to end in -*ed*. What are the base words of these verbs?

4. If you were Ms. Liang, would you have felt comfortable telling the class that you had once felt like a "nobody"? Why or why not?

Emily Dickinson

Many people like to spend time by themselves. But there are some people who withdraw entirely from society. One such person was Emily Dickinson.

Emily, the daughter of a Massachusetts politician, came from a wealthy family. In 1848, at age eighteen, she came home from what is now Mount Holyoke College, complaining of homesickness. From that point on, she never left her parents' home. Emily even refused to see visitors. Instead, she read, wrote letters, and composed over two thousand poems.

You might think that someone who never left home would have nothing to write about. But Emily did. Looking at only the things in her house, she gained new insight into life's great themes. "Tell all the truth, but tell it slant," she wrote. And that is what she did. In her private world, Emily Dickinson managed to "see" more than some of the most adventurous world travelers.

Learning from Ms. Liang

I'm nobody! Who are you?
Are you nobody, too?
Then there's a pair of us—don't tell!
They'd banish us, you know.

How dreary to be somebody!
How public, like a frog
To tell your name the livelong day
To an admiring bog!

by Juna Loch
illustrated by K. E. Lewis

PEARSON
Scott Foresman

Editorial Offices: Glenview, Illinois • Parsippany, New Jersey • New York, New York
Sales Offices: Needham, Massachusetts • Duluth, Georgia • Glenview, Illinois
Coppell, Texas • Ontario, California • Mesa, Arizona

Ms. Liang's tone was now triumphant. "But that woman believed in me and encouraged me. She forced me to see myself as a somebody. She taught me that Dickinson poem. As soon as I heard the poem, I knew I didn't need money to be somebody. I knew then that I wanted to be a teacher, and a good one. I knew I would run into students who thought they were nobodies. When I met them I could be a good teacher and tell them, 'I thought I was nobody too! Tell me about yourself, and I'll prove that you're not a nobody.'"

Everyone in the room was looking at Lisa, remembering times they had been mean to her. We all felt like nobodies for the way we had treated her. Now, because of Ms. Liang, we knew that Lisa was a somebody.

"It was the dumbest thing I've ever done," Ms. Liang said. "After dropping out, I worked ten years. Still, I was treated like a nobody. I would look at my future, and all I could see was more of the same."

Ms. Liang's tone suddenly brightened. "But then I started working for a nice lady. To my shock, she liked me. She refused to let me throw my life away. 'Go back to school,' she told me. I never would have gone back without her encouragement."

She went on, "I had to work two jobs to make enough money to live on. I studied whenever I could find the time. It wasn't easy. I often found myself behind in my studies. All I could think about was how much easier it would have been if I'd stayed in school."

On Tuesday, we found out that we were getting a new teacher. The rumor was that our old teacher, Mr. Williams, had gotten sick.

Our new teacher was supposed to start Wednesday. Wednesday arrived, but the new teacher was late. We didn't mind. The whole class was sitting around and talking excitedly about the upcoming fifth-grade chorus concert. The girls were getting new dresses. The boys were going to wear suits.

Everyone was talking about it, except Lisa Linney. She just sat at her desk, her long hair hiding her face. Everyone knew that she didn't have enough money to buy a new dress. We would often talk about Lisa in front of her. People didn't try to be mean. It was just that it was easy to forget she was there. In a way, Lisa was invisible.

The new teacher finally walked in. She wasn't all that remarkable looking, and her clothes were kind of plain. But as soon as she came in everyone stopped talking. With just a glance around the room she made you want to pay attention. Even the noisy kids who sat in the back fell silent as she walked up to the blackboard.

What's the first thing a new teacher does? She takes attendance, or writes her name on the board, right? But this new teacher didn't do that. Instead, she picked up the chalk and wrote out a poem.

I'm nobody! Who are you?
Are you nobody, too?
Then there's a pair of us—don't tell!
They'd banish us, you know.

How dreary to be somebody!
How public, like a frog
To tell your name the livelong day
To an admiring bog!

Ms. Liang sighed and looked sad. "When I was your age, I was a nobody," she told us. "There's no way I could have been anything but a nobody. I didn't fit in. Because my family was poor, I didn't have any of the toys or clothes that the other children cared about. My clothes were old, and I didn't have the money to go places with the other kids. Of course, it didn't really matter, because I was a nobody in the first place. So no one ever asked me to go anywhere with them."

Ms. Liang looked directly at Lisa. "I know what it's like to be around people who act like those proud frogs. The other students would talk about parties I hadn't been invited to. They'd talk as if I weren't there. So by the time I got to high school, I decided not to be there. I dropped out. What did I need school for? In my mind, all I needed was money. If I had money, I thought it would hide the fact that I was a nobody. The worst part was, I was so invisible that no one even noticed I had dropped out."

Ms. Liang stared out the window. No one said a word.

How could you be proud to be a nobody? We didn't understand. But Lisa Linney, our own sort of nobody, did understand. She looked at Ms. Liang like she worshipped her. Ms. Liang smiled back. It was just like the poem. Ms. Liang's face seemed to say, "Hey, Lisa, do you want to be a nobody with me?"

"You know," Ms. Liang said, looking right at Lisa, "we are *all* somebodies, though too often the world forgets it." She sighed. "When we treat other people like they are nobodies, we hurt them."

The room became very quiet after Ms. Liang said that. "I bet no one ever treated you like a nobody," Mary Alice said, breaking the silence.

"Good morning, class. My name is Ms. Liang," the new teacher said. She picked up a copy of the book we were reading. "Can someone tell me where you stopped last?"

I looked around the classroom, wondering who was going to answer. Then A.J., who always liked to challenge teachers, asked, "Aren't you supposed to learn our names before you make us work?"

Ms. Liang answered, "I'm sure we'll get plenty acquainted as time goes by. And, as a way of getting to know my students, I've always preferred reading together instead of just going around memorizing names. But since you were nice enough to speak up, maybe you could start reading out loud from where you left off?"

A.J. muttered, "I knew this would happen," and began reading.

Ms. Liang stopped him after only a couple of sentences. "No, no," she said. "Not like that. You've got to place yourself in the story. You've got to make it come alive for you and everyone else. Read as if you're telling *your* story."

A.J. looked puzzled. "What do you mean, *my* story?"

"What I mean is, read as if the book were about you. Read as if you knew everyone wanted to hear the story of your life. Imagine that you would burst if you couldn't share your story with the class."

None of us had any idea what she was talking about. Then, just out of curiosity, I looked over at Lisa. It looked like she knew exactly what Ms. Liang was talking about.

"It is essential to read with *feeling*," Ms. Liang went on. "If you read with feeling, it's guaranteed to be more interesting to the people who are listening. And it will be more interesting to you."

Nobody answered at first.

"Well," she prompted, "which would you rather be—a somebody or a nobody?"

A somebody, we all said. "Who wants to be a nobody?" A.J. added.

"Of course," said Ms. Liang. "But how does the poet talk about somebodies?"

That was when Lisa raised her hand. In the past she had always been too shy, but now her hand was high in the air.

"The poem says that somebodies are like frogs," she said. "Frogs that sit around all day doing nothing but boasting."

"Is she really talking about frogs?" Ms. Liang asked.

"No," Lisa continued. "She means that people who are full of themselves are as silly as frogs. Their talk is just like ribbeting. Because of that, Emily Dickinson is *proud* to be a nobody."

The next day, everyone was talking about the fifth-grade chorus concert again. Like last time, the girls were talking about the fancy dresses their mothers were going to buy for them. Of course, Lisa wasn't part of those conversations. But I noticed that she had stopped hiding and pretending she wasn't there. Instead, she was sitting up straight, with her homework on her desk, waiting for Ms. Liang to arrive.

I was waiting too. I wanted Ms. Liang to come in and tell us what the poem meant. When she came in, I asked.

"It's a poem by Emily Dickinson," she answered.

"But what is it? I mean, what does it *mean?*"

Ms. Liang thought for a minute before answering. "Well, what do you think it means?" she finally asked us.

"Why?" my friend Mary Alice asked.

"Because it's a scientific fact that your face affects your emotions," Ms. Liang answered.

"What's that supposed to mean?" A.J. suddenly blurted out. I could tell that he was annoyed because Ms. Liang hadn't gone over our names.

Ms. Liang explained, "Scientists have discovered that facial expressions influence people's emotions. When you make an angry face, your brain floods your body with chemicals that actually make you *feel* angry. So if you read with feeling, you will have a better chance of experiencing the characters' own feelings. Does that make better sense?"

Ms. Liang then called on Lisa to continue reading.

As soon as Lisa began reading, I thought, *she's acquainted with these feelings for sure*. But, as well as she read, her quietness made it difficult to understand her. Ms. Liang stopped her when she saw that people were having a hard time hearing her.

"What's your name?" Ms. Liang asked.

"Lisa Linney," was the mumbled reply.

"All right, Lisa," said Ms. Liang. "I want you to keep reading as you've been doing, with all that great feeling. But this time, read a little louder."

Lisa resumed her reading. Her words were full of feeling. Still, she wasn't loud enough. I realized that Lisa's quietness made people forget about her more easily.

While Lisa read, Ms. Liang stood by her desk, listening carefully. Lisa blushed in reaction to Ms. Liang's close presence.

After a while, Ms. Liang stopped Lisa. Turning to face the class, she asked, "Did you get that? The character Lisa was reading about said, 'You never understand someone until you walk around in their skin.' What did that character mean?"

I had a hard time with the assignment. I wanted to write about A.J. because he'd been mean to me. But I had no idea why he'd been mean, so I couldn't get inside his skin, like Ms. Liang wanted us to. Then I remembered the time when *I* had been mean to someone, like A.J. had been mean to me.

Mary Alice and I had been standing in the school hallway. We had been talking about Lisa's clothes and laughing at them. Right then, Lisa came around the corner. She had heard everything we said. It was awful. Lisa turned pale, and ran away.

Mary Alice and I just kept laughing. I don't know why I laughed at Lisa's clothes. I don't know why I didn't say anything to try to make her feel better so she wouldn't have run away. The memory of that time made me feel so bad that I couldn't make myself write anything.

"You might not like the person better," Ms. Liang answered, "but you might dislike the person less. Understanding people does not excuse whatever poor actions they may take. But the more you understand them, the more you might appreciate why they do what they do. It might even make you see things from their point of view, as if you were in their skin."

Ms. Liang then told us our homework assignment for that night. This time, she wanted us to sign our names because she was going to grade what we wrote. She wanted us to write a paragraph about trying to get inside the skin of someone we didn't like. To protect people's feelings, she didn't want us to use anyone's real name.

It's funny. If Mr. Williams had said the words "walk around in their skin," someone would have said "Eeew, that's gross," or made a joke. But everyone was quiet. We could tell how much Ms. Liang cared about her teaching, and nobody wanted to make trouble.

We talked about the meaning of those words for a couple of minutes. Then Ms. Liang told us to take out a piece of paper.

"Here's your assignment," she said. "You're going to find this difficult, but it's important that you understand this concept. I want you to write down what people would understand about *you* if they could walk around in *your* skin."

"What do you mean?" asked A.J.

"I'm sure there's been a time you've felt misunderstood," Ms. Liang explained. "So here's the question. Would the rest of the world understand you better if they knew what it was like to be you? That's what I mean. Does that make sense?"

The class nodded together.

"Good!" Ms. Liang said. "Then go ahead and start writing. Oh, and make sure not to sign your names."

I took out my paper and stared at it. Then I looked up at the poem on the chalkboard. I didn't know what to write. *What didn't people know about me?* I thought. *Everyone knows everything there is to know. I'm me. I'm popular. I do okay. I have a reputation for nice clothes. What else would anyone need to know?*

After a long pause, Ms. Liang answered, "What you wrote tells me that you all have a lot to learn about each other. It tells me that there are a lot of people in this class who feel like their classmates don't understand them at all. It's important that you learn more about how your classmates feel. Once you do, you'll find that you'll be treating each other better."

"What do you mean?" Mary Alice asked defensively. "Are you saying that we're mean? Are you saying that we don't treat each other well enough in the first place?"

Ms. Liang smiled. "I'm saying that all of us are mean sometimes, without even realizing it."

Mary Alice made a face. "You think that if we really knew each other, we would like each other more? I know a lot of people. I don't like them any better than other people just because I know them."

The next day the poem was back on the chalkboard. I knew it wasn't left over from the day before, because this time it was written in a different color chalk.

"Why do you keep writing that poem on the board?" A.J. asked Ms. Liang.

Ms. Liang answered, "As I told you yesterday, I find it interesting." She continued, "Now take out your assigned reading, please. Did everyone finish chapter five?"

I raised my hand. "This isn't about chapter five, but ... did you read what we wrote yesterday?" I asked.

Ms. Liang laid down her book.

"I did," she answered.

"And what did you think?" I was incredibly curious.

I'm nobody! Who are you?
Are you nobody, too?
Then there's a pair of us—don't tell!
They'd banish us, you know.

How dreary to be somebody!
How public, like a frog
To tell your name the livelong day
To an admiring bog!

Lisa was sitting in the desk to the right of me, writing quickly. I tried to peek at what she had written, but it was difficult. She had her whole body shielding the paper, as if her words were top secret.

A few minutes went by. Still, I couldn't find anything to write about. Then I heard A.J. in the back, making some mean remark about Lisa. It made me think about the times he's said mean things to me. Then I thought about the time Katie Lee Clinton and her friends had stopped talking and laughed when I came into the classroom. That had definitely made me feel like a nobody.

I looked back up at the words on the chalkboard: *I'm nobody! Who are you?* No doubt, I felt like that sometimes. There were many times when I felt like my class was filled with people who had no idea who I was. Usually that feeling disappeared after a couple of moments. But still, I knew what it was like.

My thoughts inspired me to start writing. "I know that, at times, I've felt like the person talking in the poem. Does anyone else feel that way? Do other people in the class ever feel like they've been forgotten?" I wrote.

I wrote about how those feelings were worst on days when I felt sad. Everyone's had those days. They're the days when your mother yells at you before school, or your best friend says something really mean. They're the days when you do poorly on a test. Like I said, everyone's had those days.

I wrote, "If people really knew *me*, if people could walk around in my skin and feel lonely like I do sometimes, they wouldn't say I was stuck up or standoffish. One day, Katie Lee Clinton told me that I was both of those two things. It made me feel like a nobody."

After we wrote for ten minutes, Ms. Liang collected our papers. A.J. had questions as usual.

"What's the deal with that poem?" he asked. "And why didn't you want us to sign our names?"

"I just thought you might find the poem interesting," Ms. Liang told him. "As for not signing your name, I use procedures like that to protect students' feelings. Some of the students might have felt embarrassed if I knew who had written what."

The rest of the day went by slowly. Ms. Liang went over our math and science homework. Finally, the bell rang for us to go home. As I walked out of class, an incredible thought occurred to me: *We had shared more with Ms. Liang in one day than we had with Mr. Williams in a whole year!*

Suggested levels for Guided Reading, DRA,™ Lexile,® and Reading Recovery™ are provided in the Pearson Scott Foresman Leveling Guide.

Science

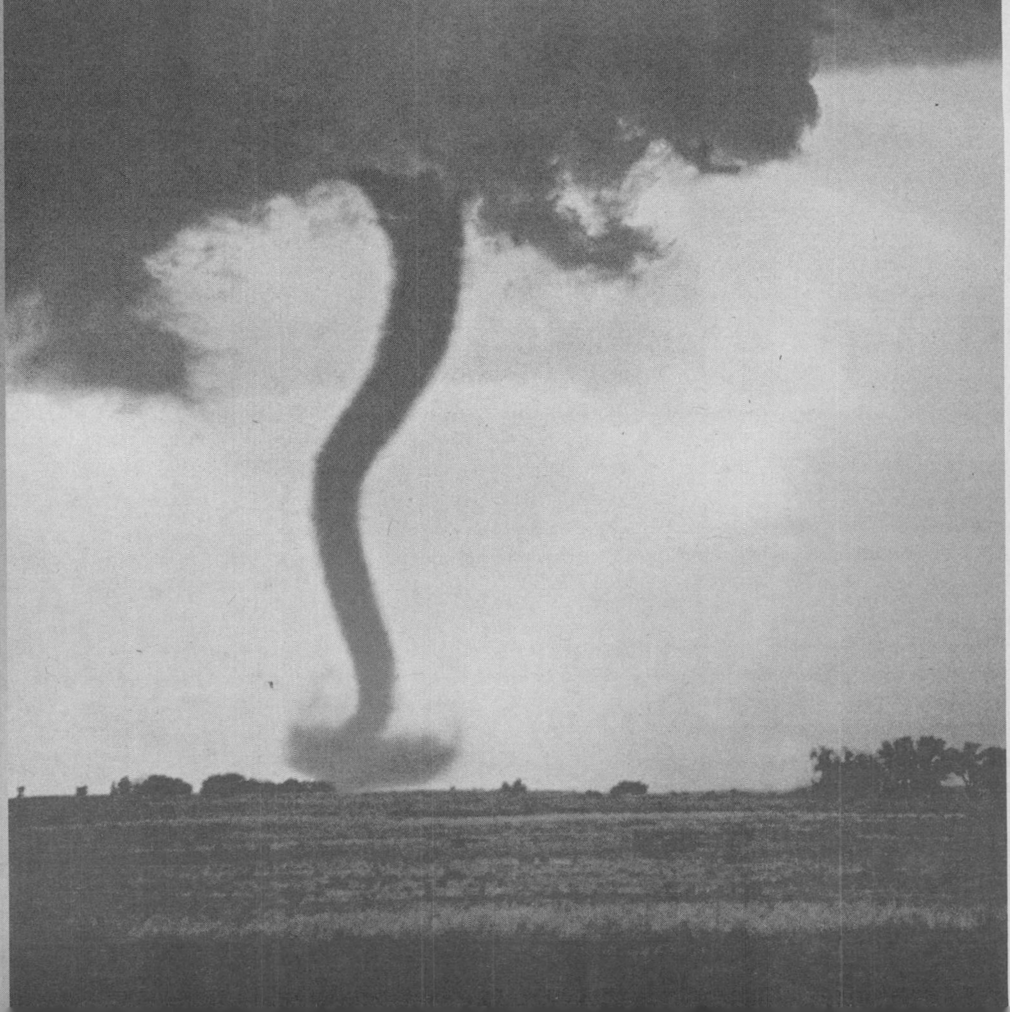

Genre	Comprehension Skill and Strategy	Text Features
Nonfiction	• Cause and Effect • Monitor and Fix Up	• Captions • Diagrams • Maps • Glossary

Scott Foresman Reading Street 5.1.2

PEARSON
Scott Foresman

ISBN 0-328-13506-2
9 780328 135066 90000

scottforesman.com

Science

Earth Science

The Challenges of Storm Chasing

by Chris Downey

Reader Response

1. What causes Tornado Alley to have lots of storms during the spring? What effects do these storms have on that area of the country?

2. What did you learn about tornadoes from reading this book? What more would you like to know? Use a chart like this one to show what you learned and what more you'd like to learn.

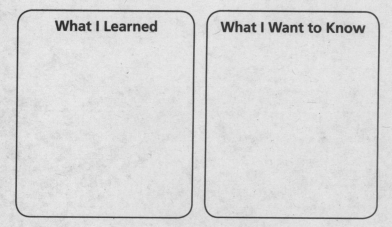

What I Learned	What I Want to Know

3. What are the root verbs in the vocabulary words *branded* and *constructed*?

4. What information did the map and caption on pages 4 and 5 give you?

Glossary

branded *v.* marked by burning.

constructed *adj.* put together.

daintily *adv.* with delicate beauty.

devastation *n.* the act of laying waste, destroying.

lullaby *n.* soft song sung to put a baby to sleep.

pitch *n.* a thick, black, sticky substance made from tar.

resourceful *adj.* good at thinking of ways to do things.

thieving *adj.* likely to steal.

veins *n.* natural channels through which water flows, or the tubes that carry blood through your body.

The Challenges of Storm Chasing

by Chris Downey

PEARSON
Scott Foresman

Editorial Offices: Glenview, Illinois • Parsippany, New Jersey • New York, New York
Sales Offices: Needham, Massachusetts • Duluth, Georgia • Glenview, Illinois
Coppell, Texas • Ontario, California • Mesa, Arizona

How do they do it?

Good storm chasers know how to reduce their risk of getting hurt. They plan out their chase ahead of time, using maps and weather reports. Good storm chasers also make sure that the car or truck that they use is in good condition. They drive carefully and stay alert, avoiding slick or flooded areas. At the first sign of lightning or very strong winds, a good storm chaser knows to seek shelter and not put him or herself in danger.

Storm chasers face many challenges. In addition to unpredictable weather, they must also contend with crowded roads and the growing number of fellow chasers. Still, many storm chasers feel that the rewards outweigh the risks. Some of the lucky ones are able to get as close to a storm as any human has ever been. Their bravery, in combination with modern technology, gives us a better understanding of how dangerous storms work!

Maps and compasses are among the many tools that good storm chasers use in order to plan the best and safest storm-chasing routes.

The Most Powerful of All

The rain from thunderstorms provides water for Earth. Without that water, trees and plants wouldn't be able to grow and life wouldn't be able to exist. Thunderstorms also have negative aspects. They can often create strong winds, hail, and lightning. These things are dangerous and can cause much damage. However, thunderstorms create one type of weather that is more dangerous than all of those things: tornadoes.

Dangerous storms most often appear in the plains of the United States. This area is known as Tornado Alley. Tornado Alley has lots of dangerous storms because of weather patterns that occur in spring. This makes spring the best season to spot a tornado, which is a funnel-shaped cloud of spinning air.

A tornado can leave a path of devastation if it touches down where there are people and buildings. But as dangerous as tornadoes are, they are amazing to look at. A few brave and curious people known as storm chasers spend their time tracking and observing these storms.

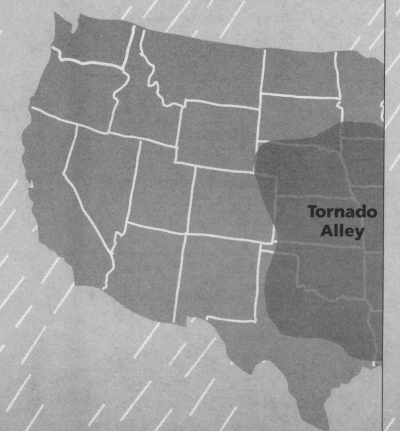

Tornado Alley

Storm chasing is becoming so widespread that storm tour groups have formed to cash in on its popularity. These groups charge people for the chance to chase storms with a tornado expert. Most of these tour groups operate in a safe, professional manner. But some of them are run recklessly enough that they cause people to question whether they should be allowed.

Obviously, it is important that storm-chasing tour groups be conducted by responsible people who know the dangers involved. Not surprisingly, people who study storms, such as meteorologists, generally make the best storm chasers. Meteorologists know more about what a storm is likely to do, and because of this knowledge they are able to chase storms with greater safety and efficiency. For instance, instead of having to drive through bad weather in order to reach a storm in progress, many meteorologists can position themselves to catch a storm that is forming.

And they're off!

At one time, only weather scientists chased storms. Now all kinds of people are doing it, including thrill-seekers and people who like being around dangerous situations. With more chasers on the move, there are many more "chaser convergences" than ever before. A chaser convergence is when a group of chasers meets in a safe place on a chase day. Another group, similar to a chaser convergence, is a chase crowd. A chase crowd is a large group of chasers who stop on open roads to watch a storm. These crowds gather in places that are not safe from storms. By doing so, they make storm chasing even more dangerous.

People who want to get into storm chasing can now go on guided tours. These tours are led by experienced storm chasers who already know the ropes and will stay safe.

Chase that storm!

Some storm chasers follow thunderstorms for scientific study, yet others do it purely for excitement. Many storm chasers are interested in weather patterns and meteorology. Meteorology is the study of the atmosphere. Very few people actually make a career of chasing storms. Many do it for the thrill of seeing a tornado and the pleasure of learning more about these amazing and powerful weather events.

States such as Oklahoma, Kansas, Nebraska, Missouri, Arkansas, and Iowa are usually included in Tornado Alley. Parts of Texas, Louisiana, Illinois, South Dakota, Minnesota, and Indiana are often added too.

Thanks to TV shows and movies, many people think that storm chasing is constant action and excitement. They might be surprised to find out that real storm chasing is very different. In fact, one of the main challenges of chasing a storm is the long time spent waiting for a possible event. In a very good year, a chaser can expect a success rate of up to 10 percent. This means that 90 percent of the time is spent waiting and looking for storms. Many chases end up as busts, missions that don't result in the chaser seeing a large storm or tornado. A chaser must be very patient.

It All Began . . .

People started chasing storms for fun in the early 1950s. Roger Jensen, a native of North Dakota, was one of the first people to follow storms for fun and to photograph what he saw. Scientist Neil Ward, now a respected tornado researcher, is also one of the pioneers of storm chasing. Ward was one of the first storm chasers to apply his observations to science. He was able to forecast weather changes based on information recorded while storm chasing.

In the 1960s, the U.S. government constructed the National Severe Storms Laboratory (NSSL) in Norman, Oklahoma. The NSSL studies storms and works to improve severe weather forecasting. Using modern technology and specially constructed equipment, scientists there work to collect data about storms.

One type of modern technology that the scientists in Norman use is termed the "Doppler on Wheels." It is a set of trucks carrying portable Doppler radar units. Doppler radar is usually used by local meteorologists to track weather changes, but the Doppler on Wheels is made for a different job. Trucks that carry the radar units are able to drive very close to tornadoes and gather data about how they form.

The Doppler on Wheels can be parked in the path of a storm so it can gather information while people are safely out of the way.

Even with help from weather reports and storm tracking equipment, a storm chaser must often make quick choices at a moment's notice. Some storm chasers use modern equipment to help forecast a storm's possible strength and direction. Satellites, radios, and laptop computers are important storm-tracking tools. Even with all of these aids, chasers are often faced with last-minute choices about when to stay put and when to move on to another location. This truck below has radar equipment that storm trackers can move from place to place to measure information about the storm at the site.

Modern equipment like laptop computers, video cameras, radios, and satellites help storm chasers learn where a storm may happen. This modern equipment also helps capture images of storms for others to see.

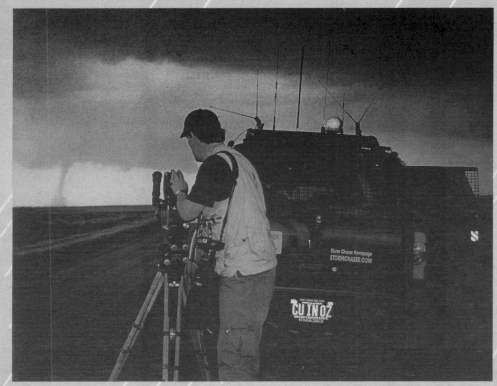

This storm chaser uses a video camera to record the tornado so he can later study its movement.

No one can be completely safe from lightning. Still, we can all use common sense in order to reduce our risk of being hurt by lightning strikes. The safest place to be when lightning strikes is inside a building. If you have to be outside during a lightning storm, stay close to the ground. Keep away from high places and avoid being near tall objects such as trees, telephone poles, or power lines. Lightning is more likely to either strike tall objects directly, or hit very close to them.

When Lightning Strikes

One of the biggest dangers for storm chasers is lightning. Lightning is a release of electricity in the atmosphere. Some lightning travels from clouds to the ground when it strikes. These strikes, also called lightning bolts, look like veins of light. Another form of lightning looks like a bright flash.

Lightning is a real threat to storm chasers. It can strike without warning and with deadly consequences. Nearly one hundred people are killed by lightning each year in the United States.

Staying Safe

Storm chasers drive many miles across the United States in search of storms. Driving in bad weather can be dangerous, even for an experienced storm chaser. Rain floods roads, often causing cars to get stuck or spin out of control. Rain, hail, fog, and pitch black can make it hard for the driver to see the road ahead. As chasing becomes more popular, the roads around storms become more crowded. First-time chasers without experience make things even more dangerous.

Some of the newer chasers have been branded as "renegades" by older chasers. The renegades start chasing for the excitement of being near a huge storm. Instead of studying the science of tornadoes, these chasers speed along roads in search of excitement and fun. Safety is very important when following a storm. Chasers who do not use common sense can make things more dangerous. They risk their lives and the lives of others just for thrills.

Chasers must be careful at all times. Not only is the weather dangerous, but many chasers carry expensive equipment to study the storms. This equipment isn't easy to replace, so chasers are very careful that it doesn't get damaged. They also pay close attention to their equipment. Those who do not can become victims to thieving people.

Some chasers take unnecessary risks in order to see a storm up close. Many seek out supercells. A supercell is a very powerful type of thunderstorm that can create tornadoes. Some chasers even go core punching. This is when a chaser drives through the center, or core, of a thunderstorm. The core of a storm has the most violent weather. Core punching is very dangerous. Many storm chasers refuse to do it, but it does give the closest view of any tornadoes that might form. Outside of the spinning core, areas of hail, heavy rain, and light rain travel around the supercell.

Heavy rain

Hail

CORE

Storm path

On May 3, 1999, a series of tornadoes with wind speeds of more than three hundred miles per hour touched down in Oklahoma. The storms, which eventually turned north into Kansas, destroyed some houses and neighborhoods around Oklahoma City.

Tornadoes never approach daintily. You can hear them coming. Their winds make a very loud roar that many people compare to the sound of a train. Many towns have special sirens that will sound a warning when a tornado is approaching.

Tornadoes can generate winds of more than three hundred miles per hour. Such powerful winds can completely destroy buildings.

A tornado can have devastating effects on buildings, property, and land. A tornado with winds moving with furious speed will rip through a town and destroy everything in its path. Houses and mobile homes may be flattened, ripped apart, or carried away completely. A tornado can even peel the bark off trees! Such violence and destruction can occur at any time, as tornadoes touch down here and there without people being able to tell where and when.

Light rain

The core is the area of a thunderstorm where the most severe weather occurs.

Tornadoes can do that?

A storm that may seem scary to you and me can look beautiful to a storm chaser. Even loud thunder claps may sound as soothing as a lullaby to a person who loves studying storms. However, this can be dangerous for storm chasers. They always have to remember that storms with lightning, driving rain, and very high winds are powerful natural events. The very same storms that chasers hope to see also threaten their lives.

High winds can flip the chaser's vehicle or blow out its windows. Heavy rain and hail can make it hard to see. Flooding and fog can make traveling harder and might strand a chaser in the path of a storm. A safe storm chaser knows to keep the car or truck in good shape and to watch the sky for any changes. Most important, a good storm chaser knows when to back off and seek safety. A resourceful chaser will plan an escape route from a dangerous storm before getting close to it.

Tornadoes form when a layer of cold air moves over a layer of warm air. The lighter air then rises up through the cold air. This makes the funnel cloud rotate as the air masses change places.

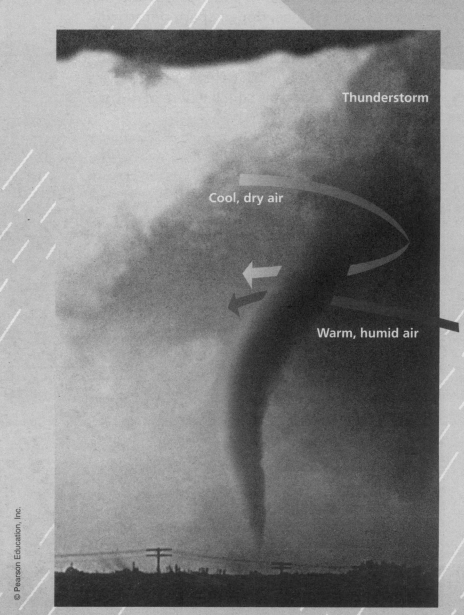

Thunderstorm

Cool, dry air

Warm, humid air

Toby's Vacation

by Christian Downey

Genre	Comprehension Skill and Strategy	Text Features
Fiction	• Literary Elements: Setting, Theme • Visualize	• Byline • Captions • Photos

Scott Foresman Reading Street 5.1.3

PEARSON

Scott
Foresman

scottforesman.com

Reader Response

1. What part of California did Toby and his family visit? What were some of the things he saw when he arrived?

2. Imagine that you are on one of the Channel Islands with Toby and his family. Visualize yourself there, and write down what you see.

3. On page 11 of the story, Toby and his family stand on the headland of the island near their ferry. If you don't know what a headland is, can you guess from the story? To be sure of the meaning, look up *headland* in a dictionary.

4. The California islands are home to many plants and animals that may soon be extinct. Think of ways that humans can help preserve them and keep them in good condition. List your ideas in the table below.

California Coast National Monument

The California Coast National Monument was established in 2000. It includes 840 miles of coastline between Oregon and Mexico. Many of the animals that live along the coast are very rare. People can be a danger to these animals. Humans who walk, swim, or ride boats too closely can cause problems. It is up to everyone to make sure that nature is protected there.

24

Toby's Vacation

by Christian Downey

PEARSON
Scott Foresman

Editorial Offices: Glenview, Illinois • Parsippany, New Jersey • New York, New York
Sales Offices: Needham, Massachusetts • Duluth, Georgia • Glenview, Illinois
Coppell, Texas • Ontario, California • Mesa, Arizona

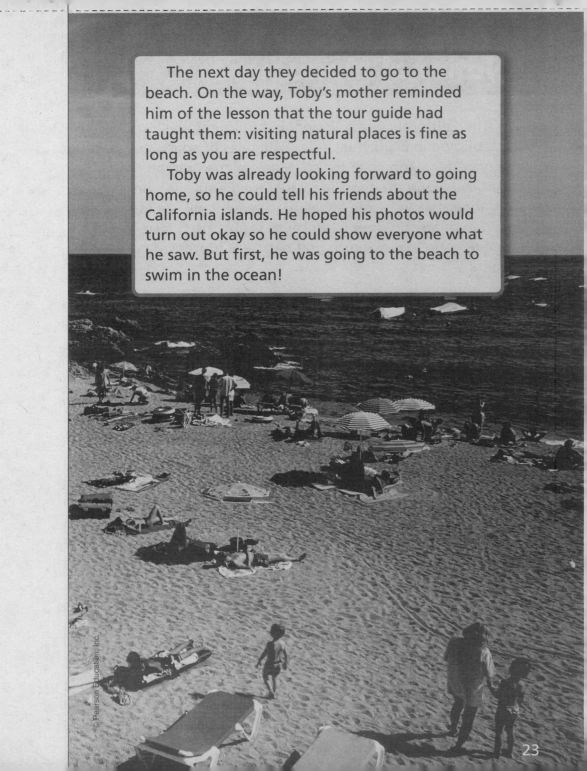

The next day they decided to go to the beach. On the way, Toby's mother reminded him of the lesson that the tour guide had taught them: visiting natural places is fine as long as you are respectful.

Toby was already looking forward to going home, so he could tell his friends about the California islands. He hoped his photos would turn out okay so he could show everyone what he saw. But first, he was going to the beach to swim in the ocean!

Toby and his parents decided to fly to California for their vacation. Toby's aunt lived in San Diego, in the southern part of California. Toby couldn't wait to visit. He had never been out West. His mom told him to pack his shorts, t-shirts, and sneakers. He also took his bathing suit, because they would visit the Pacific Ocean. Toby couldn't wait to tell his friends that he went swimming in the Pacific!

A beach in San Diego

22

3

As soon as they landed, Toby was amazed by what he saw. His mom's sister, Aunt Lee, drove Toby and his parents to her house. Out the car window, Toby saw tall buildings and palm trees. The roads were wide and he could see mountains far off in the distance.

"Toby, look!" said his mother, pointing out of her window.

Toby looked to where she had pointed and saw the ocean. People were playing and swimming at the beach. Toby couldn't wait to run in the sand and jump in the bright, blue water.

"Toby, do you want to check out some of the nearby islands?" asked his aunt.

"Of course!" answered Toby.

When they arrived at Aunt Lee's house, Toby and his family were ready for bed. Even though Toby was tired, he had trouble falling asleep. He couldn't stop thinking about all that he had learned that day. He loved seeing the islands and learning about their past. He had never seen so many animals and fish outside of a zoo or aquarium.

Downtown San Diego, CA

Alcatraz Island
Its famous prison is now a museum.

"Famous? How?" asked Toby.

"Alcatraz used to have a prison where dangerous criminals were held. There are many books and movies about it," said Aunt Lee.

"Are there still prisoners on the island?" asked Toby.

"No," said his aunt. "Now the island is a historic site. Visitors can go to see the empty prison."

The next day, they set out on their island journey. Aunt Lee told them about the islands as she drove.

"I'm taking you to see the Channel Islands," she said. "The Channel Islands are made up of eight islands off the California coast, four northern islands and four southern ones."

"What do they have on the islands?" asked Toby.

"All sorts of things," answered Aunt Lee. "They have plants and animals. There are many different kinds of birds and fish. The islands are home to all sorts of natural life. You can see for yourself, since we're almost there!"

The Channel Islands

They were all exhausted from their long day of visiting the islands. When they got off the ferry, Aunt Lee drove them to her house for the night. Aunt Lee told Toby more about California.

"You know, Toby, there are islands in the northern part of California too," she said. "San Francisco has Angel Island, Alcatraz island, and others. Angel Island used to be a fishing and hunting site. Now it is used by the Coast Guard. And Alcatraz is pretty famous!"

Angel Island is in San Francisco Bay.

The Channel Islands National Park

They ate dinner at one of the local cafes and walked around the island. It was much different than the others they had visited. This island had streets and shops. Toby thought it looked more like a town than an island.

Night had fallen. On the way back to the ferry, Toby saw a small cave-like hole by a big tree.

"What's that?" he asked Aunt Lee.

"It looks like a fox's lair. That's where the fox lives and hides from us!" she joked.

"Look," said Toby's father, pointing at the hole. "You can even see little teeth marks, where an animal gnawed at the ground."

Foxes in their lair

Toby and his family took a ferry to the islands. A tour guide described the Channel Islands National Park.

"The park is made up of five of the Channel Islands," said the tour guide. "They hold over 2,000 kinds of plants and animals. 145 of those can't be found anywhere else in the world."

"That's amazing," said Toby's dad. "What are some of the animals we might see?"

The tour guide replied. "On the islands there are seals, sea lions, foxes, owls, and many other kinds of animal life. Even though they're located close to these large California cities, the islands aren't very developed."

"So nobody bothers the animals, right?" asked Toby.

"Right," said the guide. "It's very important that the animals and plants are allowed to grow and live undisturbed."

Their first stop was Anacapa, the smallest of the northern Channel Islands. Anacapa was made up of three very small islands, called islets. Toby stood on the edge of one and looked out at the water.

"What's that brown stuff over there?" he asked his mother, pointing at the water.

"It looks like kelp. Seaweed."

"Is it bad for the animals?" asked Toby.

"Not at all, it's just a part of the environment," said his mom. "And kelp provides shelter for many sea creatures."

After they left Anacapa, Toby and his family went to San Miguel Island and then stopped for lunch. They still had a full day of sightseeing ahead of them.

Kelp

They boarded the ferry and went past Santa Barbara Island, the smallest of the Channel Islands. It was beginning to grow dark, so they went on to Santa Catalina Island, the only island with permanent residents.

"A Native American tribe used to travel here for trade many years ago," the tour guide told them. "Now conservationists work to save the plants that grow here from extinction."

"How can they be saved?" asked Toby.

The guide answered, "People work to keep the island clean and get rid of weeds. They also remove any animals that may hurt the land."

"Is it okay to have so many tourists coming to the islands?" asked Toby's mom.

"As long as people treat the island with respect, visitors are welcome," said the tour guide. "Just leave it like you found it, please!"

Avalon Bay is part of Santa Catalina Island.

After lunch, Aunt Lee wanted to visit Santa Rosa Island. Santa Rosa was the second largest of the Channel Islands. Aunt Lee was excited to see the trees. The island was known for its many kinds of trees, including a native oak.

"Toby, they found human bones on this island that were 13,000 years old. Can you believe people were here that long ago?" Aunt Lee asked.

"And now we're here too!" replied Toby.

"Think about how long these trees have been growing," said Aunt Lee.

"They look like the oak trees in your yard," said Toby. "Only much older!"

Santa Rosa Island

Western gull among coreopsis plants

Spiney Lizard

10

A loggerhead shrike

Toby's aunt told him that San Clemente was once used by fishermen and ranchers.

"What's that funny looking bird?" Toby asked his aunt, pointing up at a tall tree.

"That's called a loggerhead shrike," she told him. "It's an endangered species, which means there aren't many of them left in the world."

Toby took pictures of the bird. He couldn't wait to show everyone at home.

15

Next they traveled to San Clemente Island, located fifty-five miles out at sea. Toby's mother was feeling seasick from the long ferry ride by the time they made it to the island. Toby's father took him to the water's edge to explore.

"Look, Toby," he said, holding up a shell. "This was once part of a shellfish."

"What's a shellfish?" asked Toby.

"You remember the oyster we served you once?"

"Eww! You mean that slimy thing in a shell? It had a vein in it. Gross!" said Toby.

"That vein was its sinew, " laughed his father. "You are better off eating fish sticks."

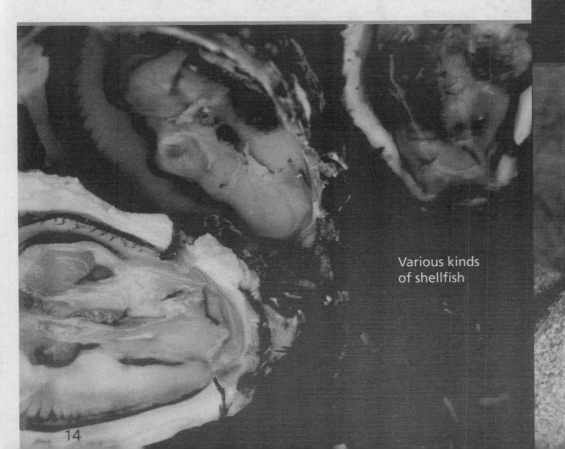

Various kinds of shellfish

Next they traveled to Santa Cruz Island, the largest of the Channel Islands. The tour guide told them all about their surroundings while they stood on the headland by the ferry.

"This island has many mountain ranges, ravines, tide pools, and sea caves. On this island alone, there are seventy-seven miles of coastline cliffs!"

"What kinds of animals are here?" asked Toby.

"So many kinds," answered their guide. "There are mammals, like deer and mice. We have over one-hundred types of birds. There are also many reptiles, like snakes and lizards."

"Snakes?" asked Toby's father, looking nervous. Toby chuckled.

The guide continued, "Santa Cruz Island is also home to many marine animals. There are dolphins, seals, and sea lions. If you're lucky, you may even spot a whale near the shore."

Island Fox

As they walked around the island, Toby and his family saw many different structures. There were adobe houses and barns, where people and animals used to live.

"People lived here many, many years ago," his aunt said. "Now the island is home to so many kinds of plants and animals. I don't want to leave!"

They had to leave, though. They boarded the ferry again to go on to San Nicolas Island.

"This island was home to an entire group of people in the 1800s," said the guide as they passed.

"What happened to them?" asked Toby.

"They became extinct," said the guide.

Toby was amazed that people had once lived on the islands. They didn't even have electricity! Years ago, people had lived without so many things. Toby wondered what it would be like to live on such a small island.

Social Studies

Social Studies

Biography

Famous Women Athletes

Genre	Comprehension Skill and Strategy	Text Features
Nonfiction	• Sequence of Events • Ask Questions	• Captions • Heads • Labels • Glossary

Scott Foresman Reading Street 5.1.4

ISBN 0-328-13512-7

90000

9 780328 135127

by Kara Race-Moore

Reader Response

1. Using a graphic organizer like the one below, place this sequence of events in the proper order: Toni Stone gets a hit off Satchel Paige; Gertrude Ederle swims the English Channel; Billie Jean King helps establish the Women's Sports Foundation; Roberta Gibb runs in the Boston Marathon; Althea Gibson qualifies to play at Wimbledon.

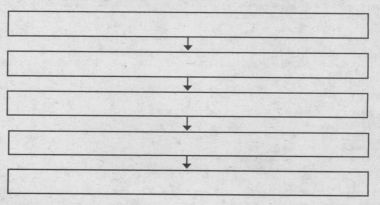

2. What questions would you have for the official who tried to drag Katherine Switzer from the marathon?

3. *Unique* starts with the letters *uni-*. What other words do you know that start with those letters?

4. Choose one of this book's photographs and explain how it adds to what you have learned from the text.

Glossary

confidence *n.* firm belief in yourself.

fastball *n.* a pitch thrown at high speed with very little curve.

mocking *v.* the act of laughing at; making fun of.

outfield *n.* the part of a baseball field beyond the diamond or infield.

unique *adj.* having no like or equal; being the only one of its kind.

weakness *n.* a weak point; slight fault.

windup *n.* a swinging movement of the arms while twisting the body just before pitching the ball.

Famous Women Athletes

by Kara Race-Moore

PEARSON
Scott
Foresman

Editorial Offices: Glenview, Illinois • Parsippany, New Jersey • New York, New York
Sales Offices: Needham, Massachusetts • Duluth, Georgia • Glenview, Illinois
Coppell, Texas • Ontario, California • Mesa, Arizona

Six months later Mingxia finished first in the ten-meter platform competition at the 1991 world championships. At twelve years old she had become the youngest world champion ever. Next she won a gold medal at the 1992 Olympics. She was the youngest person to win an Olympic gold medal since 1936. She was the youngest Olympic diving champion ever.

At the 1996 Olympics, Mingxia won both the ten-meter platform and three-meter springboard diving event. Mingxia took the next few years off for school. Then, in the 2000 Olympics, Mingxia again took home gold in the three-meter springboard diving event. Training and competing brought injuries and hardship, but Mingxia always pressed on.

Over the past hundred years, female athletes have broken down many barriers. From Ederle's swimming to Mingxia's diving, they have inspired us with their feats. Thanks to their pioneering efforts, today's women can participate in and excel at whichever sports they choose!

Mingxia Fu: Diving Into Success

Mingxia Fu was born in 1978 in Wuhan, China. She started diving before she knew how to swim. To help, her coaches tied a rope around her waist so they could pull her out of the water after her dives.

Mingxia said that when she first started diving she was "scared to death." According to the rules, a diver could not climb back down the ladder once he or she had climbed up. Mingxia was always afraid, but never climbed back down the ladder.

When Mingxia was eleven she was selected for the Chinese Junior diving team. Shortly after she won a gold medal in platform diving at the 1990 Goodwill Games. Mingxia's career as a world champion diver had been launched.

Mingxia Fu conquered her fears to become an Olympic diver.

Women in Sports: A Brief Overview

In the 1800s women were allowed to play very few organized sports. They could play croquet and badminton or enter archery tournaments. Most other sports were restricted to men only. And only men were allowed to compete at the the first modern Olympic Games, held in 1896.

By the beginning of the 1900s, change was in the air. Women were working for the right to vote, own property, and work for the same wages as men. They were also fighting for the right to compete in sports. The 1900 Olympics showed signs of progess. At those Olympic Games, women were allowed to compete in tennis, golf, sailing, equestrian events, and croquet. Today, girls and women participate in all sports, at all levels.

In the early 1900s, golf was one of the few sports that women were allowed to play.

Trudy Ederle: The Super Swimmer

Gertrude "Trudy" Caroline Ederle was born in 1906. She was a child of German immigrants living in New York City.

Ederle learned to swim when she was very young. At the age of twelve, she swam the eight-hundred-yard freestyle in thirteen minutes and nineteen seconds This made her the youngest person to break a world record.

Trudy held eighteen world swimming records by the time she was seventeen. She was also a member of the United States Olympic swimming team. She won a gold medal and two bronze medals at the 1924 Olympics.

Newspaper photographers took pictures of Switzer while the marathon official tried to drag her away. Despite this event, marathon officials still refused to allow women to run. This led to a five-year legal battle. Finally, in 1972 Nina Kuscsik became the first woman to officially run in the Boston Marathon.

Meanwhile Switzer continued to work for female athletes' rights. She convinced Avon, the world's largest cosmetics corporation, to sponsor a series of women's races. Today Switzer continues to run and fight for equality.

Trudy Ederle

Female Marathoners: Fighting to Race

Women such as Althea Gibson, Billie Jean King, and Rosemary Casals fought for equality on the tennis courts. At the same time, women such as Roberta Gibb, Katherine Switzer, and Nina Kuscsik fought for the right to run.

In the 1960s women were not allowed to run in the Boston Marathon. Roberta Gibb decided to test this. In 1966, after putting on a hooded sweatshirt to hide her identity, she joined the race. She ran the entire race. Afterward, officials refused to acknowledge that a woman had run the Boston Marathon.

The next year Katherine Switzer decided that she wanted to run the race. On the race application she wrote her name, 'K. V. Switzer,' so officials wouldn't know she was a woman. They sent her an official number.

Four miles into the marathon, a race official realized Switzer was a woman and tried to drag her out of the race. She outran him while other runners deliberately ran in front of the official to prevent him from stopping her. Switzer finished the race.

Katherine Switzer had to fight off this race official in order to finish the 1967 Boston Marathon.

In 1925 Trudy tried to swim across the English Channel. Although she failed, she refused to admit weakness. On August 6, 1926, she set off again from the coast of France. She was nineteen. The water was very rough that day. Trudy would not quit and swam on despite big waves and seasickness.

It took Ederle fourteen hours and thirty-one minutes to swim the thirty-five miles that separated England from France. Her time was two hours faster than the previous record set in 1875 by a British Navy captain.

Trudy had proven that she was a great swimmer. She became an international celebrity overnight. She returned home to America as the first major sports heroine. Thousands of people lined the streets of New York City to cheer when she arrived home.

Ederle was inducted into the International Swimming Hall of Fame in 1965. She joined the International Women's Sports Hall of Fame in 1980. She was one of the first women athletes to be recognized. But she quickly was followed by others.

Babe Didrikson

Babe Didrikson: The Great Athlete

Mildred "Babe" Didrikson was born in 1914 in Port Arthur, Texas. She was given the nickname "Babe" because people thought she played baseball as well as Babe Ruth. As a child Didrikson played basketball, golf, and baseball. She also did track and field, diving, swimming, tennis, and bowling.

Babe won two gold medals for track and field in the 1932 Olympics. She would have won a third but was disqualified by the high jump judges. They disqualified her because they thought her style of diving headfirst over the bar was inappropriate!

After the Olympics, Babe became a professional golfer. She was the first American woman to win the British Women's Amateur Tournament. As a golfer Didrikson broke the standards for how a "lady" played golf. She hit long drives when women were expected to take dainty shots.

After knee surgery in 1978, Casals took a break from playing tennis. Since 1981 she has been president of Sportswomen, Inc. This is a California company she formed to promote tennis tournaments for older female players. In 1990 she teamed up again with Billie Jean King to win the U.S. Open Senior women's doubles championship.

Historically, tennis had been a sport for the wealthy. Players wore expensive white outfits, and the crowd would clap only rarely and very quietly.

Casals wore brightly colored outfits and expected the crowd to show more enthusiasm for her hard work. She was almost excluded from her first Wimbledon games for not wearing white. Today, bright outfits and cheering crowds are found at most tennis tournaments. This is thanks in part to the trailblazing work of Rosemary Casals.

In 1966, Casals started playing in doubles tournaments with Billie Jean King. Casals and King became one of the best doubles teams in the history of women's tennis.

Casals and King were a great match as teammates. Casals also fought for the rights of female tennis players. She worked with King to get female tennis players the same prize money that male tennis players received. Throughout her career Casals worked to better the sport of women's tennis.

Rosemary Casals created a sensation in the world of tennis with her brightly colored outfits.

Didrikson didn't care that people were shocked by her long drives. She was determined to win. She knew that she would do better by hitting the ball as far as she could. She won fifty-five tournaments, including ten majors. Three of them were U.S. Opens.

Didrikson was never afraid to speak her mind. Then she'd show people what she could do. In 1949 she helped form the Ladies Professional Golf Association to support women's golf.

Babe spent the last three years of her life battling cancer, but she kept playing golf. She had surgery to try to remove the cancer. Afterward, she returned to the golf course and won the U.S. Open in 1954. Didrikson died in 1956. She is still remembered as one of the greatest athletes ever, male or female.

Babe Didrikson changed women's golf forever with her long drives.

Women's Baseball: A League of Their Own

While Babe Didrikson was changing women's golf, other women were breaking into baseball. During World War II many major league baseball players went to war. Chicago Cubs owner Phil Wrigley set up the All-American Girls Baseball League (AAGBBL) in 1943. He was worried that there weren't going to be enough men to play baseball during the war.

Dorothy Kamenshek, born in 1925, was one of the AAGBBL's best players. Kamenshek played first base. She won back-to-back batting titles in 1946 and 1947. She was an excellent hitter and rarely struck out. Dorothy could bunt the ball or smack it deep into the outfield. She could make any hit her team needed. Her team, the Rockford Peaches, won four championships during her ten-year career.

Women's baseball enjoyed great success during the 1940s.

Despite coming from a poor background, Rosemary Casals rose up to achieve tennis greatness.

Rosemary Casals: Rising to Greatness

Rosemary Casals, an Hispanic tennis player, energized the sport of tennis as she fought to prove herself on the courts.

Rosemary was born in 1948 in San Francisco, California. Her parents were immigrants from El Salvador. When Casals was only a year old, her parents felt they were unable to care for her. So she was raised by her Uncle Manuel and Aunt Maria. Manuel taught Rosemary to play tennis. He remained her coach throughout her career.

Casals felt different because she was poor. Other children arrived at the public tennis courts dressed in fancy clothes and carrying brand new rackets. Rosemary did not have these things. She was also at a disadvantage because she was shorter than almost all the other players. Casals had to prove herself through her game. And she did.

Rosemary rebelled against the traditions of tennis. She played against older girls. She rebelled against the "feeling" that tennis had at that time. She was not what the fans or the players expected.

In 1950 the Peaches lost the sixth game of the championship series. Kamenshek rallied her teammates to win the final game. She hit two singles, a triple, and a home run, driving in five runs. Dorothy had to wear a back brace because of injuries in her final season in 1951. Even so, she was able to hit for a .345 batting average while stealing sixty-three bases.

Ticket sales to women's baseball games began to decline in the early 1950s. In 1954 the AAGBBL was shut down. Still, their memory lived on. Kamenshek and the Peaches became the inspiration for the hit movie *A League of Their Own*.

Toni Stone: Good Enough To Hit Paige

Toni Stone was another baseball player who proved women could play what had been a men's only game. She also had the added obstacle of being African American. Toni was born Marcenia Lyle in St. Paul, Minnesota, in 1921. She later adopted the name Toni Stone.

Toni loved baseball. When she was ten she played in a league sponsored by a cereal company. She would practice anywhere, even in old ball parks with rickety benches and no markings on the field.

Stone became the first woman to play for a men's big-league team. Syd Pollack was the owner of the Negro American League's Indianapolis Clowns. He signed her to play second base in 1953. Pollack signed her up partly as a gimmick to attract more sales. But Stone soon proved to be one of the team's best players.

Toni had to put up with the mocking from other players. Teammates would tell her that she belonged in the kitchen. But Toni refused to quit the game she loved.

Then, in 1974, King played a key role in helping to establish the Women's Sports Federation, or WSF. The WSF works to make it possible for all girls and women to participate in sports.

Billie Jean King won thirty-nine Grand Slam titles and 695 match victories during a sports career that lasted two decades. By helping to found the WSF, King ensured that the women who followed her would have an easier time entering the sports world. Even now King still helps promote women's athletics.

Billie Jean King's win against Bobby Riggs was nationally televised.

Billie Jean King: A Tennis King

Billie Jean King was born in 1943. She was the daughter of a fireman and a homemaker. She grew up to become a successful professional tennis player. It angered her that men earned larger prizes for winning tennis tournaments than women did. In 1970, King and several other women tennis players were upset that the tournament judges were still not giving equal prizes. So, they founded the Virginia Slims Tour.

In 1971 King became the first female athlete to win more than $100,000 in annual prize money. Her most famous moment as a tennis player came in 1973. That year she beat Bobby Riggs in a tennis match titled the "Battle of the Sexes." The game was nationally televised. King's win proved to the whole country that women could excel at sports too. King had been nervous before the match, but she found the confidence to play, and won.

Toni Stone was a good enough batter to get a hit off the legendary Satchel Paige in 1953.

In 1953 Toni had the chance to bat against the legendary pitcher Satchel Paige. It was her most memorable moment playing baseball. Paige had a fastball that almost no one could hit. He would ask batters how they wanted him to throw the ball—high, low, or down the middle. He would complete his windup and throw what the players asked for. They still couldn't hit the ball.

When Stone went to bat against Paige, she jokingly asked only that he not hurt her. Yet Toni got a hit right over second base! She was the only player to get a hit off of Paige during that game.

Stone was inducted into the International Women's Sports Hall of Fame in 1993. Three years later she died.

Althea Gibson: Pioneer in Women's Tennis

Another African American woman athlete who broke records and expectations was Althea Gibson. Althea was born in South Carolina in 1927. She grew up in New York City.

As a young girl, Gibson often played paddle tennis. She once won a tournament. Buddy Walker, a Harlem jazz musician, noticed her playing and suggested she might do well at regular tennis.

Althea learned to play at Harlem's Cosmopolitan Tennis Club. She became very good. She went on to win the American Tennis Association's women's singles tournament ten years in a row.

By 1951 Althea was at the top of her game. That year she qualified to enter the English tournament at Wimbledon. She became the first African American to play at Wimbledon.

In 1955 Gibson toured the world as a member of a national tennis team supported by the U.S. State Department. Later, she won many international events, including the French, English, and U.S. championships. In 1957 she won the doubles and singles events at Wimbledon. She returned home a national heroine. Her hometown greeted her with a ticker tape parade.

Althea Gibson was inducted into the National Lawn Tennis Hall of Fame, the International Tennis Hall of Fame, and the Black Athletes Hall of Fame.

Gibson died in 2003 knowing of the tennis victories of Serena and Venus Williams. The Williams sisters' successes are possible because of the groundbreaking work of Althea Gibson. Gibson was a unique athlete who broke through many barriers in women's sports.

Althea Gibson was a dominant tennis player during the 1950s.

Social Studies Social Studies

A NATION OF MANY COLORS

BY JOSHUA NISSENBAUM

Genre	Comprehension Skill and Strategy	Text Features
Nonfiction	• Cause and Effect • Summarize Text	• Table of Contents • Captions • Labels • Glossary

Scott Foresman Reading Street 5.1.5

PEARSON
Scott
Foresman

scottforesman.com

ISBN 0-328-13515-1

90000

9 780328 135158

Reader Response

1. Using a graphic organizer such as the one below, write down the main cause of the civil rights movement, along with one of its effects.

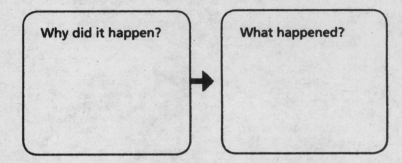

Why did it happen?   What happened?

2. Summarize the main reasons why people immigrate to the United States.

3. On page 14, it says, "In some ways, African Americans today are still forced to elbow their way to equality." How is the word *elbow* used in this context?

4. Which one of this book's pictures did you think best portrays what the immigrant experience is like? Why?

Glossary

advice *n.* opinion about what should be done; suggestion.

advised *v.* gave advice to.

circumstances *n.* conditions that accompany an act or event.

elbow *v.* to make your way by pushing.

hustled *v.* to get or sell in a hurried way.

immigrants *n.* people who come into a country or region to live there.

luxury *n.* something pleasant but not necessary.

newcomer *n.* person who has just come or who came not long ago.

peddler *n.* person who travels about selling things carried in a pack or in a truck, wagon, or cart.

A NATION OF MANY COLORS

BY JOSHUA NISSENBAUM

PEARSON
Scott Foresman

Editorial Offices: Glenview, Illinois • Parsippany, New Jersey • New York, New York
Sales Offices: Needham, Massachusetts • Duluth, Georgia • Glenview, Illinois
Coppell, Texas • Ontario, California • Mesa, Arizona

Conclusion
Our Diverse Country

Never before has there been a country as diverse as the United States. In the past, cities such as London, Rome, and Hong Kong have attracted diverse populations. But the United States has *many* cities, such as Chicago, New York, and Los Angeles, with lots of different ethnic groups living in them. In New York alone there are more than one hundred different languages spoken!

The ethnic groups that you have read about have done much to contribute to the United States' diversity. At times they have experienced tension both among themselves and with other ethnic groups. But overall they have made our country a far more exciting and interesting place to live!

23

Some Jewish American peddlers were very successful and used their profits to open stores. Jewish immigrants opened famous department stores such as Filene's in Boston. Other Jewish immigrants moved into selling luxury goods such as diamonds and fur coats. These early business ventures allowed Jews to move into positions of power and wealth in American society.

During the 1900s much of the Jewish American community moved from the cities to the suburbs. In the process, they blended into mainstream American culture. Jewish Americans were so successful at blending in that in a short time they were seen as being more American than Jewish. Today, many in the Jewish community have called upon American Jews to revive their ethnic heritage.

The United States is a nation of immigrants. Its constant stream of newcomers has given it the most diverse population in history.

CONTENTS

Introduction
The Melting Pot

Have you ever heard of the phrase "the melting pot"? No one knows when it was first used. But it first became popular in 1908 when Israel Zangwill wrote a play titled *The Melting Pot.* The play, which attracted a lot of attention, focused on the experiences of early twentieth-century American immigrants.

Ever since Zangwill's play, people have used "melting pot" to describe the many different ethnic groups that have immigrated to the United States. The United States' melting pot grew rapidly in the late 1800s, when millions of immigrants came into the country. These newcomers brought along with them their customs, cultural products, languages, and values, which changed American culture.

The United States' diverse population earned it the nickname the melting pot.

Some Jews took the skills they learned as peddlers to become successful business people.

From Peddlers to Business People

Despite these difficulties, the Eastern European Jews often had a slight advantage over other immigrants groups. Most other European immigrants had been farmers. However in parts of Europe, Jewish people were not allowed to own land. This forced them to become business people. In Manhattan, which had no farming and focused on business, it helped to have such a background.

As much as the Eastern European Jews were helped by their business experience, they still faced enormous challenges upon arriving in New York. Most of the jobs available to immigrants were already taken. As a result, many Jewish people became peddlers. They would buy something small and then sell it on the street for a modest profit. Being a peddler was tough work. Peddlers hustled their goods throughout the city to attract customers.

In time Jewish Americans would overcome their cultural differences to embrace their common heritage. But in the late 1800s, these differences caused tension. The German Jews considered the Russian Jews to be inferior. The Eastern European Jews felt that the German Jews had given up their Jewish identity.

The majority of Jewish immigrants from Eastern Europe settled in New York City. They lived in a compact community centered in Manhattan's Lower East Side. Life there was very different from what they expected.

Many of the Russian Jewish immigrants had expected life to be easier in America. However, many found themselves living in poverty upon arriving in the United States. They struggled to find work. Many lived in crumbling apartments crammed with dozens of people.

New York's Lower East Side, where many Eastern European Jews lived during the early 1900s.

Many Cubans have reacted to Cuba's government by immigrating to Florida.

Immigrants come to America for all sorts of reasons. Many arrive looking to acquire an education. Others come hoping to find jobs and gain civil rights. Millions journey to the United States to escape from war, starvation, and the cruel government policies they experienced back home.

Immigration to the United States often occurs in waves, as many people of the same ethnic background arrive over the course of several years. For example, from 1959 to 1962, 200,000 Cuban immigrants came to Florida. They came because they felt threatened by Fidel Castro's communist form of government. They were also looking forward to obtaining better jobs, civil rights, and educations.

New York City's Chinatown contains block after block of Chinese-run shops and businesses.

Immigrant Communities

Immigrants to the United States are sometimes unprepared for parts of American life. To ease their transition, those that belong to the same ethnic group often settle in the same area, forming a small community. Such communities are spread across the United States. They exist in many major cities, especially the seaports of the East and West Coasts. Immigrant communities are often given names such as "Chinatown," "Koreatown," or "Little Italy," based on the ethnic groups that live in them.

For a newcomer, these communities provide many of the features of home. They also offer a newcomer the chance to adjust to the United States gradually and to keep his or her ethnic identity. Within these communities, immigrants speak their native language, and restaurants, shops, and businesses sell traditional ethnic foods, goods, and services.

Friction Between Different Jewish Groups

In the late 1800s, people from all over Europe immigrated to the United States. Among them were many Jewish people. From 1880 to 1920 approximately two million Jews entered the United States. Many of them were Eastern European Jews escaping the anti-Semitism that flared up in Eastern Europe during the late nineteenth century.

The Jewish Americans who had immigrated in the early 1800s from Germany resented the later Eastern European Jewish immigrants. These earlier Jewish immigrants had worked hard to blend into American society. They feared that the newcomers would upset their position in America and cause anti-Semitism. Most of the Jewish people from Eastern Europe were uneducated and needed assistance in adapting to life in the United States.

Many Russian Jews faced poverty when they first arrived in New York.

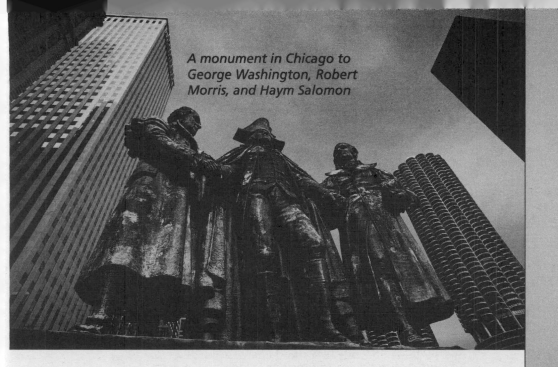

A monument in Chicago to George Washington, Robert Morris, and Haym Salomon

Chapter Three
Jewish Americans

Jewish people have been in the United States since the 1600s. In Europe, Jews faced anti-Semitism. Anti-Semitism is a form of prejudice that singles out Jewish people. It caused many Jewish people to come to the United States.

From early on, Jewish Americans were eager to assist with the country's development. Haym Salomon, a Polish Jew, helped finance the American Revolution. Such efforts inspired George Washington to send a letter in 1790 to Rhode Island's Jewish American community, promising that they would always be safe in the United States.

Washington's letter was important, given how few Jews lived in the United States at that time. The two thousand Jewish people living in the United States in 1790 made up less than one percent of the country's total population.

Among the most famous immigrant communities are San Francisco's Chinatown, Detroit's Greektown, New York's Little Italy, and the Koreatown in Los Angeles. Each of these immigrant communities has a long and proud tradition. They all feature restaurants and shops that specialize in the foods and products of their residents' homelands. They are also famous for celebrating the holidays of their residents' native cultures.

An immigrant community's restaurants, shops, and other cultural attractions can make it an attractive place to live. This can lead to *gentrification*. Gentrification happens when wealthier people move into a poorer neighborhood. Since wealthier people are willing to pay more for things, they cause the cost of living to go up. The residents of immigrant communities need to work together with local politicians to help solve the problems created by gentrification.

Celebrations of the Chinese New Year include colorful parades.

Immigrants to the United States have to deal with many issues other than gentrification. They need to find places to live. They need to find jobs that can pay for necessities such as food, clothing, and shelter. They have to learn the laws and customs of American society.

Each of these issues creates challenges that immigrants have to overcome in order to be successful. The rest of the book describes the challenges that three separate ethnic groups–Hispanic Americans, African Americans, and Jewish Americans–have faced in the United States. Each of these three groups arrived in the United States under different circumstances. Each brought along with them different sets of values and beliefs. But as you will see, the hardships they faced have given them much in common.

Condoleeza Rice has played an important role in giving foreign policy advice to President George W. Bush.

The ceremony in which immigrants become citizens marks the end to a long and challenging process.

In 2001, President George W. Bush named Colin Powell to serve as Secretary of State and Condoleezza Rice to serve as National Security Advisor. In 2004, Rice replaced Powell as Secretary of State. Both Powell and Rice have advised President Bush on how to deal with major foreign policy issues. And both are African American.

Many African American politicians of less fame than Powell and Rice are working to improve the lives of African Americans. Groups such as the Congressional Black Caucus (CBC), formed in 1969 to give added strength to African Americans in Congress, have helped reduce inequality over the past few decades by drawing attention to issues affecting African Americans. The CBC and similar organizations will continue to play a major role in guiding African Americans towards a better future.

African Americans in Politics

African Americans account for only 13 percent of the U.S. population. This makes them a minority. Despite this disadvantage in numbers, African Americans have been elected mayors in major cities such as Los Angeles, Philadelphia, Chicago, and New York City. They have also won elections in cities where there are very few African Americans, such as Augusta, Maine, and Denver, Colorado.

African Americans have also gained ground in the federal government. In 1992, Carol Moseley Braun was elected senator of Illinois, making her the first female African American senator. The following year, Ron Brown, was named Secretary of Commerce. Before Brown, only Robert Weaver, who was Secretary of Housing and Urban Development during the 1960s, had held such a position.

Willie Brown served as San Francisco's mayor from 1996 to 2004.

Many Mexican citizens became Americans as a result of the Mexican-American War.

Chapter One
Hispanic Americans

The first Hispanic Americans came from Mexico. They became Americans in an unusual way. From 1846 to 1848 the United States and Mexico fought the Mexican-American War. The United States won the war in 1848. As a result it took control of land that had belonged to Mexico. This land included parts of what are now the states of California, New Mexico, Nevada, Wyoming, Utah, Colorado, and Arizona.

The Mexicans living on this land were given the choice of staying and becoming Americans, or moving south to Mexico. For various reasons, most Mexicans who found themselves in this situation decided to stay on the American-controlled land. In a sense, these Hispanic Americans didn't "come" to the United States. Rather, the United States came to them!

Spain

South America

Mexico

A Fast-Growing Ethnic Group

People from Mexico make up more than half of all Hispanics living in the United States. The 2000 Census reports that there were 20,640,711 Mexican Americans living in the United States at the time. The number of Mexican Americans increases each year as more Mexicans immigrate to the United States.

You've now seen the phrase "Hispanic American" used a few times. But do you know what it means? The Census Bureau states that Hispanic Americans are people who have come from Spain and Mexico. Hispanic Americans also come from the Spanish-speaking countries of Central and South America. Hispanic Americans have been one of the country's fastest-growing ethnic groups for several decades. In 2000, an estimated thirty-five million Hispanic Americans lived in the United States.

The 1960s also saw a renewed interest in African cultural traditions. In 1966, the holiday Kwanzaa was created by an African American political activist named Maulana Ron Karenga. Karenga created Kwanzaa so that African Americans could enjoy elements of traditional African culture. Kwanzaa is celebrated during the last six days of December, ending on New Year's Day. Nearly five million African Americans took part in Kwanzaa in 1990.

After years of struggle, African Americans have created a strong ethnic identity. Music, fashion, sports, and entertainment are all areas that have benefited from African American involvement. In addition, African Americans have made major contributions to science and literature.

The March on Washington, held August 28, 1963, was a highlight of the civil rights movement. Martin Luther King, Jr. gave his famous "I Have a Dream Speech" at this rally.

The Civil Rights Movement

Since the abolition of slavery, African Americans have had to battle severe prejudice, or racism, of white Americans. White Americans have had difficulty accepting the fact that African Americans deserve equal rights. In some ways, African Americans are still forced to elbow their way to equality.

After World War II, African Americans decided they were no longer going to tolerate racism. Out of their determination grew the civil rights movement. The movement used peaceful methods to promote equality among all Americans. It caused many white Americans to reconsider their views towards African Americans and others. The movement united African Americans as never before, producing leaders such as Martin Luther King, Jr.

Of those thirty-five million Hispanic Americans, almost three-quarters lived in Texas, California, New York, and Florida. The population of Hispanic Americans living in California is particularly large. It is estimated that 1.7 million Hispanic Americans live in the city of Los Angeles alone. As high as that number is, it does not include the large number of Hispanic Americans living in the cities surrounding Los Angeles. In comparison, Madrid, Spain, has approximately three million Spanish-speaking residents.

Jennifer Lopez: Star for the Ages

Hispanic Americans are active in politics, the arts, civil rights, and other areas. Perhaps the most well-known Hispanic American is Jennifer Lopez, who has enjoyed success as an actress, singer, and businesswoman. Lopez is Puerto Rican by background. Born in 1970, she grew up in New York City's Bronx neighborhood.

Jennifer Lopez has created a business empire from her career as an entertainer.

Lopez has starred in several movies and sold millions of recordings. She even has her own perfume! Lopez is currently the highest paid Hispanic American actress. She is also the first woman to have a movie and record album reach number one at the same time.

César Chávez: Fighting for Farmworkers

Before Jennifer Lopez, the most famous Hispanic American might have been César Chávez. Chávez was born in 1927 to a family of migrant farmworkers. His childhood was made difficult by his family's constant moves. When Chávez became a farmworker in the 1950s, he began organizing farmworkers. He advised them on ways to gain better pay and improved working conditions. For years, Chávez fought for farmworkers' rights. He died in 1993. The following year, President Bill Clinton awarded Chávez's family the Presidential Medal of Freedom.

César Chávez worked tirelessly to improve conditions for migrant farmworkers.

African Americans were enslaved until 1865. They have struggled to obtain equal rights ever since.

Chapter Two
African Americans

In the history of the United States, African Americans are unique. They are the only immigrant group to come to the United States against their will.

Enslaved Africans were first brought to what would become the United States in 1619. By 1700, the colony of Virginia was importing about 1,000 enslaved Africans each year. The Southern economy depended on enslaved Africans for the labor they provided.

The growth of the cotton and tobacco industries encouraged white Americans to import more and more enslaved Africans. By the start of the Civil War there were about 3.5 million enslaved African Americans. In 1865, slavery was abolished, freeing the enslaved African Americans.

Social Studies

Social Studies

Using Special Talents

Genre	Comprehension Skill and Strategy	Text Features
Nonfiction	• Compare and Contrast • Answer Questions	• Captions • Charts • Glossary

Scott Foresman Reading Street 5.2.1

PEARSON

Scott
Foresman

scottforesman.com

ISBN 0-328-13518-6

9 780328 135189

90000

by Sharon Franklin

Reader Response

1. Using a graphic organizer like the one below, compare and contrast how Lee and Miguel helped other people.

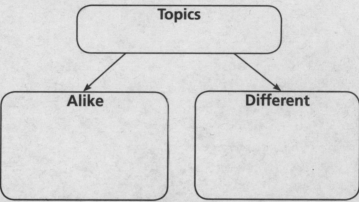

2. Go back to the chart on page 18. After reading it, what questions do you still have about how to get involved in helping others?

3. Which of the vocabulary words contain prefixes?

4. This book contains charts on pages 11, 18, and 22. Which of the charts was most helpful and why?

Glossary

caterpillar *n.* the wormlike larvae of insects such as butterflies and moths.

cocoon *n.* case of silky thread spun by the larvae of various insects, to live in while they are developing into adults.

disrespect *n.* a lack of respect for someone or something.

emerge *v.* to come into view or into the open.

migrant *n.* a worker, especially a farm worker, who travels from one area to another in search of work.

sketched *v.* to have made a rough drawing of something.

unscrewed *v.* to have loosened by having taken off or turned.

Using Special Talents

by Sharon Franklin

PEARSON
Scott Foresman

Editorial Offices: Glenview, Illinois • Parsippany, New Jersey • New York, New York
Sales Offices: Needham, Massachusetts • Duluth, Georgia • Glenview, Illinois
Coppell, Texas • Ontario, California • Mesa, Arizona

Hallanah decided to profile a different student each week on her Web site. For her first profile she decided to pick someone who was especially inspiring and who had made a big difference.

Hallanah picked Melissa Poe. When Melissa was nine, she wrote a letter to the President, asking him to help clean up the environment. Her letter soon appeared on more than 250 billboards across the country. Melissa even went on television to get her message out. Her club, Kids For a Clean Environment, or Kids F.A.C.E., grew and grew. Today, it has chapters all over the world, and its members have helped plant more than a million trees! It's all thanks to a young girl who wrote a letter. As you can see, students can accomplish pratically anything when they decide to help out!

Hallanah Makes Her Picks

Hallanah had to do a lot of research about national organizations. She visited more than twenty-five Web sites and looked at the kinds of activities they sponsored. She also compared them with each other to see how the opportunities they offered were both alike and different. Hallanah thought that displaying that kind of information on her Web site would help students find just the right project! The chart below lists the national organizations that Hallanah recommended the most, based on the opportunities for volunteering that they provide.

Hallanah's Top Picks

- American Red Cross
- Boys and Girls Club of America
- Girl Scouts of America
- Great American Bake Sale
- Make a Difference Day
- National Park and Recreation Association
- Youth Service America

Students Helping Across America

Did you know that every day in cities across the United States, students like yourself are helping others?

Each year in Louisiana, a young student and her younger brother have gone around collecting stuffed animals for children who live in a homeless shelter.

In New York City, seventy-six students from Harlem teamed up with four Olympic athletes to transform a run-down park into a playground featuring a daffodil garden.

And each year in Indiana, a young student has gone around collecting hundreds of bundles of baby clothes and other baby items. In the fall she delivers them to a home for mothers who are having tough times.

Students from Harlem transformed a run-down park into a playground using daffodils.

Harriet Hanson's Story

The United States has a long history of young people making a difference. It was American children from the past whom you have to thank for your education! Some courageous children in the 1800s helped change laws governing child labor. By doing so, they helped ensure that children in the future would not be denied an education.

In 1835 Harriet Hanson had her tenth birthday. That was also the year she began working in a textile factory. Harriet had to be at work at five o'clock in the morning. She worked fourteen hours a day from Monday to Friday. On Saturday she worked eight hours.

Several years before Harriet started working, factory owners began paying girls less in order to keep profits high. In 1836 Harriet, along with other girls, decided to stop working temporarily, to protest the unfair wages.

When the girls who had stopped working lost their jobs, Harriet joined the Factory Girls' Association. Members of this association helped other young people strike for better wages. They also raised money to help pay for food and shelter for the children on strike.

Hallanah worked on her Web site for several weeks. She found that making a Web site about volunteering took a lot of the same skills as being a volunteer.

She had to talk to a lot of people to gather information about volunteer opportunities in her community. She talked with people who work for the city. These people work in the library, the parks department, the police department, and the public works department. They all wanted to be listed on Hallanah's Web site.

Hallanah also talked to the directors of several nonprofit organizations. The director of the hospital, several preschools, and the homeless shelter all had volunteer opportunities for her to list.

Hallanah's Web site soon blossomed with opportunities for students to help out and volunteer! Below are some of the opportunities that Hallanah's Web site offered.

Hospital looking for students to play games with young patients.

New Beginnings Shelter looking for tutors for young children.

Police Department looking for a few good girls and boys to advise police on problems that affect young people in our community.

How Hallanah Helped Out

After school Hallanah rushed down to the computer room. She asked her computer teacher if she could create her own Web site.

Her teacher liked the idea! He agreed to let Hallanah make a site that would help students become volunteers. Her site would have information about volunteer opportunities with all different kinds of organizations. Hallanah also decided to include stories about young people who volunteered. Those young people would be able to see pictures of themselves and their projects on the Web site. They would also be able to read about how others got started and the success they've had.

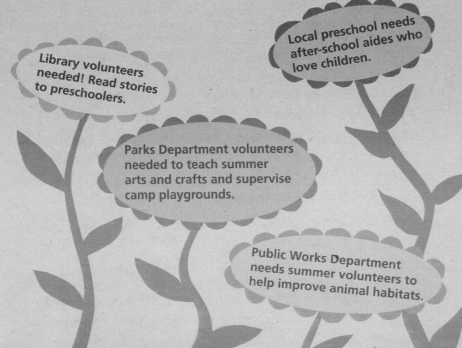

Library volunteers needed! Read stories to preschoolers.

Local preschool needs after-school aides who love children.

Parks Department volunteers needed to teach summer arts and crafts and supervise camp playgrounds.

Public Works Department needs summer volunteers to help improve animal habitats.

In the nineteenth-century, young girls worked long hours in factories that were dangerous and unhealthy. Their factory work kept them from getting a good education.

How Your Resources Can Help

You have now read about several young people who worked hard to help others. Can you think of times you've helped someone? Maybe you've helped a family member. Perhaps you've taken the garbage out for your mom or helped a brother or sister with homework.

Or maybe you've helped a friend. Have you ever lent a book to a friend who was sick in bed? Or simply helped a friend with chores? We often help people we know. But have you ever helped someone you didn't know?

You might be afraid of helping someone you don't know because you're not sure whether you have enough resources to help them. Resources are things that help you do a job. Money is a good example of a resource.

These students are using their time and energy to help with this garden. Time and energy are resources.

In contrast to Annie, Miguel, and Lee, Hallanah is an experienced volunteer. In kindergarten her mom encouraged her to join her on walk-a-thons. Since then she has walked more than fifty miles. For each mile Hallanah walked, friends and family members donated money for cancer and cerebral palsy research. Last year she signed up a for a National Youth Service Day car wash that raised money for a local preschool.

Hallanah had been thinking about her talents and interests. Her friends and teachers tell her she is a good communicator. Hallanah also loves computers. She wanted to combine her talents and interests in a way that would help others.

On the way to school one morning, a big smile spread across Hallanah's face. She had realized what she wanted to do! Before Hallanah did anything else, she knew that she would first have to speak with her computer teacher.

Reviewing How It's Done

You've now seen how three young people who had never volunteered before got started. All of them wanted to do something they were interested in. Annie wanted to use her baking talents and found out about the Great American Bake Sale by talking with her mother. Miguel's teacher found out about an organization that helps build houses. Miguel did research on the organization and the work it does. Now he will be able to help build a house! Lee went to the library. There, he looked up projects on the Internet that interested him. All of these students had to do research and contact people and organizations.

Look at the chart below. It shows the steps to take to start helping others. If you're unsure about any part of the process, you can always refer back to the chart to refresh your memory.

Seven Steps To Get Started on Helping Others

1. Identify my interests and talents.

2. Talk to other people.

3. Find out what is happening in my community.

4. Find out about needs in my community.

5. Research projects and organizations.

6. Contact people to get involved.

7. Get started!

Money can certainly come in handy. But think about the young people you read about earlier in the book. They made a big difference by using resources that everyone has: time, desire, willingness, good ideas, and hard work.

What are some resources you could use to help other people?

What are your special talents?

A resource can also be something like a special talent or interest. Are you a great dog trainer with a well-behaved dog? Perhaps you and your dog could pay a weekly visit to a senior care facility. You and your dog could help a lonely senior to begin to open up, like a butterfly that is set to emerge from a cocoon.

If you are very interested in something special, you can become an expert on the topic. Being an expert can make you a resource for others. Are you a computer whiz? Try tutoring people who don't know a lot about computers. Are you an artist? Maybe some of the things you've sketched could become a mural for your school.

Some people think they don't have special talents or interests that can help other people. Sondra Clark disagrees. Sondra is a young author who has received many national awards for helping other people. She believes everyone can do something to make others feel good.

In order to help on the project, Lee needed to call the person responsible for organizing the volunteer collectors. This made Lee nervous. He decided to go home and ask his parents what to do.

When Lee got home, he thought about waiting for another day to make the phone call. Then he remembered that it takes courage to make a difference. Lee asked his mom's permission to call. She said it was OK, and together they practiced what he would say.

Lee's nervousness ended as soon as he called. The person he talked to was very happy to hear from him! She invited him to a meeting to learn more and to help clean caterpillar collection jars. The jars' lids had been left unscrewed, so they had to be cleaned.

8

17

The next day, Lee went to the library to continue his research. The librarian told him about an organization called Youth Service America. This organization sponsors National Youth Service Day, a special day when students work together to make a contribution in their communities.

Lee visited the organization's Web site on the library computer. The site instructed Lee to type in his zip code. When Lee did the site showed him what projects were happening in his area.

Lee, who is very interested in animals and the environment, saw three activities scheduled for the spring. One project involved collecting caterpillars for a scientist who is trying to figure out why many butterflies are disappearing. It looked perfect for Lee!

By logging on to a Web site, Lee found an interesting project that involved finding caterpillars (like the one shown below) and cleaning jars (like the ones shown to the right).

For Sondra it started when she entered an essay-writing contest. In her essay, Sondra described why her dad was great. When she won, she told the contest sponsor to donate the money to charity. The sponsor was so impressed that he asked Sondra to be a young spokesperson for a group dedicated to helping poor and hungry children in foreign countries. Sondra's work helped relieve the suffering of children around the world.

Using Your Special Talents

Every one of your talents and interests can be used to help others and to make a difference in the world. You can use them in many ways.

What you do depends on your personality and how you want to use your talents. Some people like to work closely with only one person. These people might want to be tutors or read to a person who is blind.

Other people might prefer to work with groups. These people might want to start a campaign to fight the disrespect and prejudice among students in schools. Others might like to organize a drive to collect food or blankets for people in need.

The chart on page 11 shows some activities that you can do to help others. These activities all help other people. They also require your time and effort. Can you think of any others?

Think about whether you want to work with an individual or a group. Are you interested in helping people by teaching them something? Maybe you would prefer to use your time fundraising or collecting items.

Lee Helps Out

Lee is having a hard time deciding on a project. He has so many interests that it is hard for him to choose.

Annie told Lee to check out two Web sites. The first site was for a program called Make a Difference Day. Lee found a page called "Project Ideas" and took a quiz. The quiz had Lee answer questions about whether he wanted to work alone or with a group. Lee answered questions about his skills and interests and filled in some boxes about things his community needs.

When Lee submitted his answers, more than a dozen project ideas came up on the screen. Lee liked three of them, but he wanted to look for more ideas.

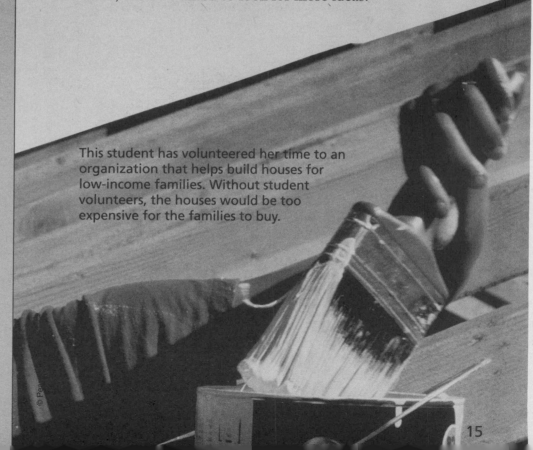

This student has volunteered her time to an organization that helps build houses for low-income families. Without student volunteers, the houses would be too expensive for the families to buy.

Miguel Helps Out

Meanwhile, Annie's friend Miguel has decided to work on a different project. Miguel's family came to the United States from Mexico. His parents have told him about the hardships they faced as migrant workers and how difficult it was to not have a permanent home.

Miguel's teacher told him about an organization that helps build houses for low-income families. Miguel did a lot of research at the organization's Web site. He talked with people at the organization and asked former volunteers questions about the work they did. This summer, through the organization, Miguel is going to help a family of migrant workers build a house!

Education (Helps people learn and understand new things)	Donations (Provides needed items to people who might not have them)	Political (Influences decision-makers and leaders)	Social (Helps solve a problem in our society)
Volunteer to be a guide for a special event in your town.	Collect cans and bottles. Donate the proceeds to a childcare center.	Write a letter to your state senator about something you think should be done to make people's lives better in your state.	Volunteer to help build a park in a part of town where children don't have a place to play.
Create a Web site about an important topic that lots of people are interested in.	Contact local businesses for holiday gift donations for less fortunate children.	Organize a petition drive to tell city officials about things you'd like to change.	Start a school newspaper with kids' stories and artwork.
Volunteer to read at your library's preschool story time.	Join a national walk-a-thon to raise money for a good cause.	Take a poll of your classmates to find out what kinds of problems you could help them solve.	Contact a high-school student organization to see if you can work together on a project.

Getting Started on Helping Others

There are lots of fun and interesting ways to help others. But how do you get started?

The first step is to talk to your parents and other adults, along with your friends. Ask about what is going on in your school and community. Talking with people will also make your activity more fun. When people see how excited you are about helping others, they might want to join you. Then you can share the work and satisfaction.

Once you get an idea of what needs to be done, you'll have to decide whether you want to join a group or start your own.

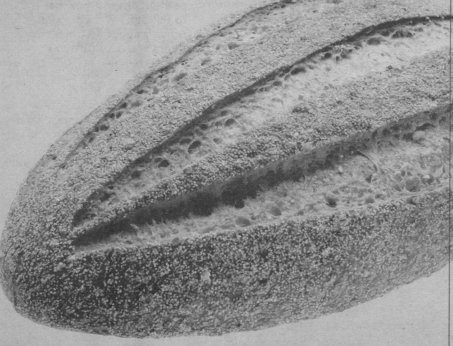

The Great American Bake Sale is an organization that helps arrange bake sales for people who want to fight hunger in the United States. By selling baked goods like the ones shown here, these sales have raised $1.5 million to help feed hungry Americans.

Annie Helps Out

For some ideas on how to get started, let's follow four friends while they choose their first projects. Meet Annie, Miguel, Lee, and Hallanah.

Annie is a great cook. She hopes she will be able to put her talent for cooking to work someday.

A few weeks ago, Annie's mother showed her an article about kids having a bake sale. A national organization called The Great American Bake Sale had helped the kids get set up. The kids raised money to fight child hunger.

Annie liked the idea that her baking could help fight hunger in our country! She is now logging onto the Great American Bake Sale Web site to find out how to join in.

Social Studies   Social Studies

Holocaust Rescuers

by Gretchen McBride

Genre	Comprehension Skill and Strategy	Text Features
Nonfiction	• Author's Purpose • Monitor and Fix Up	• Headings • Captions • Glossary • Cutaway Diagram

Scott Foresman Reading Street 5.2.2

PEARSON

Scott
Foresman

ISBN 0-328-13521-6

90000

9 780328 135219

Reader Response

1. Why do you think the author included information about the *Kindertransport*? Use a graphic organizer like the one below to identify words you thought of when you read about *Kindertransport*.

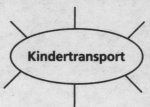

Kindertransport

2. Raoul Wallenberg is remembered for saving the lives of thousands of Jewish people. He is described on page 17 as having used "any means he could" to save their lives. What methods did he use? Why might it have been unusual for a diplomat to use them?

3. Choose three words from the glossary that you did not know the meanings of before reading the book. Write each word in an interesting sentence.

4. Which photo captures your attention more than the others? Why?

Glossary

agreement *n.* harmony in feeling and opinion.

cable *n.* a message sent through wires by electric current or electronic signals.

diplomat *n.* someone who manages the relations between his or her nation and other nations.

issue *v.* to send out; put forth.

refugees *n.* people who flee for refuge or safety.

representatives *n.* people appointed or elected to speak for others.

superiors *n.* people of higher position, rank, or ability.

visa *n.* an official signature or endorsement upon a passport.

Holocaust Rescuers

by Gretchen McBride

PEARSON
Scott Foresman

Editorial Offices: Glenview, Illinois • Parsippany, New Jersey • New York, New York
Sales Offices: Needham, Massachusetts • Duluth, Georgia • Glenview, Illinois
Coppell, Texas • Ontario, California • Mesa, Arizona

This Holocaust memorial sculpture (below) is located in Berlin, Germany.

Remembering: Yad Vashem

The Hebrew phrase *yad vashem* can be translated as "an everlasting name." The Israeli government founded Yad Vashem to help preserve the memory of Holocaust victims. The organization is in charge of many museums, libraries, memorials, and monuments. Yad Vashem's Avenue and Garden of the Righteous Among the Nations, in Jerusalem, Israel, honors the non-Jewish people who risked their own lives to save Jews during the Holocaust.

The Hall of Remembrance (below) is found in the Holocaust Memorial Museum in Washington, D.C.

Adolf Hitler, shown here in this calendar, ruled Germany from 1933–1945.

Campaign of Hate

Adolf Hitler seized power in Germany in 1933. He died in 1945. From 1933–1945, he carried out a brutal plan to eliminate Europe's Jewish people. Hitler and his Nazi Party claimed that Jews were an "inferior race." He convinced many Germans that the Jews were responsible for Germany's economic problems.

Hitler was able to spread his message of hate by holding huge rallies and giving speeches on the radio. Radio provided an inexpensive way to reach millions of people. Still, there were many people who refused to believe Hitler and the Nazi Party's lies. Some of those people tried to save Jewish people from the certain death that awaited them at Nazi concentration camps.

The Holocaust

Holocaust means complete destruction by fire. The word is used today to describe the Nazis' plan to wipe out Europe's Jews.

About six million people died in the Holocaust. Among the victims were people of many different beliefs and backgrounds. However most of those killed were Jewish. The Holocaust destroyed lives, families, and whole villages. It came close to ending Jewish life and culture throughout all of Europe.

The Jewish population was *concentrated*, or brought together in one place, at camps such as the one above.

A Jewish family from Denmark shares Christmas dinner with a Christian family in Sweden. The Danes saved approximately seven thousand Jewish people during World War II.

The Danes

The Nazis occupied Denmark during most of World War II. Despite the occupation, many Danes refused to help the Nazis murder the Jews. A courageous German diplomat, Georg Ferdinand Duckwitz, secretly told the Danes that the Nazis were about to deport all of the Jewish citizens of Denmark. The Danes acted quickly. They hid some Jewish people. They helped others leave the country. For two weeks, Danish fishermen ferried Jewish people across the water to Sweden. Almost every Dane helped in this effort. More than seven thousand Jewish Danes were saved.

Georg Ferdinand Duckwitz

This Danish fishing boat was used to rescue Jewish refugees. It is on display at the Holocaust Memorial Museum in Washington, D.C.

Did people know?

Life became harder for the Jewish people as soon as Hitler took power. Many were taken from their homes and forced into ghettos. These ghettos were areas of cities cut off from the rest of the people. The ghettos were crowded and dirty. The Jewish people were not allowed to leave them. But soon the Nazis came up with a "final solution" to the "Jewish question." They sent the Jewish people to concentration camps to be killed.

People in the United States suspected that something was happening to the Jewish people in Europe. But there was no proof of the Holocaust until 1942. In that year the United States government received a cable from representatives of the World Jewish Congress in Switzerland. The cable revealed that Hitler was planning to kill millions of Jewish people in Europe.

American President Franklin Roosevelt learned about the Holocaust in 1942.

You might be wondering why the Jews did not leave as soon as Hitler took power. There are several reasons. First, they had no idea of the horror that was to come. The Nazis kept their plans secret. That helped prevent the Jews from fighting back. Most people did not want to leave their homes. It is scary to leave everything behind in order to start a new life somewhere else. The Jewish people did not want to be refugees. However, as things got worse, many of them tried to get out of Europe.

Symbols of the Jewish faith such as these were destroyed wherever the Nazis went.

© Pearson Education, Inc.

In January 1945 the Nazis planned to kill the last remaining Jews of Budapest's largest Jewish ghetto. At this point, it was clear that Germany would be defeated. Raoul Wallenberg threatened the general who had been ordered to carry out the killings. Wallenberg said that if the order were carried out, he would have the general executed as a war criminal following Germany's defeat. Thanks to Wallenberg's brave threats, the people of the ghetto were saved at the last minute.

When the Soviet troops marched into Hungary, Wallenberg asked permission to visit their military headquarters. He was never seen again. Wallenberg's fate is unknown. Nevertheless this courageous man was able to save as many as 100,000 Jewish people from the Nazi concentration camps.

The Nazis transported people to concentration camps on freight trains such as this one.

The Nazis would fill train cars with Jewish people to take them away to concentration camps. Wallenberg climbed onto the tops of the train cars and passed protective passes to the people inside them. He then would jump to the ground and demand that the people with passes be released. The guards had orders from their superiors to shoot Wallenberg. But they were so impressed by his amazing courage that they allowed him to escape unharmed.

It was not easy for the Jews to leave. Jewish families often had to leave their money behind when they left. The Nazis stamped Jews' passports with the letter "J" so they would be questioned by other countries' officials. Jews also needed a visa. A visa is a pass that allows people to enter a country. Many countries would issue only a few visas per year.

Did non-Jewish Europeans know what was happening to their Jewish friends and neighbors? Many people did not know how bad the situation was. Others knew that terrible things were happening but did nothing to help. Still, there were a few very brave people who did what they could to help the Jewish people. You will learn about some of those people later in this book.

The Nazis forced the Jewish people to wear the Star of David on their clothing so everyone could tell that they were Jews.

Into Hiding

A small number of Jewish people went into hiding in Germany and the other countries that the Nazis took over. Of them a young girl named Anne Frank became the most famous. You may have read *The Diary of Anne Frank*. It tells the story of Frank's years spent hiding in a Dutch family's attic. The Nazis found Anne and her family. She did not survive.

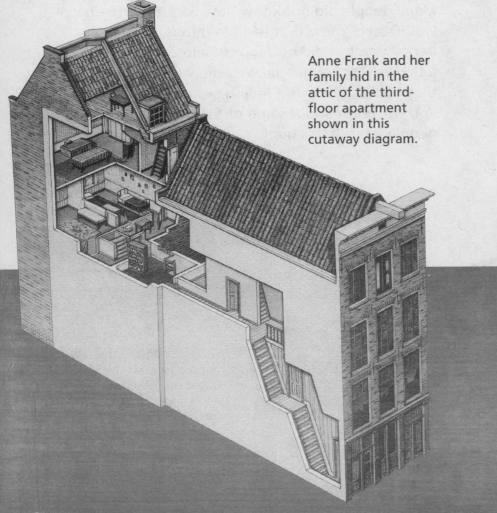

Anne Frank and her family hid in the attic of the third-floor apartment shown in this cutaway diagram.

At the time, the Nazis were losing control of Hungary to the Russian army. The Russians were taking over very quickly. So the Nazis worked as fast as they could to deport Hungary's Jews to concentration camps. Raoul Wallenberg felt there was no time to follow the usual rules of diplomacy. He used any means he could to save Jewish people.

The people who worked under Wallenberg issued thousands of protective passes. Wallenberg also had "Swedish houses" built in the city. He used his position to declare the houses Swedish territory. Jews were safe at the "Swedish houses" because Sweden, like Switzerland, was neutral. That meant it wasn't involved in the war. Soon diplomats from other neutral countries followed Wallenberg's example.

Jewish people going to one of Wallenberg's "Swedish houses" in Budapest

Raoul Wallenberg, Heroic Diplomat

More than anyone else, Raoul Wallenberg is remembered for having saved Jewish people from the Holocaust. Wallenberg was born in in Sweden in 1912. He came from a wealthy family. In 1935 he graduated from the University of Michigan with a degree in architecture. Wallenberg had difficulty finding architectural work in Sweden. So he went to work in Palestine (now Israel). There he met Jews who had escaped from Nazi Germany.

In 1944 the United States established the War Refugee Board (WRB) to help save Jewish people. The WRB's representative in Sweden brought together a group of people who wanted to organize a rescue mission in Budapest, Hungary. The group asked Wallenberg (now a diplomat) to lead the rescue mission. He accepted.

Raoul Wallenberg

There were other Jewish children and adults who were hidden by non-Jewish people. Jews were hidden in attics, cellars, and other places. The people who hid them shared their own food, which during the war was often hard to find.

Some Jewish people tried to "hide in plain sight." This meant they continued to go out in public. However, they hid their Jewish identity. They removed the yellow Star of David that the Nazis made them wear. By doing so they hoped to blend in more. But as "illegals" they could not buy food. This caused many Jewish people to starve to death. Many of those that hid were captured and killed. Often the people who protected them were also killed. And yet some Jewish people escaped because brave people helped them.

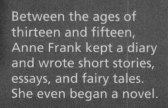

Between the ages of thirteen and fifteen, Anne Frank kept a diary and wrote short stories, essays, and fairy tales. She even began a novel.

Kristallnacht opened the world's eyes to the horror unfolding in Nazi Germany.

Kindertransport: Children's Transport

November 9, 1938, was a turning point for Nazi Germany. On that night the Nazis smashed the windows of Jewish homes and businesses throughout Germany. That night is now known as *Kristallnacht* (KRIS-tahl-nahkt). In English it means the "Night of Broken Glass." *Kristallnacht* alerted the world to the danger facing the Jews of Europe. People realized that something had to be done to help the Jewish children trapped in Germany.

After *Kristallnacht*, groups in Britain asked their government to change the laws so that more Jewish children from Germany could enter the country. The British government responded by issuing visas for ten thousand children. Seventy-five hundred of the visas were for Jewish children.

responded by allowing Jews to hide in their homes. Other Jews were given shelter by Catholic Christians in Catholic buildings near the village. The villagers also helped some Jews obtain fake visas to enter Switzerland. Switzerland was not involved in the war. That made it safer for Jews to live there.

The people of Le Chambon-sur-Lignon did not feel that they were doing anything heroic. They simply made an agreement with Pastor Trocme to do the right thing. In doing so, they helped almost five thousand Jewish people survive the Holocaust.

A postcard from 1942 (left) showing a children's home in Le Chambon-sur-Lignon.

Refugee children with their guardian (below) outside of a children's home in Le Chambon-sur-Lignon.

Le Chambon-sur-Lignon

The French village of Le Chambon-sur-Lignon (ler shahm-BOHN ser lin-YOHN) gave shelter to Jews during the war. The people of the village were mainly Protestant Christians. This made them a minority in France, where most people were Catholic Christians. As minorities the Protestants sympathized with the Jews and wanted to help them.

Andre Trocme, a church pastor, urged the people to give aid to their Jewish neighbors. The people

The *Kindertransport* saved many Jewish children from certain death.

Children who were homeless, orphaned, or had parents in concentration camps were the first to get visas. But only children who had found people to pay their living costs in Britain were issued visas. The rescue effort was called *Kindertransport*. The word meant "children's transport."

The children traveled by train and then by ship to Britain. Upon arriving in Britain some went to live with foster families. Others were housed in hotels and on farms. The rescuers who organized the *Kindertransport* hoped that the children would rejoin their parents after the war. But when the war ended an awful truth was revealed. Almost all of their parents had died in concentration camps. After the war the children became citizens of Great Britain, Israel, the United States, Canada, and Australia.

Emergency Rescue Committee: Varian Fry

In 1940 a group of New Yorkers formed the Emergency Rescue Committee (ERC). The ERC was concerned about the safety of Jewish writers, artists, and educators. Many of them had fled to France before the war. But then the Nazis conquered most of France in May 1940. The Nazis' control of France placed these Jews in danger. The ERC responded by deciding to try a secret rescue mission.

The journalist Varian Fry was sent by the ERC to Marseille (mahr-SAY). Marseille was located in a part of France that the Germans had left alone. Fry opened an office in Marseille. He pretended that he was running a charity. In reality Fry used the office to help Jewish people escape to safety. The French government soon became suspicious of Fry. They made him leave France in 1941. But in just thirteen months, Varian Fry had helped over two thousand people leave Nazi-occupied France. Among them were some of the most famous artists and thinkers of the twentieth century.

"All of his hearers were greatly interested and impressed by what he said. . . . It is evident that Mr. Fry is exceptionally well informed regarding the France of today and the most prominent Frenchmen. Mr. Fry has a good voice and a pleasant delivery."

—ROBERT ERSKINE ELY, *Executive Director, The Economic Club of New York*

"Immediately after his return from France, Mr. Fry spoke at several Foreign Policy Association meetings. He was uniformly enthusiastically received by the audience. His sincerity and effective platform manner combine to make him an excellent speaker."

—FRANCES J. PRATT, *Director, Speakers Bureau, Foreign Policy Association*

© Fabian Bachrach

VARIAN FRY

Fifteen Months in France and Portugal
European Director, Emergency Rescue Committee

—LECTURES—

FRANCE UNDER PETAIN

AFTER THE WAR, WHAT?

AMERICA'S FOREIGN POLICY TOWARD FRANCE

WANTED BY THE GESTAPO
Rescuing Refugees in France, Spain and Portugal

© Pearson Education, Inc.

Varian Fry (above) saved almost two thousand Jews during World War II by setting up a pretend charity fund in Marseille, France (left).

While under the patronage of the Medicis, Michelangelo blossomed as a sculptor. He studied the family's collection of statues from ancient Rome to learn more about sculpture. The sculptor Bertoldo, a friend of the Medicis, taught Michelangelo during this time.

The Medicis' money did more than assist artists such as Michelangelo. It helped the family become the rulers of Florence. However, in 1494 the Medicis were overthrown by a rival, a priest named Savonarola.

Savonarola created a serious problem for Michelangelo. The powerful priest hated the art of the Renaissance, feeling that it made people less devoted to religion.

Michelangelo left Florence when Savonarola rose to power. After a brief stay in Bologna, he moved to Rome. There he was able to study the ruins of the ancient Romans. The ruins inspired him to carve *Bacchus* in 1497. It was his first large-scale sculpture.

St. Peter's Basilica in Rome

Ancient ruins in Rome

Donatello's *David*

Detail of Lorenzo de Medici, from the *Tomb of Lorenzo de' Medici* by Michelangelo

Painting of Lorenzo de Medici, patron of the arts

MICHELANGELO: THE SCULPTOR

Michelangelo was supposed to study with Ghirlandaio for three years. But he left after just one year. One source says this was because the young artist had "nothing left to learn."

As talented as he was, Michelangelo still needed other people to support him. So he went to study sculpture with financial assistance from Lorenzo de Medici, head of the Medici family.

The Medicis were one of Italy's wealthiest families. They used some of their fortune to fund talented artists such as Michelangelo. They helped create the system of *patronage*. Under this system, wealthy families sponsored promising young artists. Patronage led to the creation of some of the Renaissance's most famous sculptures, paintings, buildings, and works of literature.

MICHELANGELO: THE STUDENT

Michelangelo is one of the most famous Renaissance artists. He was born in 1475 near Florence, Italy, to a family of bankers. Michelangelo was interested in art from an early age. When he turned thirteen, Michelangelo went to study with Ghirlandaio, Florence's greatest artist of the time. Michelangelo studied the art of the fresco. This method of painting on wet plaster became popular during the Renaissance.

Ghirlandaio's *Madonna della Misericordia*

Michelangelo's *Persian Sybil,* from the Sistine Chapel Fresco Series

DONATELLO

Like Michelangelo, Donatello achieved fame for the statues he sculpted out of marble and bronze. Also like Michelangelo, Donatello was born in Florence and worked there. He, too, worked for the Medicis.

Donatello was born in Florence around 1386. His career as a sculptor began around 1400 when he first learned stone carving. His teachers might have been sculptors who were then working on Florence's main church. Around 1405 Donatello found work as a sculptor in the workshop of the artist Lorenzo Ghiberti. Ghiberti influenced some of Donatello's early sculptures.

In contrast to Michelangelo's art, Donatello's work showed a closer connection to the religious art of the later Middle Ages. Donatello specialized in statues of saints. Like Michelangelo, Donatello was famous for his statue of the biblical hero David. But Michelangelo's *David* was carved out of marble, and Donatello fashioned his out of bronze.

Donatello died in 1466. Although he did not achieve fame as an architect and painter, as Michelangelo did, he is remembered as one of the Renaissance's great artists because of his wonderful sculptures.

RAPHAEL

Unlike Michelangelo and Donatello, Raphael never worked as a sculptor. He spent some time in Florence and was influenced by its artists, but he was not born there.

Raphael was born in Urbino in the year 1483. By that time Urbino had become a center of the Italian Renaissance. Raphael's father, a painter, died when Raphael was only eleven. But before he died he was able to teach Raphael some things about painting.

By 1500 Raphael had moved to the city of Perugia, where he painted the inside of churches. Raphael's work attracted a lot of attention. At the age of fifteen he was already being called a "master."

In 1504 Raphael moved to Florence. There he studied the works of Michelangelo. Later on, when Raphael moved to Rome to paint frescoes in the private rooms of the Sistine Chapel, he became a rival of Michelangelo's.

Raphael's most famous work is *The School of Athens.* The painting, which is one of the frescoes he painted for the Sistine Chapel, depicts some of the greatest ancient philosophers, including Plato and Aristotle.

THE ITALIAN RENAISSANCE

The ideas and styles of the Renaissance spread all over Europe. The Renaissance had a major impact in England, France, and Germany. But it had the greatest influence in Italy.

Not only did the Renaissance have the greatest influence in Italy, but it also began there. As the birthplace and heart of ancient Rome, it made sense that Italy should be where the Renaissance first took hold. The palaces, public buildings, and cemeteries of Italy were filled with art and architecture created by the ancient Romans. Italians who were interested in learning more about the culture and history of ancient Rome could look to these artifacts. They inspired great Renaissance artists, such as Donatello, Michelangelo, Raphael, and da Vinci.

These artists, using the works of the ancient Romans for guidance, shifted the focus of art away from religion. Their paintings were less about religious teachings and more about the emotions and drama of everyday human life. Historians now use the term *humanism* to describe this style of art.

A room in Florence, Italy. The Italian Renaissance was based in Florence.

6

The School of Athens by Raphael

19

LEONARDO DA VINCI

Michelangelo, Donatello, and Raphael were all great artists of the Renaissance. But none of them came to represent the Renaissance the way Leonardo da Vinci does. For many people, da Vinci *is* the Renaissance.

As a painter, da Vinci was one of the first Italian artists to experiment with oil paints instead of egg-based paints. Using oil paints allowed artists to layer colors and to cover mistakes. Leonardo created the famous *Mona Lisa*, which still attracts many visitors to the Louvre museum in Paris, France. Da Vinci also worked with the fresco method. His painting *The Last Supper* is one of the most famous frescoes in history.

Da Vinci was fascinated with the natural world. He had a passion for science and anatomy, and he studied the human body. His interest in science inspired his work as an artist, writer, philosopher, and inventor. Leonardo studied the nature of water, animals, and plants. He was especially interested in horses.

Leonardo da Vinci died almost four centuries ago. Like Michelangelo, Donatello, and Raphael, da Vinci was a great artist. Unlike the others, da Vinci is also well known for his achievements outside the arts.

The Parthenon in Greece and the Coliseum in Rome are examples of architecture that influenced the Renaissance.

THE CHANGE BEGINS: THE END OF THE MIDDLE AGES

With this new focus and organization, life in Europe seemed calmer toward the end of the Middle Ages. This improvement led to a major change in peoples' attitudes about what was important in life. During the Middle Ages, people focused more on religion, partly because it promised that their suffering would end. But with life in Europe getting better, people began looking to other things beside the Church.

Religion continued to play an important role in European life long after the Middle Ages ended. However, at the end of the Middle Ages, artists and scholars began to look back to ancient Greece and Rome for ideas. They felt that they had much to learn from everything that the Greeks and Romans had achieved. Interest in the work of Greek and Roman thinkers, writers, and artists fueled an explosion of new thinking.

BEFORE THE CHANGE: THE MIDDLE AGES

Every period in human history is influenced by the attitudes and ideas of the time that came before it. The Renaissance was no exception. In European history the time before the Renaissance is called the Middle Ages.

The Middle Ages began around A.D. 500, after the fall of the Roman Empire. After the Empire collapsed Europe was plunged into a period of disorder.

The Roman Catholic Church responded to the disorder by becoming the new authority in people's lives. Its rules helped create stability. Its teachings gave people comfort. And its celebrations brought joy.

Artists and writers reacted to the Church's new role by focusing their works on religion. The great thinkers of the Middle Ages devoted their time to studying Church history and to teaching about its faith.

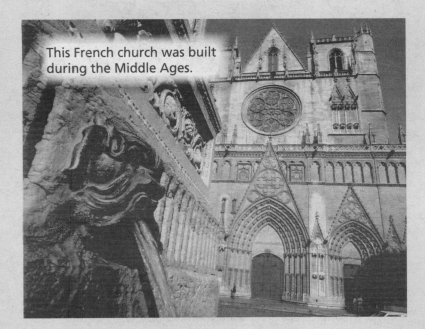

This French church was built during the Middle Ages.

Da Vinci's *Mona Lisa*

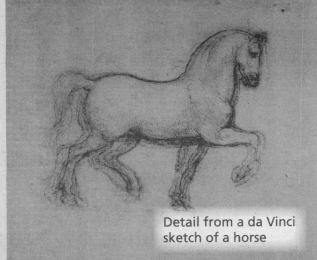

Detail from a da Vinci sketch of a horse

WRITERS OF THE RENAISSANCE

The great writers of the Renaissance, like the great artists of that time, looked to ancient Greece and Rome for their inspiration. The poet Petrarch wrote romantic poems called sonnets to celebrate the great love of his life. One of Petrarch's friends, Boccaccio, is known as one of the Renaissance's great storytellers. His most famous work, the *Decameron*, is a collection of tales from the time of the plague called the Black Death. The Black Death was a deadly illness that killed many people during the Middle Ages.

Petrarch, Renaissance poet

Has anything ever happened to you to make you change your mind? Between the years 1300 and 1600, things happened that caused many European artists, philosophers, architects, and scientists to change their minds dramatically. Historians now describe those events and the changes they caused as "the Renaissance."

The new ways of thinking during the time of the Renaissance changed life in Europe. The changes were seen in architecture and poetry. In the sciences, too, people such as Galileo (pictured below on the right) caused many people to question their beliefs about humanity and the universe. Art was another area of great impact and change. Renaissance artists such as Michaelangelo changed the world with their art!

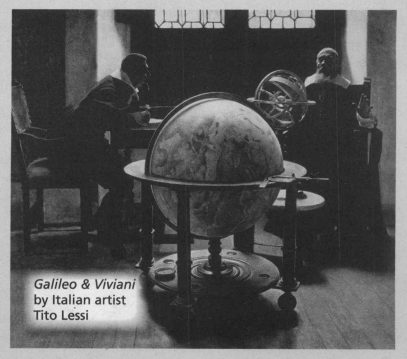

Galileo & Viviani by Italian artist Tito Lessi

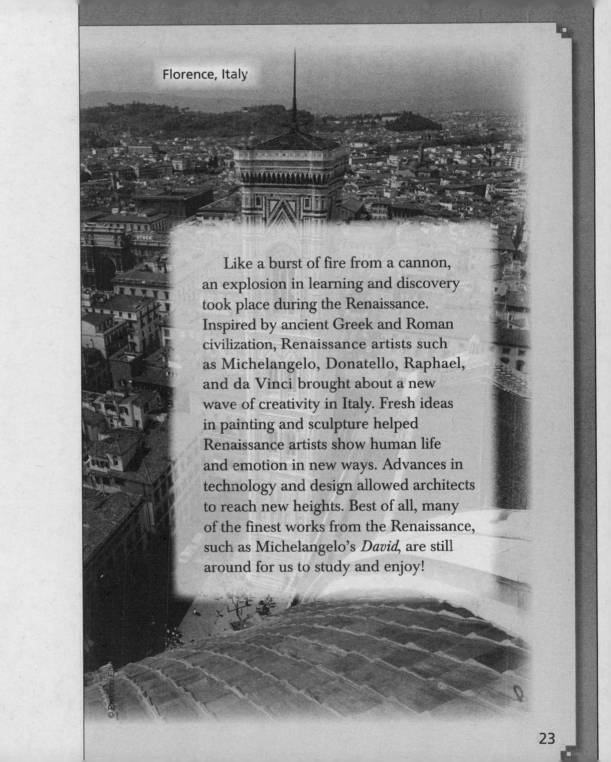

Florence, Italy

Like a burst of fire from a cannon, an explosion in learning and discovery took place during the Renaissance. Inspired by ancient Greek and Roman civilization, Renaissance artists such as Michelangelo, Donatello, Raphael, and da Vinci brought about a new wave of creativity in Italy. Fresh ideas in painting and sculpture helped Renaissance artists show human life and emotion in new ways. Advances in technology and design allowed architects to reach new heights. Best of all, many of the finest works from the Renaissance, such as Michelangelo's *David*, are still around for us to study and enjoy!

Glossary

achieved *v.* accomplished something.

architect *n.* someone who designs and makes plans for buildings.

bronze *n.* type of metal made by combining copper and tin.

cannon *n.* big gun, especially one that is mounted on a base or wheels.

depressed *adj.* very gloomy or sad.

fashioned *v.* made something.

midst *n.* the middle of something.

philosopher *n.* person who seeks wisdom by observing the world and asking questions.

rival *n.* person who attempts to do better than someone else at the same task.

Michelangelo *and* The Italian Renaissance

by Liz Murray

PEARSON

Scott Foresman

Editorial Offices: Glenview, Illinois • Parsippany, New Jersey • New York, New York
Sales Offices: Needham, Massachusetts • Duluth, Georgia • Glenview, Illinois
Coppell, Texas • Ontario, California • Mesa, Arizona

Reader Response

1. What is the main idea discussed on page 13? Using a graphic organizer like the one below, write down the main idea of page 13, along with supporting details.

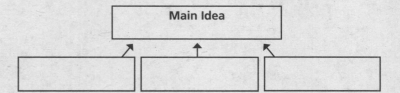

2. Write a paragraph summarizing the kinds of materials Michelanelo used to create his art during his career.

3. *Depressed* is formed from the prefix *de-* and the word *pressed*. Can you think of other words that are made by combining the word *pressed* with a prefix? Write them down on a separate piece of paper and use a dictionary to list their definitions.

4. The style of Renaissance art called *humanism* is described on page 7. Which one of the images in this book do you think best displays this style? Why?

Social Studies

Social Studies

Michelangelo *and* The Italian Renaissance

by Liz Murray

Genre	Comprehension Skill and Strategy	Text Features
Nonfiction	• Main Idea • Summarize	• Captions • Labels • Glossary

Scott Foresman Reading Street 5.3.2

PEARSON

Scott
Foresman

ISBN 0-328-13536-4

90000

9 780328 135363

scottforesman.com

Following the achievements of Curtiss and the Wright brothers, airplanes began to change American society. Some people started going to air shows to see airplane stunt pilots perform exciting and entertaining feats while flying. Others thought about designing airplanes that the public could travel in. The age of aviation had begun.

Then, in 1914, World War I began. Airplane designers scrambled to design warplanes for the warring countries. Both the Allied Powers (consisting of England, France, Russia, Italy, and the United States) and the Central Powers (made up of Germany, Austria-Hungary, and Turkey) used planes to spy on enemy territory and gain information about troops and weapons. Military leaders used their countries' air forces to help plan attacks.

World War I military leaders also started using airplanes, such as bombers, in their attacks. The first bombers were small and could only carry grenades and other light bombs. Soon, however, both sides were building bigger planes that carried larger loads of bombs. But bombers had a fierce foe in the sky: fighter planes.

The first fighter planes were simple military planes loaded with large guns. The pilot fired the guns from within the cockpit. Airplane designers soon improved the designs of fighter planes, building aircraft that carried machine guns mounted in front of the pilot. A special gear allowed the guns to fire in between the planes' spinning propeller blades.

Thousands of feet in the air, enemy planes battled in "dogfights." They circled, chased, and dodged each other. To gain the upper hand, they swooped down on or snuck up behind the enemy. Some pilots were able to shoot down five or more planes. One German ace, known as the "Red Baron" because of his red plane, shot down eighty Allied planes before he was shot down himself in 1918.

The British Sopwith Camel was one of the legendary fighter planes of World War I.

Chapter 4 *The Many Uses of Airplanes*

World War I ended in 1918. In the years that followed, aviation became even more popular as the improvements made to airplane designs during the war were applied to peacetime aircraft.

With the war over, there was a reduced need for pilots, but many wanted to keep flying. The United States military helped these pilots by selling warplanes, minus their weapons, for low prices. Many pilots bought their own planes and traveled from town to town putting on air shows. Called "barnstormers," those daring fliers performed breathtaking stunts such as dips, loops, and rolls.

Barnstormers thrilled the American public in the years following World War I by putting on incredible flying displays.

Chapter 3 *Early Airplanes and War*

Several months after the Wright brothers demonstrated their airplane, Glenn Curtiss won a trophy for making the first successful airplane flight in front of the public (remember that the Wright brothers had conducted their flights in secret). Curtiss's one-mile flight in the *June Bug* appeared on the cover of newspapers and in newsreels. During that time, airplanes also made big news in Europe, where pilots competed for flying "firsts."

Glenn Curtiss and the Wright brothers were rivals. This photo shows Curtiss's airplane, the *June Bug*.

The Wright brothers continued to improve their airplane. Over the next few years, they flew hundreds of trips. Some lasted for more than twenty miles. Afraid that a scoundrel would steal their ideas, the Wrights made their flights in secret. Finally, in 1908, they demonstrated their airplane to the U.S. Army. By then, other inventors in the United States and Europe were trying their hands at building their own airplanes.

The stunning feats of the barnstormers fascinated Americans. When the barnstormers weren't putting on flying shows, they competed in air races for world records, personal glory, and cash prizes.

Of all those pilots, people looked most admiringly upon Charles Lindbergh. He was known as "Lucky Lindy" because he survived several airplane crashes. Lindbergh wanted to be the first person to fly solo across the Atlantic Ocean. He began by taking off from New York City on May 20, 1927, in his famous plane, the *Spirit of St. Louis*.

Lindbergh battled storms, fog, cold, and sleepiness during his flight. A little more than thirty-three hours later, he landed in Paris and was greeted by cheering crowds. Overnight, Lindbergh became an international hero.

Amelia Earhart earned the nickname "Lady Lindy" for being the first woman to fly across the Atlantic Ocean. She showed the world that women could fly planes too.

Amelia Earhart was a pioneer among female pilots.

Soon people realized that airplanes could be used for more than barnstorming shows and record-setting flight attempts. On May 15, 1918, a full six months before the end of World War I, pilots hired by the U.S. Postal Service began flying mail between New York City and Washington, D.C. Demand was so great that within months, the post office expanded service to include the entire country.

The DC-3 began carrying regular passengers in 1936. About one thousand DC-3s still fly today.

Orville Wright flew into history on December 17, 1903, by piloting the *Flyer*.

Orville's brother, Wilbur, gave the *Flyer* the push it needed to take to the skies.

Chapter 2 *The Wright Brothers*

Europeans were not the only people inventing flying machines. In the United States, Orville and Wilbur Wright also set their sights on taking to the skies. The Wright brothers had been interested in flying since they were young. As adults, they owned a bicycle shop. Building and repairing bicycles helped them learn how to design machines.

By the late 1890s, after having studied gliders and aeronautics, the Wright brothers started work on an airplane. They designed and tested wings, propellers, and ways to control the aircraft. Not all of their tests worked. But they learned something from everything they tried, ensuring that none of their experiments were worthless.

By late 1903, the Wright brothers' airplane, which they named the *Flyer*, was ready. Powered by a small gasoline engine, the *Flyer* had two sets of wings and propellers, and two movable rudders. These devices worked together to permit the pilot to control the plane.

On December 17, 1903, at Kitty Hawk, North Carolina, Orville lay on the *Flyer*'s lower wing while Wilbur pushed the plane along a track. Wilbur watched as the *Flyer* rose into the air. Twelve seconds and 120 feet later, Orville set the plane down safely. The Wrights had just completed the world's first controlled airplane flight!

In the mid-1920s, the U.S. Postal Service began hiring private companies to fly the mail. To earn extra money, these companies sometimes sold tickets to passengers, thereby becoming some of the earliest passenger airlines. Early passengers put up with a lot to experience the thrill of flying. They were forced to sit on mailbags and often had to get off the planes to make more space for mail!

Although passenger airlines began during the mid-1920s, the first passenger flight took place a decade earlier in 1914, when a plane flew tourists between Tampa and St. Petersburg in Florida. Still, air travel didn't become popular in the United States until the 1930s. During that decade, airplanes improved dramatically. The newest planes traveled longer distances, carried more passengers, and flew at night.

Because of these changes, airplanes could deliver passengers in safety throughout the country and across Europe. The airlines also made air travel enjoyable. When passengers climbed aboard, flight attendants showed them to comfortable seats and served them food and drinks.

Airmail cut the time taken to deliver mail by almost seventy hours!

German dirigibles were called zeppelins in honor of their inventor Count von Zeppelin. The *Hindenburg* zeppelin, shown here flying over New York City, was the most famous.

While these changes were occurring, inventors were also experimenting with other types of flying machines. By the 1920s, designers had developed the airship. Also called blimps or dirigibles, airships were long, gas-filled balloons that had covered cabins for their passengers and crews. Huge German airships traveled across the Atlantic during the 1920s and 1930s. Passenger airship travel ended in 1937, however, when the *Hindenburg* exploded as it tried to land at a docking station in Lakehurst, New Jersey.

Flying boats were also popular in the 1930s. They had regular wings, but their bodies were shaped like the hull of a ship. They landed and took off at sea. As airlines and airports improved, airlines stopped using flying boats.

Igor Sikorsky built the first successful helicopter during the 1930s. Helicopters could fly sideways, backwards, and straight up or down, making them very popular.

One of those inventors was an Englishman named Sir George Cayley. Cayley earned the nickname "Father of Aeronautics" for his studies of the motion of air. He spent much of his life designing gliders. These machines looked similar to modern planes, with wings in front and a tail in the back. In 1853, Cayley tested one of his gliders by sending his chauffeur into the air. Upon landing, the driver quit!

A German named Otto Lilienthal, who was inspired by Cayley's work, designed and built a series of gliders during the 1890s. Lilienthal's gliders looked very similar to the hang gliders of today. Lilienthal tested out his designs by going to the top of a hill, strapping on his cloth-covered wooden wings, and jumping! In this way, Lilienthal "flew" as far as one thousand feet.

Otto Lilienthal, who influenced the Wright brothers, steered his gliders by swinging his legs and shifting his weight.

On November 21, 1783, in the presence of King Louis XVI, Queen Marie Antoinette, Benjamin Franklin, and many a loyal French subject, two men took to the air in a Montgolfier balloon. The flight lasted twenty-five minutes, during which time the balloon traveled five miles and rose three thousand feet into the air. At last, people could fly!

By the end of the 1800s, people were traveling long distances in balloons. Photographers took pictures from ballons, joyriders rode them for pleasure, and armies used them for spying on their enemies.

At the same time, inventors were developing new types of flying machines. In contrast with balloons, these machines were "heavier than air," meaning that they did not use hot air or other gases to keep them aloft.

Chapter 5 *More Warplanes*

By 1939, when World War II broke out, warplanes had advanced. The German air force, known as the *Luftwaffe*, or "air weapon," launched speedy attacks known as *blitzkriegs*, or "lightning wars," that helped Germany conquer most of Europe. As the war progressed, German and Japanese warplanes bombed many areas in Europe and Asia.

During World War II *Luftwaffe* warplanes conducted bombing raids on major European cities such as London, Rotterdam, Warsaw, and Belgrade.

To fight back, Great Britain and the United States built thousands of new fighter planes and bombers. These new warplanes were very different from the ones flown during World War I. Planes now had radios so pilots could coordinate their attacks and warn each other of approaching enemy planes. Another key development was radar. Radar operators told pilots the locations of enemy planes.

Much of World War II took place over the Pacific Ocean. To support planes in the Pacific, huge ships called aircraft carriers were built. Also known as "flattops," they stretched over eight hundred feet long and could carry one hundred aircraft. Planes landed, refueled, and took off from the decks of these floating airfields.

Military planes helped England, the Soviet Union, and the United States defeat Germany and Japan. Bomber attacks deep within Germany caused serious damage to German industry. When two B-29 bombers dropped atomic bombs on Japan in August 1945, the War in the Pacific ended. Airplanes played a key role throughout the war.

A painting showing the launch of the Montgolfiers' hot-air balloon.

Two brothers, Joseph-Michel and Jacques-Etienne Montgolfier, owned a paper factory in France in the late eighteenth century. One day, while experimenting in their factory, they realized that a paper bag rose as it filled with hot air and descended as the air cooled. This discovery inspired the brothers to build a large cloth balloon with a basket underneath. A fire inside the basket heated the air, causing the balloon to rise.

Chapter 1 *Early Dreams and Attempts*

Since the dawn of time, people have dreamed of flying. An ancient Greek myth describes a man who flew through the air on wings made of feathers and candle wax. The ancient Chinese may have attempted to fly using the kites they invented. And during the Middle Ages, people jumped off towers with "wings" made of cloth in unsuccessful attempts to fly!

Despite such early failures, people refused to give up on the idea of human flight. Leonardo da Vinci was one person who did not hesitate in his belief that humans could fly. The great fifteenth-century artist and inventor, after spending hours studying birds in flight, filled his notebooks with sketches of flying machines such as the ornithopter. The pilot was to steer it by moving his head and neck, and power it by flapping its large mechanical wings.

Sadly, da Vinci never built his ornithopter, and over the next few hundred years, little progress was made on flying machines.

Da Vinci filled his notebooks with designs for all kinds of flying machines.

Chapter 6 *Speedy Airplanes*

In the years after World War II, air travel became more common. Because of the war, many countries had new airports, more large planes, and skilled pilots. Planes traveled faster and could fly long distances more easily. The development of the jet engine at the end of World War II marked a major advance in airplane technology. Jet engines made planes go much faster than ever before.

The underside of a Boeing 747. Each 747 engine is more powerful than all four engines on a Boeing 707 combined!

Jet engines also had a huge effect on air travel. In 1958, the new Boeing 707 carried passengers nonstop across the Atlantic Ocean from New York City to Paris. This jet airliner was remarkable for its speed and size. It had room for up to 181 passengers and could travel 600 miles per hour. That year, more than one million people flew between the United States and Europe. For the first time in history, more people crossed the Atlantic by plane than by ship.

In the 1970s, British and French airplane designers came up with the Concorde, a supersonic (faster than the speed of sound) passenger jet. From 1977 through 2003, the Concorde flew passengers every day at speeds approaching 1,400 miles per hour, cutting the flying time from the United States to Europe in half!

The newest passenger jet is the Airbus A380. This massive new plane, designed with the latest technology, can carry up to 840 passengers. The plane has enough space to install bedrooms, bars, gyms, and lounges!

The Boeing 747 (shown in both images) is also known as the "jumbo jet." The Airbus A380 is designed to compete with 747s for control of the market for the largest jet airliners.

CONTENTS

It's hard to believe that the first airplane flight took place only a little more than one hundred years ago. Since then, planes have changed greatly. And they've changed the world in which we live. Airplanes do a lot more than carry passengers and fight in wars. Planes help water crops, fight fires, monitor weather, and also make for a fun hobby.

Who can say what the future of flight holds? Perhaps someday, everyone will be able to strap on wings and fly through the air, just as da Vinci dreamed. Or maybe one day, most homes will have an airplane parked in the garage next to the family car! One thing is certain: as long as people gaze at the sky and dream about flying, we will continue to design new and exciting flying machines.

In only one hundred years, airplanes have evolved from the Wright brothers' tiny and basic *Flyer* to the massive and advanced jet airliners of today.

Glossary

admiringly *adv.* with respect and awe.

permit *v.* to make possible or allow.

scoundrel *n.* a dishonest person.

subject *n.* a person who lives under the rule of a king or queen.

worthless *adj.* someone or something that has no value or use.

The Story of Flight

by Rena Korb

PEARSON

Scott Foresman

Editorial Offices: Glenview, Illinois • Parsippany, New Jersey • New York, New York
Sales Offices: Needham, Massachusetts • Duluth, Georgia • Glenview, Illinois
Coppell, Texas • Ontario, California • Mesa, Arizona

Reader Response

1. What was the author's purpose for writing *The Story of Flight*? Did you adjust your reading rate at any time while reading? Why?

2. The author used time order to structure the book. Using a graphic organizer such as the one below, make a timeline showing major dates in the history of flight.

Major Dates in the History of Flight

first manned balloon flight

1783

3. Make a web with the word *flight* in the center. Around it, write words from the selection that relate to flight.

4. Review the table of contents. Which chapters would you turn to if you wanted to learn more about the use of airplanes in battle?

Science

Science

Physical Science

The Story of Flight

by Rena Korb

Genre	Comprehension Skill and Strategy	Text Features
Nonfiction	• Author's Purpose • Text Structure	• Table of Contents • Captions • Sketches • Glossary

Scott Foresman Reading Street 5.3.1

PEARSON

Scott Foresman

scottforesman.com

ISBN 0-328-13533-X

90000

9 780328 135332

Scientists have identified approximately fifty "dead zones" along the world's coasts, where ocean creatures can no longer live.

Water Habitats in Danger

Land habitats are not the only ones in danger. Marine habitats, and the animals that live in them, are threatened as well. There are about fifty "dead zones" along the world's coasts, for example. These are areas in which those coastlines' ocean creatures simply can no longer live. The largest dead zone in the Western Hemisphere is along the Gulf of Mexico. There, excess phosphorus and nitrogen from the Mississippi River flowed into the Gulf and damaged the ecosystem.

A specific example of the harm caused by dead zones involves the Mexican gray whale. In 1999, fifty gray whales were reported killed off the coast of Mexico. It was found that they had died from excess salt in the water. The salt had come from salt-making operations near the coast.

Mexican gray whale

Of all the whale species that swim the coast of the United States, the humpback whale is probably the most famous. Its fame comes from the dazzling leaps and displays that it makes. Today, there are perhaps ten thousand humpbacks worldwide. This is estimated to be 8 percent of the original humpback whale population. In the mid-1800s, about 125,000 humpback whales lived worldwide. Like other whales, they were hunted for their meat, oil, and a substance called baleen attached to their jaws. At that time, whale oil was used in street lamps and baleen was used to make women's dresses.

In 1966 the International Whaling Commission gave all humpbacks protected status, by prohibiting people from hunting them. However, some countries have ignored the ban and continue to hunt. Humpbacks have also been hurt by becoming entangled in fishing gear and ocean debris. Ship collisions have resulted in humpback whales being stranded, and jet skis and parasails near Hawaii have been hazardous to humpbacks and their ecosystem.

Growth in farming has hurt natural habitats.

Unfortunately, Mexico is not the only country where the clearing of land for crops has hurt habitats. There are many examples of habitats that have been damaged or destroyed to make room for farmland. In the United States alone, more than 90 percent of our native prairies have been lost to farms.

Changing habits and demands of humans can forever change an ecosystem. For example, worldwide demand for rice, wheat, and corn is expected to grow 40 percent by 2020. This means that the demand for irrigation—changing the paths of waterways to get water to crops—is expected to rise 50 percent or more. In all likelihood this will lead to increased pressure to transform many areas into agricultural regions.

Monach butterflies are as small as Asian elephants are large. But as with Asian elephants, human activities have severely affected their migration patterns. Migrating monarch butterflies fly from North America to Mexico for the winter. There they rest before returning north for the summer. Part of Mexico's evergreen forest is a protective shelter for the butterfly.

In spite of this, the forested region is losing trees at an alarming rate. Once the tourists and butterflies have left for the season, loggers come to clear the land. In Mexico there is an increasing demand for wood and the crops that can be planted on cleared land.

Habitat loss in Mexican forests has caused major problems for the monarch butterfly.

The overeating of sea otters by orcas led to the reduction of kelp forests in Alaskan coastal waters.

The hunting of whales can have a domino effect on other species' habitats as well, as an investigation into changes in Alaska's coastal ecosystems revealed. Off the coast of Alaska, from the 1940s through the 1970s, overfishing of many of the species of large whales, such as fins and humpbacks, caused orcas to seek prey other than the large whales that they normally ate. Orcas began to prey on harbor seals, then fur seals, then sea lions, and, at last, sea otters for food. The sea otter population was reduced to such a low level that there were not enough of them to feed on all the sea urchins. This caused the sea urchin population to grow by a huge amount. Sea urchins overgrazed, which led to the reduction of Alaska's kelp forests in its coastal waters.

Coral reefs are one kind of ocean habitat. Like kelp forests, they have experienced trouble. In fact, coral reefs are considered endangered. A reef is a fragile limestone framework in which corals, other types of animals, such as jellyfish, sea urchins, and sponges, live. It is believed that up to 25 percent of the world's coral reefs have already been destroyed. Overfishing, marine pollution, and an increase in viral and bacterial diseases that can kill coral are to blame.

Tropical storms, such as cyclones and hurricanes, make reefs weaker and more prone to habitat destruction. Reefs have also been affected by human activities. Australia's Great Barrier Reef is one such reef. Its population of nesting loggerhead turtles has decreased by 80 percent since the 1960s. It is believed that this can be directly traced to increased farming and material deposited in the ocean through runoff.

Like orangutans, Asian elephants are threatened by habitat loss. Asian elephants live on forest-covered lands. But those lands are also used by 1.5 billion people, leading to an uneasy mix. In India, Thailand, and Sumatra, the clearing of forests—in many cases to make space for growing human populations—has placed Asian elephants in serious trouble.

Forest clearing has resulted in a loss of Asian elephants' natural habitat. This loss is especially troubling for Asian elephants because they are migratory. Now, when Asian elephants migrate, they become trapped in small forest pockets.

Just as groups are working to save the habitats of orangutans, others are working to protect forests that elephants call home.

Like their Asian cousins, African elephants are threatened by habitat loss.

Many other species of marine life in the world's oceans are also in trouble. For example, it is estimated that since the 1950s tuna and marlin populations have been reduced by 90 percent, due to overfishing and harmful fishing methods.

Overfishing has been so harmful that, even when fishing has been reduced, it has taken several years for the fish to "catch up." For example, Canada and New England's cod populations dropped so low in the 1990s that only 1 percent of their original population remained. The Canadian government closed cod fishing areas for several years to allow the species to recover. Still, the cod population remains very low.

Red snapper, which lives off the west coast of the United States, is another fish that is now in danger. Overfishing is to blame, along with the fact that shrimp trawlers often capture 10 to 20 million very young red snappers every year.

Fishing trawler

The polar bear is the largest of the eight bear species on Earth. It lives along the Arctic Circle, in North America, Russia, and Norway. The polar bear is considered the world's largest land predator. It is the only bear that eats mostly meat. But today polar bears are under pressure. The gradual warming of their habitat has caused ice packs to break up across the Arctic.

The melting of the polar ice caps means the bears are often stranded onshore and have less time to fatten up each summer. As a result, some female bears cannot produce enough milk for their cubs and fewer cubs are able to survive the harsh winters. Polar bears are also threatened by oil spills. Oil partially strips the polar bear's fur of its warming properties and covers the bear's prey as well. Toxic chemicals and air pollution also threaten the Arctic region.

Habitat destruction has caused orangutan populations to decline.

Another forest-dwelling animal whose habitat is at risk is the orangutan. Its homes are the island of Borneo and the neighboring Indonesian island of Sumatra. This huge ape (ranging from sixty to three hundred pounds) needs large areas of forest in which to roam. Unfortunately, humans have taken over land for mining, logging, and various types of farming, so less than 20 percent of the orangutan's original habitat remains.

When a habitat is destroyed, the animal's food supply decreases and it can no longer thrive. During the past one hundred years, orangutan populations have decreased by about 90 percent. Some researchers estimate that there are fewer than thirty thousand orangutans on the islands today.

Many organizations are concerned about the survival of orangutans. Orangutan Foundation International is one group working to protect the tropical forests that orangutans call home.

The black bears of Yosemite National Park have learned that it is easier to find scraps of food in the cars and trash of the park's visitors than it is to wander around looking for berries.

Park officials have developed regulations to help visitors avoid contact with bears. These regulations warn visitors to hide their food. Without these regulations, bears would continue to depend on humans for food instead of relying on their natural environment. Sometimes, a black bear becomes so dependent on humans that park officials are forced to move the bear to another part of the park.

Some black bears are too dependent on humans for food.

Air Troubles

The air quality of an environment can affect habitats too. In parts of Inner Mongolia, mining activities and accidents have sparked numerous fires in underground coal mines. The fires have put harmful chemicals into the air. These chemicals have polluted the groundwater that animals drink and produced acid rain that destroys the plants that some animals eat.

Although Inner Mongolia probably has the worst problem with coal fires, they have also occured in India, Indonesia, and even the United States. In 1962 an abandoned mine in Centralia, Pennsylvania, was used to burn trash. The fire from the burning trash grew out of control. As a result, the fire is still burning, and has caused devastation and destruction of many habitats.

Wind farms such as this are a great source for clean energy, but they have led to the deaths of many birds.

Land at Risk

The black bear is one animal whose habitat has been deeply impacted by humans. Black bears like to live in old forests filled with hardwood trees. In spring and summer they feed on the forest's berries and leaves. In the fall they remain deep in the woods, where the plant growth is thick, as they prepare to hibernate for the winter.

Black bears are shy by nature and avoid humans. Many of their habitats, however, have been destroyed due to the construction of houses and roads. In many regions, bears have had to learn to become more comfortable around humans in order to survive.

Near Lake Tahoe, California, black bears discovered that they could feed and rest comfortably in an environment controlled by humans. Now, the black bears of Lake Tahoe feed on scraps of food from garbage cans and campsites and sleep under people's porches.

Black bears' lives have changed dramatically in places where humans have altered their habitats.

Natural disasters can destroy peoples' homes and animals' habitats.

What would you do if your home was destroyed? Families who survive natural disasters, such as tornadoes and hurricanes, sometimes face this question. Fortunately, it is only rarely that people lose their homes due to natural disasters. For animals, however, habitat loss occurs much more often. Nature sometimes destroys animals' habitats. A beaver's dam can be ruined in a rainstorm, and a sudden snowstorm can wreck a bird's nest.

Scientists called ecologists have found that increasing human populations and their daily activities directly contribute to the loss of many animal habitats. Today, about 50 percent of the world's land surface is considered destroyed or disturbed. By 2032 that level may reach 70 percent. Destruction of animal habitats threatens to ruin entire ecosystems, or environments, and the animals that live in them. We must discover and learn about new ways to protect these ecosystems.

Windmills, in contrast to coal, are a source of clean, renewable energy. Unlike power plants, they do not pollute while generating electricity. Unfortunately, despite these benefits, the windmills on modern wind farms have killed many birds. Near San Francisco, California, it is estimated that 22,000 birds have been killed by the turbines on windmills. The windmills have only been around for a couple of decades. Because of that, California's birds have not yet learned to change their flight paths, thereby avoiding the turbines. One suggestion that people have made to help birds adjust is to paint the blades of the windmills in colors and patterns that birds can see more easily. This might encourage the birds to fly farther away from the machines.

Factories and power plants are a major cause for habitat loss and destruction.

Helping Habitats

You have just read about many habitats and ecosystems that are in danger. Habitats can be spoiled in two main ways. Either the amount of habitat is reduced, such as when a wetland is paved for a highway, or the quality of the habitat is changed. A company that dumps toxic wastes into a waterway is reducing the quality of that ecosystem.

In 1995 the United States Geological Survey documented the extent to which habitats in our country were in danger. Altogether it listed 126 ecosystems as being either critically endangered, endangered, or threatened.

Technological improvements, while mostly positive, also have the unfortunate side effect of causing large-scale damage to happen more quickly than it did in the past. But what can we do to halt and repair this damage?

Habitats as Homes

What is a habitat? It is an environment in which a living thing, such as an animal, grows and thrives. Every animal has special requirements of its environment. An animal's habitat must contain enough food, water, shelter, and nesting places for it to survive. A habitat is its home.

Habitats are found all over the world. Your own backyard is a habitat. Oceans, rivers, and freshwater lakes are water habitats. Forests, deserts, and prairies are land habitats. Habitats are all around us, and they are at risk.

Fortunately, there are many successful examples of states, organizations, and individuals working to preserve habitats. For example, the states of Delaware and Virginia have programs that encourage citizens to understand ecological resources. West Virginia allows its residents to adopt birds at its Raptor Rehabilitation Center. South Dakota is a leader in preserving prairie lands. A conservation program there has encouraged ranchers to return farmland to native grassland while still allowing cows and other animals to graze.

You, too, can help in many ways. Visit your local library or historical society to see some before-and-after photographs of development in your area to understand how the habitat around you has changed. Be an enthusiastic supporter of efforts to save local habitats and the animals that live in them. Talk to your family. Put your habitat-saving ideas into action!

Glossary

conservation *n.* preservation from harm or decay.

contribute *v.* to help bring about.

enthusiastic *adj.* full of enthusiasm; eagerly interested.

environment *n.* the circumstances or conditions of air, water, and soil.

investigation *n.* a careful search.

Habitats
In Need Of Help

by Jane St. John

PEARSON

Scott Foresman

Editorial Offices: Glenview, Illinois • Parsippany, New Jersey • New York, New York
Sales Offices: Needham, Massachusetts • Duluth, Georgia • Glenview, Illinois
Coppell, Texas • Ontario, California • Mesa, Arizona

Reader Response

1. You have read about habitat loss. Much of what you have read is fact, having been proven by scientists. But some of what you have read is opinion. On a chart similar to the one below, list three facts and three opinions about how habitats have been destroyed.

Fact	Opinion

2. In this book, the author talks about land, water and air pollution, and habitat loss. Can you think of other, more specific habitats? What kinds of pollution is harming those habitats? How do you think you could help save them?

3. Use the words from the glossary to write a short newspaper article that urges readers to protect a habitat in your neighborhood.

4. In three to five sentences describe what is happening in the photograph on page 11 and how it relates to habitat loss.

Science

Suggested levels for Guided Reading, DRA,™ Lexile,® and Reading Recovery™ are provided in the Pearson Scott Foresman Leveling Guide.

Genre	Comprehension Skill and Strategy	Text Features
Nonfiction	• Fact and Opinion • Ask Questions	• Captions • Labels • Glossary

Scott Foresman Reading Street 5.2.4

PEARSON
Scott Foresman

ISBN 0-328-13527-5
9 780328 135271 90000

scottforesman.com

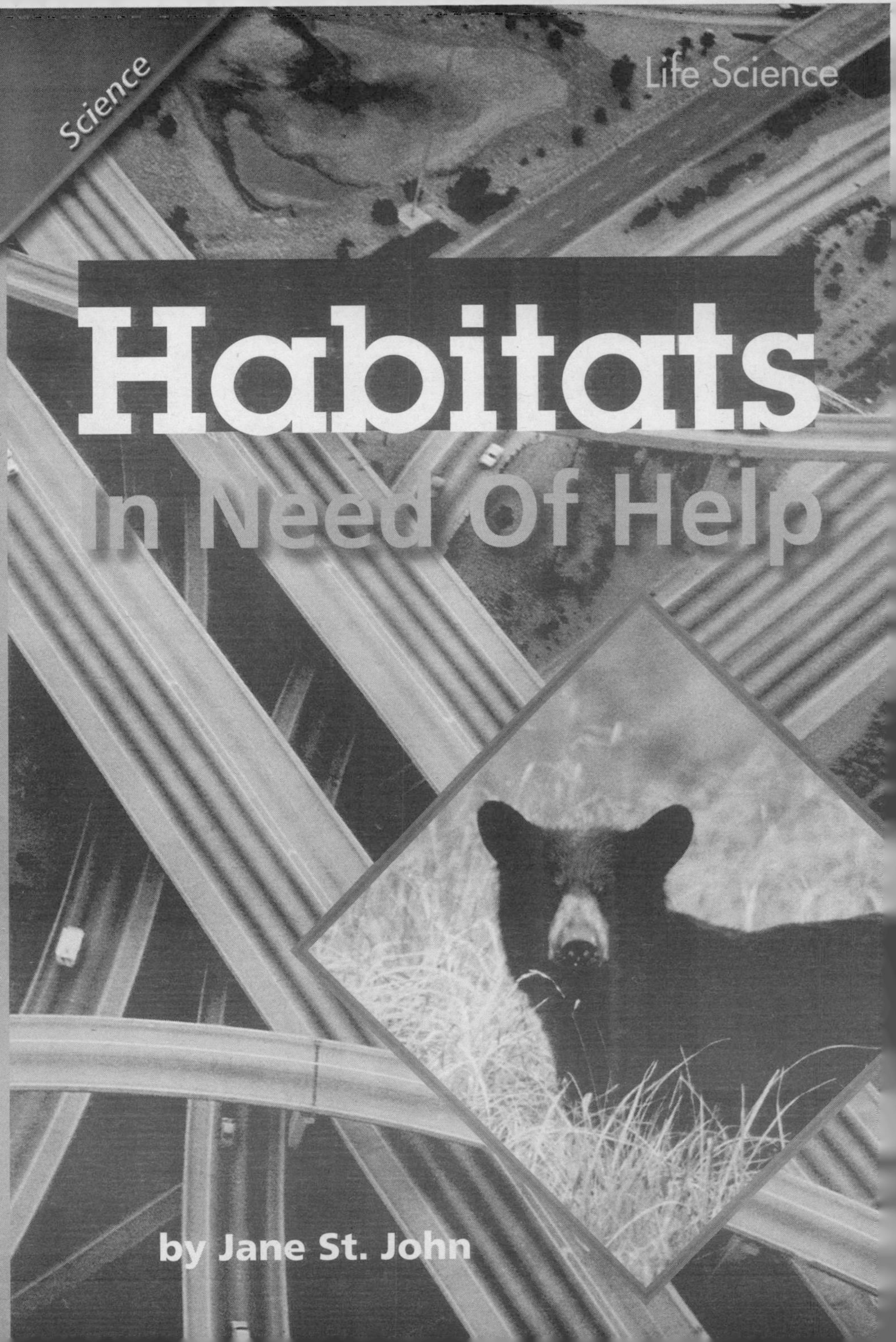

Science

Life Science

Habitats
In Need Of Help

by Jane St. John

Lupe finished her treat. Soon after Abuela asked Lupe to go with her to the market. They needed to pick up ingredients for the Rosca de Reyes. Lupe lost no time in getting ready. She told her mother that she was going out and grabbed her notebook along with Abuela's basket.

Lupe always carried her little notebook around when she was cooking with Abuela. She took notes to make sure that she didn't miss anything. Lupe wrote down exactly which ingredients were used and in what amounts. She even wrote down where she bought everything. That way, she could go shopping on her own some day at Abuela's market!

The outdoor market was buzzing with activity. It seemed as if everyone in town was there. There were brightly colored Christmas decorations everywhere. Here and there stood equally colorful displays advertising the different foods. Phoenix had nothing that could compare to the market. Because of this Lupe was sad whenever the shopping was done.

Lupe loved to wander up and down the market's aisles smelling the wonderful scents of the fruits, spices, fish, breads, and meats. Best of all, Lupe could try out her Spanish with the vendors. Lupe's Spanish was already good. But she knew she could always use more practice!

After a while the hearth became too warm to sit by. So Lupe got up and bounced into the warm and inviting kitchen, following the scent of the chocolate. Abuela stood waiting in the kitchen. She knew that her granddaughter would show up there eventually!

Lupe said to Abuela, "I could smell the chocolate as soon as I entered the house!" Abuela smiled. She said, "I had remembered how much you liked my hot chocolate. So I prepared some for you, along with another of your favorite treats. Try some!"

Abuela handed Lupe a steaming mug of hot chocolate and a *churro*. *Churros* are made of dough and covered in sugar and cinnamon. They had a crispy, crunchy taste that Lupe found irresistible. And dunking them in Abuela's hot chocolate only made them better!

As soon as Lupe entered Abuela's home, memories of all the previous Christmas celebrations came rushing back to her. The smell of Abuela's famous hot chocolate filled the air, blending with the sweet smell of the wood stove. Lupe could hardly contain her excitement as she said hello to everyone and unpacked all of the gifts she had brought.

Lupe sat down by the hearth afterwards. This was another of her favorite activities at Abuela's house. The hearth had a wonderful smell that was nearly as good as that of the hot chocolate. Lupe loved to stare at its glowing coals and soak up their warmth.

Lupe and Abuela made their way to the fruit and nut stand. There Abuela picked out the candied fruit she needed for the Rosca de Reyes. Lupe could never get enough of the fruits' amazing colors. Many of them shimmered with a thick coating of sugar. Lupe couldn't wait to try them all!

Abuela took out her purse to pay. As she did the fruit vendor said, "Remember to get the baby Jesus. I recommend the bakery down the street." Lupe didn't understand what he meant. Abuela explained that a small figure of the baby Jesus is usually baked into the Rosca de Reyes. Whoever finds the figure in their piece has to host the next holiday party.

"It works like a lottery," Abuela described. "Everyone at the dinner table gets very excited about it. It adds more fun to the tradition."

Abuela visited the bakery on the way home. There she bought two of the baby Jesus figures. Lupe placed them into the basket. Then she slipped her hand into Abuela's for the walk back to her house.

Abuela and Lupe made one last stop on the way home to buy spices. Lupe felt like she was carrying around a basket full of treasures. She couldn't wait to start cooking!

The next morning, Abuela and Lupe got to work right away on baking the Rosca de Reyes. Abuela read the ingredients out loud. Lupe carefully wrote them down in her notebook. Then she measured them out and put them into the bowl. Later on Lupe's mother joined them to help prepare the rest of the meal.

While they were cooking together Lupe's mother talked about what it was like when Abuela had taught her how to bake Rosca de Reyes. Then Abuela told the story of how *her* mother had taught her how to bake Rosca de Reyes.

Hearing these stories made Lupe feel special. She saw how she was connected to a tradition that stretched back way beyond Abuela. Abuela and her mother's stories made it sound like the family had been baking Rosca de Reyes since the beginning of time!

You couldn't make Rosca de Reyes without telling the story of the Three Kings. It was a story that Lupe had heard many times. Twelve days after Christmas, on January 6, people in Mexico celebrate the procession of the Three Kings, Caspar, Melchior, and Balthasar. These three kings had brought gifts of gold, frankincense, and myrrh to the baby Jesus. In Mexico, January 6 is the day set aside for the distribution of the childrens' Christmas gifts.

On the eve of the festival, Mexican children leave their shoes on the windowsill. They fill the shoes with hay for the kings' camels. This ensures that the camels are happy and that the kings will leave the children gifts. Lupe always left her shoe on the windowsill, hoping to please the camels.

Lupe enjoyed the procession of the Three Kings. At times she felt sad, because so few families in Phoenix celebrated the wonderful holiday. But here in Mexico, Abuela's entire community took part in the event. It made Lupe feel like she was connected to something special.

8

While they cooked, the rest of the family sat around in the living room, catching up on what they had been doing over the past year. Now and then Lupe's cousins would visit the kitchen to chat with her. At times they could be a little wild, but at Christmas they made sure to be on their best behavior.

Lupe loved to see her family so happy together. She felt proud that she was old enough to share responsibility for making the family meal.

Lupe's mother finished making the rest of the meal and helped serve the dinner with Lupe and Abuela. Lupe listened to the adults' conversation while she ate. They talked about the differences between life in Mexico and life in the United States. Lupe knew it was difficult to have the family living in two different countries. But she knew that they handled it as best they could.

Another family tradition involved the baking of the Rosca de Reyes. Rosca de Reyes is a pastry. Made from sweet bread, it is twisted into a round braid and decorated with candied fruits. The fruits and round braid make it look like a king's crown.

In Mexico, the Rosca de Reyes is made to celebrate the sacred Festival of the Three Kings, which happens at Christmas. The Rosca de Reyes is always the centerpiece of the Mexican holiday dinner table.

In years past, Lupe had not been old enough to help bake the Rosca de Reyes. This year would be different. Abuela and Lupe's mother knew that Lupe was now ready to help with the baking. It was a difficult dish to make. But Lupe's mother had learned how to make the Rosca de Reyes when she was Lupe's age, as had Abuela. So now was the time!

The family finished eating dinner. At last it was time for dessert! Lupe helped bring all kinds of sweets out to the table. Lupe's mother had prepared her famous *flan*, a rich and dense egg custard. Her aunt had prepared *arroz con leche*, a type of rice pudding. There was more of the steaming hot chocolate and cinnamon-covered *churros*.

Finally, Lupe carried in the Rosca de Reyes. It looked beautiful! Its golden brown crust was sprinkled in sugar and covered in clusters of candied fruits. Lupe had worked hard on the pastry dish. Everyone at the table gave her compliments on how well she had done baking it. Lupe beamed.

For Lupe, the best part of visiting Abuela was the time they spent together in the kitchen. Abuela's kitchen was a very special place. There were always wonderful smells wafting around in it. And you could always find a variety of delicious Mexican treats tucked away here and there.

As much as Lupe liked those things, what she cherished most of all about her time in Abuela's kitchen were the hours when Abuela would tell her stories about Mexico. For as long as Lupe could remember, Abuela had told her stories. The stories had become family tradition.

Abuela made sure that each person took a generous slice. Lupe's mother found the baby Jesus in her piece. That meant she would have the honor of hosting the next holiday party! Everyone congratulated Lupe's mother for her good luck.

The family sat around the dinner table talking for a while after dessert. Then they moved over to the living room to exchange Christmas gifts. Soon it was Lupe's turn to run and get Abuela her gift.

Suddenly shy, Lupe presented Abuela with the recipe book that she had made. Everyone fell silent as Lupe explained how she made it, describing all the different notes she had to take down in her notebook in order to get the recipes just right. Lupe also talked about how much she enjoyed Abuela's storytelling and cooking.

This year, Lupe had decided that her Christmas gift to Abuela would be a special book of recipes. She wanted to show her gratitude for all the wonderful times she had spent cooking dishes in Abuela's kitchen. Lupe had worked hard to write down each recipe using her best handwriting. Next to each entry she had added a photograph. Each photograph showed Lupe at home holding up the dish that she had prepared from each recipe.

Lupe had had a fun time putting together her special book of recipes. Every week she cooked something new from her recipe collection. Every week she had her mother take a picture of her in front of her latest creation. Lupe was astonished at how well her book had turned out.

Lupe's family lived in Phoenix, Arizona. Her abuela lived in northern Mexico, a short distance from Phoenix. Every year at Christmas Lupe's family drove to see Abuela.

Lupe loved the drive. She would pack the trunk with gifts for her cousins, aunts, and uncles. The gift that she got for Abuela was always the most special. Lupe would spend lots of time thinking about it. She missed her Abuela greatly and wanted to make sure she knew how much she loved her.

The Christmas celebration was important in Lupe's family. It was the only time of year that they got to see Abuela. That made Lupe put even more effort into selecting her abuela's present.

Abuela's wrinkled face broke into a big smile. She held Lupe close as she leafed through the pages, showing everyone the photos. In each one Abuela could see that Lupe had worked hard to get the recipes prepared exactly right.

"What a beautiful book!" Abuela said. "And what a wonderful way to remember our recipes. Now if you'll just wait a minute, I have a gift for you."

Abuela excused herself and disappeared into her bedroom. She returned a few moments later holding a very big and very old-looking book in her hands. Abuela explained that it was the greatest gift she ever received. It was a family scrapbook that Lupe's great-great-grandmother had started when she was a little girl. She had passed it down to Abuela when she thought the time was right. Now Abuela was passing it down to Lupe!

Abuela opened the book and started turning the pages, showing them to the family as she went. They saw old, yellowed wedding invitations and photographs from past holiday parties. Lupe noticed her own birth announcement and a picture of her on the first day of kindergarten. At the very back of the book there was a carefully drawn family tree that went back for many generations. Abuela closed the book and held it out to Lupe.

Looking seriously into her granddaughter's eyes, she said, "This book is yours now, but it comes with an important responsibility. Now you are in charge of keeping our traditions alive. My gift to you will become your gift to the rest of the family as you record our history for years to come."

Lupe ran home from the school bus stop. It was the last day of classes before winter break, and she was very excited about her family trip. She was going to Mexico to visit her grandmother for Christmas. It had been a whole year since she had seen her *abuela*, which means grandmother in Spanish. The trip was always fun for Lupe because she got to practice her Spanish and visit many different fun places in Mexico. She also got to spend time with her cousins and hear stories about when her mother was a little girl.

That Christmas in Mexico was one Lupe would remember for the rest of her life. She spent the entire drive back to Phoenix thinking about the gift that Abuela had given her. She felt honored to be trusted with the responsibility of keeping the family traditions alive. But she also was a little scared. What if she couldn't do well at her new task?

Lupe's mother reassured her that she could.

"Think about all the hard work you put into learning the recipes from Abuela," she said.

Lupe smiled as she stared out of the car window, imagining all the stories and recipes she would add to her great-great-grandmother's special book.

Different Countries, Different Gifts

Different cultures have different traditions of gift-giving. In China, gift-giving is surrounded by etiquette and ceremony. There are certain days when gifts are required, such as birthdays and weddings. It is considered rude not to offer a gift on these days.

Gift-giving takes place on January 6 during the Mexican celebration of Christmas. Some Mexican children receive gifts on both Christmas Day and January 6. This is due to the influence that the American Christmas celebration has had in Mexico.

In both the Mexican and Chinese cultures, gifts represent the respect and admiration that the benefactor has for the person receiving his or her gift. What do you feel like when you receive a gift?

Traditional Chinese wedding gifts

The Gift

by *Isabel Sendao*
illustrated by *Durga Bernhard*

PEARSON

Scott Foresman

Editorial Offices: Glenview, Illinois • Parsippany, New Jersey • New York, New York
Sales Offices: Needham, Massachusetts • Duluth, Georgia • Glenview, Illinois
Coppell, Texas • Ontario, California • Mesa, Arizona

Reader Response

1. Compare and contrast Lupe's gift to Abuela with Abuela's gift to Lupe. Use a graphic organizer like the one below to write down your answer.

2. Do you predict that Lupe will do a good job at keeping the family scrapbook? Explain your answer.

3. The word *benefactor* contains the Latin root *bene-*. Can you think of any other words that have this root? What do you think the root means?

4. Imagine you were Lupe. What would you do if the scrapbook started falling apart because of its age?

Social Studies

The Gift

by Isabel Sendao

illustrated by Durga Bernhard

Genre	Comprehension Skill and Strategy
Fiction	• Compare and Contrast • Predict

Scott Foresman Reading Street 5.2.3

PEARSON

Scott Foresman

scottforesman.com

ISBN 0-328-13524-0

9 780328 135240

90000

MICHELANGELO: THE ARCHITECT

In 1546 Michelangelo was made chief architect of St. Peter's Basilica, a grand church in Vatican City. At the time, St. Peter's was being rebuilt. The project had already lasted forty years. The people of Rome wanted Michelangelo to help finish the job.

Michelangelo was in his seventies when he accepted this huge assignment. This was during a time when few people lived to the age of fifty. Even more impressive, Michelangelo refused to be paid for his work. He believed he was fulfilling a duty to the Roman Catholic Church by working on St. Peter's Basilica.

Michelangelo's work on St. Peter's was as breathtaking as his sculpture of David and the Sistine Chapel frescoes. Its design influenced the design of the U.S. Capitol building in Washington, D.C, and other buildings throughout the world. However, Michelangelo died before he was able to complete the project.

Michelangelo was not perfect. When he became depressed he would often leave his work unfinished. He was very critical of his patrons. Still, Michelangelo is rightly thought of as one of the great artists of the Renaissance. The following pages will explore the works of other great artists of the Renaissance.

The people of Florence soon grew weary of Savonarola's rule. They overthrew the priest in 1498, and Michelangelo returned to Florence.

Soon after Michelango came back, he received an opportunity to sculpt a fourteen-foot statue for Florence's main church. The statue would be of the biblical hero David. Michelangelo started work in 1501, using an old and damaged block of marble.

Michelangelo finished his *David* in 1504. The people of Florence loved it, hailing Michelangelo as a genius. To this day, *David* is Michelangelo's most famous sculpture. Except for da Vinci's *Mona Lisa,* it is the most famous work of art from the Renaissance.

Michelangelo's *David*

Detail of Sistine Chapel

MICHELANGELO RETURNS TO PAINTING

The success of *David* made many people want to hire Michelangelo. In 1508 the Pope asked him to come to Rome. He had a special project for Michelangelo.

The Pope wanted Michelangelo to paint fresco scenes for the ceiling of the Sistine Chapel, in Rome's Vatican City. In order to do the project, Michelangelo was forced to master the art of painting. He had given up painting early in life to concentrate on sculpture.

It was not easy for Michelangelo to learn how to paint again. At times the size of project threatened to overwhelm him. Supposedly, Michelangelo became so frustrated early on in the project that he erased his work and fired all of his assistants. From then on, it is thought that he worked alone to finish the frescoes.

Michelangelo took four years to paint the Sistine Chapel ceiling. When it was done, people again hailed him as a genius. They marveled at the beauty and massive scale of the frescoes he had painted. The work still exists today. It has undergone painstaking restoration since the time of its creation.

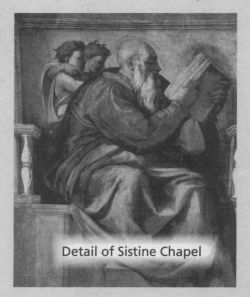

Detail of Sistine Chapel

Science

Science

Earth Science

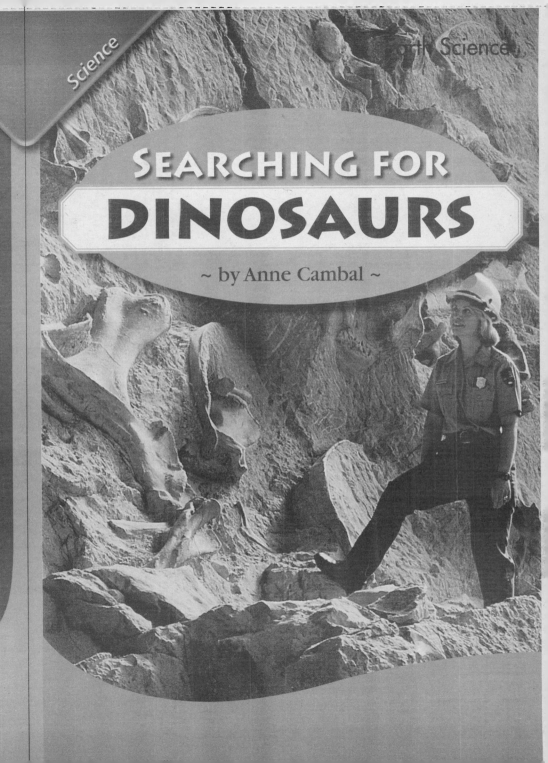

SEARCHING FOR
DINOSAURS

~ by Anne Cambal ~

Genre	Comprehension Skill and Strategy	Text Features
Nonfiction	• Fact and Opinion • Predict	• Captions • Labels • Map • Glossary

Scott Foresman Reading Street 5.3.3

PEARSON

Scott
Foresman

ISBN 0-328-13539-9

90000

9 780328 135394

Reader Response

1. Each of the two paragraphs on page 11 contains at least one fact and one opinion. Use a graphic organizer like the one below to write down two facts and two opinions found on page 11.

Facts	Opinions

2. What do you predict the future of animatronics will be like?

3. Make a list of words used in the selection that have Latin and Greek roots.

4. Which of the photos of the animatronics process did you find most helpful to you in understanding how animatronics works?

Glossary

erected *v.* to have been put straight up; to have set upright.

foundations *n.* bases; part on which other parts rest.

mold *n.* a hollow shape into which anything is formed or cast.

occasion *n.* particular times.

proportion *n.* a proper relation among parts.

tidied *v.* to have put in order; to have made neat.

workshop *n.* shop or building where work is done.

SEARCHING FOR DINOSAURS

by Anne Cambal

PEARSON

Scott Foresman

Editorial Offices: Glenview, Illinois • Parsippany, New Jersey • New York, New York
Sales Offices: Needham, Massachusetts • Duluth, Georgia • Glenview, Illinois
Coppell, Texas • Ontario, California • Mesa, Arizona

7. Test, Test, and Retest

Once the entire dinosaur model has been erected, the final stage of testing begins. The purpose of these tests is to make sure that all the systems work, that the dinosaur figure will hold together, and that the color and texture of the dinosaur will look good on film. The dinosaur remains in the workshop, where the equipment and materials are available for making changes.

After the dinosaur model has passed the tests, it is moved from its workshop to a new location, where it either becomes part of a museum exhibit or is filmed in a movie or television show. This process usually requires the use of cranes and trucks. Obviously, none of the scientists, artists, or engineers involved in building the model have ever seen a living dinosaur. But they've done their best to create the best possible model for the museumgoers or moviegoers to see, hear, and enjoy!

Workers assembling a full size model of a tyrannosaurus rex.

6. Assemble It All

Once work on the molded figure and its animatronics is complete, everything is assembled and tested. As each new part of the dinosaur model's frame is connected, its machinery and fit are also tested. By testing each section while it's being assembled, problems can be identified and fixed before it is too late.

FASCINATING FOSSILS

Why are we so fascinated by dinosaurs? Dinosaurs have been extinct for at least 65 million years. Human beings will never be able to study live dinosaurs. Not only will we never be able to study live dinosaurs, but it's incredibly difficult to study *dead* dinosaurs! Fossils are very hard to find. Those that are found are often fragile.

Also, fossils are most often found in remote deserts, where the wind blows away the thin soil to reveal dinosaur remains. These deserts are hard to get to. Their harsh climates create tough working conditions. So what keeps people motivated to keep searching for fossils?

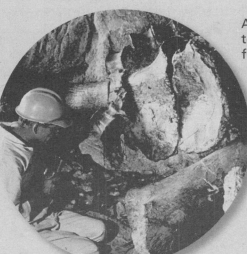

A scientist using excavating tools to carefully remove fossil remains from rock.

Two of the tools used to excavate fossils

A DINOSAUR NAMED SUE

One reason why people become fossil hunters is that they are very curious about living things from the past. This curiosity drives fossil hunters to go on searches that many people would consider risky or even dangerous.

Fossil hunters know full well that most of their searches will come up empty, and they will not discover a new fossil. But sometimes they get lucky. In 1990 the fossil hunter Sue Hendrickson, working in the harsh semidesert of western South Dakota, found what may be the most famous dinosaur fossil of all time.

Named "Sue" in honor of its discoverer, it is the largest and most complete tyrannosaurus rex fossil that has ever been found. Sue is believed to be about 67 million years old. It's estimated that Sue weighed 7 tons when she was alive and that her skull alone weighed 600 pounds.

Sue Hendrickson hunts fossils because she loves doing it. She excels in finding fossils trapped in amber. Amber is hardened tree sap. Insects and other small animals become trapped in tree sap. Over millions of years the sap turns into amber, preserving the animal caught inside.

How long have people been fossil hunting? No one can say for sure. But the first fossils that we know to have been dug up by humans were discovered just 200 years ago.

Engineers test the machinery that controls the movements of a dinosaur model's tail.

5. Make the Parts for the Animatronics

At the same time that the molds are made, the animatronics machinery that controls the final model's movements is designed and built. Four different types of systems are used to create the machinery. These systems are called the mechanical, structural, surface, and electronic systems. They work together to move the dinosaur's head and jaws. They also support the weight of the figure each time its body (or tail) moves. The systems also make the skin look realistic and coordinate things so that the dinosaur model moves in a lifelike way.

3. Sculpt a Full-Sized Model

The finished miniature model serves as the basis for the full-sized model. Sometimes the full-sized model is created by hand. Other times it is built using a process called CAM, which stands for **Computer-Assisted Manufacturing**. Any marks or flaws in the finished full-sized model must be tidied up before the final details are carved onto its surface.

4. Make a Mold and Cast the Figure

Once the full-sized model is complete, artists use it to make a mold of the final product. Since the final model is usually very large, it is often molded in several smaller sections. These sections must fit together perfectly for everything to work. At this step the machinery that controls the final model is placed inside the mold. This is done to make sure that the machinery will fit properly into what will become the final model.

An artist assembles a cast of a dinosaur head.

When was the last time you spent a day with a dinosaur? If you live in the Midwest, you can visit Sue at the Field Museum in Chicago, Illinois.

EARLY FOSSIL HUNTERS

Georges Cuvier developed the first system for classifying animals based on their anatomy, or body structure. He was a French scientist and zoologist who lived from 1769–1832. Cuvier also developed the science of paleontology.

Paleontology is the study of the fossils, or remains, of plants and animals from prehistoric times. It includes the study of Earth's layers, which are called *strata*. These layers help preserve fossils and provide clues to their age.

Georges Cuvier

Most scientists no longer use Cuvier's system of paleontology. However, Cuvier's ideas and studies helped greatly in making paleontology a respected science.

These bands of rock layers, or strata, might contain fossils.

1. Make a Drawing

To save time and money, the artist first draws a sketch of the dinosaur. The sketch is much smaller than the animatronics model that will be built from it. However, the artist draws the dinosaur in proportion to the final model. This means that the drawing, if made many times larger, would be equal in its dimensions to the final model.

The initial drawing serves as the final dinosaur model's foundations. It must be done as accurately and completely as possible, because all the other steps are based on it.

2. Build a Miniature Model

The artist then makes a small model so that everyone can see how the dinosaur will look from various angles. The model also helps determine whether the original drawing of the dinosaur can actually be transformed into an animatronics model.

Designer Edgar Martinez uses a computer to draw a blueprint for a new model of a dinosaur.

HOW TO MAKE AN ANIMATRONIC DINOSAUR:

1. Make a drawing of the dinosaur model you have in mind.
2. Build a miniature model using the drawing as a guide.
3. Sculpt a full-sized model using the miniature model as a guide.
4. Make a mold from the full-sized model. Pour the material used to make the skin of the finished dinosaur into the mold.
5. Design and make the parts that will control the model's animatronics.
6. Combine the molded figure with the animatronics to create the finished product.
7. Test everything to make sure it works!

Gideon Mantell, an English doctor who lived during the early 1800s, was one of the world's first fossil hunters. He became interested in fossils as a teenager and corresponded with other early fossil collectors. They exchanged both ideas and some of the fossils they found.

Gideon Mantell

Sir Richard Owen was nicknamed "the British Cuvier" for his work in zoology and paleontology. He lived from 1804–1892. In 1842, Owen first used the word *dinosauria*, from which "dinosaur" comes. *Dinosauria* is based on the Greek words for "terrible" and "lizard." Owen used the word to refer to a group of extinct reptiles.

Today, Mantell and Owen are known as the first people to find, identify, and classify dinosaur fossils. They helped turn dinosaur paleontology into a major field of study.

Sir Richard Owen

Mary Anning, another nineteenth-century English fossil hunter, discovered several new fossils when she was a child. At the time, only the rich could afford to be fossil hunters. But Anning's family was poor. Still, she became an excellent fossil hunter and examiner.

Barnum Brown began his career in 1897 at New York's Museum of Natural History. In 1902 he won fame for discovering the first *tyrannosaurus rex* fossil. Brown worked as a paleontologist for sixty-six years, leading fossil hunts all over the world.

Barnum Brown marks the boundary between early and modern dinosaur paleontology. His discoveries greatly advanced the study of dinosaur fossils. But he lacked the modern equipment of today's dinosaur paleontologists. Now let's look at the work of some modern dinosaur paleontologists.

Barnum Brown

Without computers it would be impossible to do modern animatronics. But animatronics is very different from the special effects that are made using computers. When computer artists create special effects, they use computer programs to draw images that you see later as part of the film. In many cases the special effects made by computers have made it unnecessary to build models.

In contrast, animatronics engineers create actual models. Animatronic models cost a lot of money and take many hours to design and build. Paleontologists, painters, sculptors, movers, technicians, photographers, and movie directors must all work together in order to create realistic animatronic models. The following pages describe in detail how an animatronic model of a dinosaur actually gets made. Just turn the page to find out more!

MODERN VIEWS OF DINOSAURS: ANIMATION TO ANIMATRONICS

Anyone who has watched cartoon shows is familiar with animated cartoons. Animation was first developed as an art form during the early 1900s. It is similar to regular filmmaking. But while regular filmmakers film people or the natural world, animators film clay models, drawings, or computer images.

Computer technology has given a big boost to animation. It has also helped develop animatronics, which is like animation. *Animatronics* is a technology used to build robot models. Animatronics artists create special electronic devices that make the body parts of their models move.

ANIMATRONICS VOCABULARY

animatronics, n.
A technology that uses electronics to animate or move puppets or other figures. Robotic models are designed to move at certain times. Dinosaur animatronics often include recordings of the sounds that scientists believe dinosaurs made.

animate, v.
To make, design, or produce something visual (a cartoon, for example) that creates the illusion of motion.

animation, n.
An animated cartoon, or the art or process of making animated cartoons.

STUDYING DINOSAURS TODAY

Today the field of dinosaur paleontology is thriving, thanks to the efforts of scientists worldwide. Modern communications instantly spread news of each new discovery. They also make it easier for dinosaur paleontologists to resolve disputes regarding how dinosaur fossils should be classified. Since the early 1800s, scientists on several continents have discovered more than three hundred species of dinosaurs!

Some of the areas where paleontologists have discovered dinosaur fossils

A TEAM OF FOSSIL HUNTERS

Paul Sereno is a famous fossil hunter. While in college at Northern Illinois University, he was granted a behind-the-scenes tour of New York's Museum of Natural History. The museum's displays of dinosaur fossils fascinated him. Sereno was so impressed that he decided to study for a career in dinosaur paleontology.

Sereno worked hard to make his dream a reality. He studied collections of dinosaur fossils in China and Mongolia and earned a doctorate, or special degree, in geology from Columbia University. Sereno also married Gabrielle Lyon, a fellow paleontologist. Together, they became a team of great fossil hunters and have made many important discoveries in the field of dinosaur paleontology.

Paul Sereno

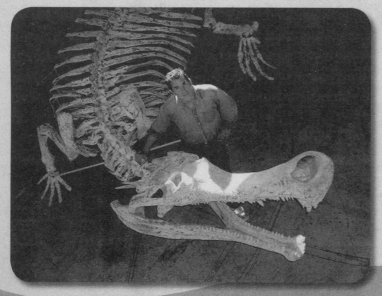

Joan Wiffen showed those who doubted that New Zealand had any dinosaur fossils that they were wrong.

On one occasion while out rock collecting, Wiffen bought a fossil of a trilobite, a small extinct marine animal, at a roadside stand. The trilobite made her even more interested in extinct animals. From then on Wiffen spent much of her time hunting for dinosaur fossils.

At first Wiffen had difficulty earning respect as a serious hunter of dinosaur fossils. The scientific community ignored her because she lacked a degree in paleontology. They also doubted that any fossils could ever be found in New Zealand, an island they thought was too small to have supported the huge prehistoric creatures.

Wiffen worked hard to overcome the scientists' lack of faith. She read endlessly about fossils and dinosaur paleontology, studying the latest theories and discoveries. Her breakthrough came in 1974, when she found her first dinosaur fossil. It was the first ever found in New Zealand!

You have now read about some of the most well-known dinosaur paleontologists and fossil hunters. Nowadays, many dinosaur paleontologists are involved in a new kind of technology called animatronics. Keep reading to find out what animatronics is all about!

Scientists assembling a massive fossil head of carcharodontosaurus.

In 1995, Sereno and Lyon led a fossil-hunting team to Africa. The trip's highlight occurred when Sereno discovered a fossil skull of a dinosaur species named *carcharodontosaurus*. Based on the skull, the team estimated that a living carcharodontosaurus would have been forty-five feet long! Lyon also discovered a new dinosaur fossil during the trip. Her find was named *deltadromeus agilis*, or "agile delta runner."

Sereno's most important discovery occurred in 1997 in the West African country of Niger. David Varricchio, a member of Sereno's team, spotted a fossil claw sticking out of the desert sand. It was a great find, but even more lay in store. Eventually, more than *four hundred* pieces of dinosaur fossil were found scattered around the claw!

What Varricchio had found was a whole new species of dinosaur. It was named *suchomimus*, which means "crocodile mimic." The skull of suchomimus shows that it was not a meat-eater, as most such dinosaurs were believed to be. Instead, it ate fish. Suchomimus was given its name because scientists believe that it ate like a crocodile.

People around the country were excited by the discovery of suchomimus. It was mentioned on the front page of the *Chicago Tribune* and in *Time* magazine. *National Geographic* even gave the discovery its own television special!

Paul Sereno and Gabrielle Lyon will always be known primarily as fossil hunters. But they have done more than go digging around for fossils. In 1998 the couple cofounded Project Exploration. The organization has two main purposes. It tries to educate people about the latest discoveries in dinosaur paleontology. At the same time, it wants to get children interested in careers in science.

Claw from a *suchomimus*

Joan Wiffen, the first person to find a dinosaur fossil in New Zealand, digging at an excavation site

JOAN WIFFEN: AMAZING FOSSIL FINDER

So far you have read about American fossil hunters, but interest in fossil hunting is worldwide. Joan Wiffen is just one of many fossil hunters based outside of the United States. She specializes in fossil hunting in New Zealand.

Wiffen first became interested in dinosaurs when she read stories about them to her young children. It was an interest that suited her well. She was already an expert rock collector, having traveled around New Zealand for years looking for and identifying minerals and gemstones. During her rock-collecting trips, Wiffen gained a vast knowledge of New Zealand's landscape and geology. She also developed a scientific mindset and the keen eye of someone who spends her life hunting for objects buried in the ground.

Social Studies

Social Studies

Biography

LEGENDS of the BLUES

by Stephanie Wilder

Genre	Comprehension Skill and Strategy	Text Features
Nonfiction	• Main Idea and Details • Graphic Organizers	• Captions • Labels • Heads • Glossary

Scott Foresman Reading Street 5.3.4

PEARSON

Scott Foresman

ISBN 0-328-13542-9

90000

9 780328 135424

scottforesman.com

Reader Response

1. What is the main idea of the second paragraph on page 13? What are two supporting details?

2. Make a chart similar to the one below. List the four musicians included in *Legends of the Blues* and at least one major accomplishment of each.

Ma Rainey	Bessie Smith	Ray Charles	Aretha Franklin

3. *Appreciate* has another meaning, one that relates to money. Look that meaning up in the dictionary. Then write a sentence using that meaning.

4. Which one of this book's photographs did you find the most interesting? Why?

Glossary

appreciate *v.* to think highly of; to recognize the worth or value of.

barber *n.* someone whose business is cutting hair and shaving or trimming beards.

choir *n.* a group of singers who sing together, often at a church service.

released *v.* permitted to be published or sold.

religious *adj.* interested in the belief, study, and worship of God or gods.

slavery *n.* the practice of holding people against their will and making them work without pay.

teenager *n.* a person in his or her teens.

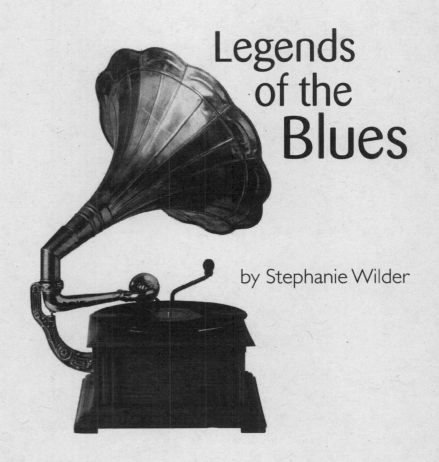

Legends of the Blues

by Stephanie Wilder

PEARSON
Scott Foresman

Editorial Offices: Glenview, Illinois • Parsippany, New Jersey • New York, New York
Sales Offices: Needham, Massachusetts • Duluth, Georgia • Glenview, Illinois
Coppell, Texas • Ontario, California • Mesa, Arizona

Back to Where It All Began

The first blues music was played in the American South during the early 1900s. The blues was a product of major cities, such as Atlanta and St. Louis. It also sprang up from the countryside in places such as the Mississippi Delta.

The blues had its roots in both African culture and the time when African Americans were enslaved. Even so, it was a new form of music. It had a sound and style that was uniquely American. African American singers, such as Ma Rainey and Bessie Smith, made the music popular during the 1920s. They sang about their experiences as African Americans in ways that touched the lives of their listeners. Their powerful music helped many people work through the challenges in their lives.

Segregation and slavery no longer exist in the United States, but blues music lives on. Modern legends, including Ray Charles and Aretha Franklin, created music that owed much to the blues. They took the early blues sound and mixed it with other musical styles to create soul music, which reached an even wider audience. Thanks to these musical legends, blues music remains popular today and continues to inspire many talented musicians.

A shot of Memphis's Beale Street, famed for its blues music.

A scene from the American South, where the blues was invented.

The Roots of The Blues

Much of African American history is filled with sadness. That sadness, however, is often mingled with hope for the future. These two emotions, sadness and hope, are at the heart of the great American musical traditions of the blues.

The United States' enslaved African Americans were freed in 1865. Before then slavery existed throughout the American South. For centuries the South's African Americans were made to work without pay. They were free to do only what they were told.

The end of slavery did little to improve African Americans' lives. Most remained poor, and what work they could find didn't pay enough. A special set of laws known as Jim Crow laws were written to keep African Americans from having many of the rights that other Americans had.

The blues were inspired partly by the songs sung by sharecroppers.

Aretha Franklin continued to record major hits during the 1970s, including "Spanish Harlem," "Bridge Over Troubled Water," and "Daydreaming." In 1977 she sang at President Jimmy Carter's inauguration. Then, in 1980, Aretha appeared in the smash hit comedy movie *The Blues Brothers*, which also starred Ray Charles and other notable blues artists. The movie made Aretha popular with a whole new generation of fans and helped revive her career.

In 1985 Aretha won a Grammy award for her hit song "Freeway of Love." It was Aretha's first Grammy award in a decade and showed that she could still produce hits a quarter-century after her first recordings. In 1987, Aretha was inducted into the Rock and Roll Hall of Fame, becoming the first female artist to earn an induction.

Aretha Franklin's most recent albums have focused mostly on her roots in gospel and religious singing. Although they have not sold as well as her works from the 1960s and 1970s, Aretha continues to earn respect as a legendary singer of the blues.

Aretha Franklin performing in Washington, D.C., with the Capitol Building in the background

Taking Strength from Music

When slavery ended, many African Americans became sharecroppers, or farmers who rent their land from others. While laboring in the fields, they often sang songs to pass the time. These songs had their roots in the music of Africa.

African music didn't originally have the blues' sad and mournful feel. But it changed to reflect the hardships African Americans faced. African Americans also sang hopeful songs, usually when they met together in church. Eventually these two types of songs came together to form the blues.

The blues first became popular with sharecroppers in the lower South. Soon everyone was playing or listening to the blues, from the local barber to national audiences. White listeners also embraced the new style of music, and in the 1950s, musicians combined it with country music to create rock 'n' roll. Almost every kind of popular music played in the United States today is based partly on the blues. But it all started with just a handful of African American musicians. This book will tell their story.

Ma Rainey:
Mother of the Blues

On April 26, 1886, Gertrude Pridgett was born in Columbus, Georgia. She began performing at the age of fourteen when she participated in a local talent show. A few years later, while in St. Louis, she heard some music that was totally new to her. What she heard was an early form of the blues. Ms. Pridgett was greatly influenced by the music and made it the focus of her singing.

In 1904 she married William "Pa" Rainey. From that point on she was known simply as Ma Rainey. She traveled and performed with her husband all over the South. Ma Rainey is known as the first female blues singer. Her nickname is "Mother of the Blues."

Ma Rainey was named "Mother of the Blues" for having been one of the first female blues singers.

As a child and young teenager Aretha Franklin sang gospel in her father's church choir. She came to appreciate gospel for its power and beauty, and it would influence the rest of her singing career.

Aretha's father had a national radio show and was an important figure in African American culture. He was able to introduce Aretha to several important gospel singers, who helped guide her young career. In 1956 she recorded her first album, *The Gospel Sound of Aretha Franklin* for the Checker label.

Aretha moved to New York at the age of eighteen. There she began performing live at both clubs and concert halls, singing for primarily African American audiences.

In 1966 Aretha began recording for Atlantic Records, and her career took off. She had a series of hits with Atlantic, including "I Never Loved a Man (the Way I Loved You)," "Chain of Fools," "Dr. Feelgood," "Baby, I Love You," and "Respect."

Of all these hits, "Respect" had a unique status. Leaders in both the feminist and African American civil rights movements embraced "Respect" for the way it seemed to symbolize women's and African Americans' struggle for equal rights.

Aretha Franklin: The Queen of Soul

Aretha Franklin is another great soul singer. Her music has earned her the title "Queen of Soul."

Franklin was born on March 25, 1942, in Memphis, Tennessee. She grew up in Detroit, Michigan, where her father was a church minister.

Aretha Franklin honed her amazing voice singing gospel music in her father's church.

Ma Rainey had a powerful voice that brought meaning and emotion to her songs. Although primarily a singer of rough, country-style blues songs, she also added some polished, city-style blues to her singing.

During the 1900s men usually sang in the country style and women in the city style. Ma Rainey mixed the sounds and themes of both styles. She gained respect for writing her own songs and made things easier for other female blues singers by proving that women could sing the blues.

Ma Rainey's Recordings

During the early 1900s Ma Rainey traveled with a group called Tolliver's Circus and Musical Extravaganza. Ma's voice and singing became known and liked by more and more people as the group toured around the country. However, Ma Rainey's fans were limited at first to those who saw her live performances. This is because she had to wait many years to record any of her music.

In 1923 Ma Rainey finally released her first phonograph recording. This meant that people could listen to and enjoy her music at home on a phonograph, or record player, a machine that was used before the invention of tape and compact disc players. They no longer had to travel to a live performance to hear her.

Ma Rainey's recordings sold well. In response, she recorded ninety-two songs over the next five years.

People played Ma Rainey's records on phonographs such as this.

Ray Charles sold millions of records over his career, which spanned almost seven decades.

Ray's New Sound

People called Ray's new style of music soul. Soul combined the blues, jazz, gospel, and country, and audiences loved it.

Ray enjoyed a string of hit songs in the 1950s, starting with 1951's "Baby Let Me Hold Your Hand." His song "Things That I Used to Do" sold a million copies in 1954. In that same year, Ray made the song "I've Got a Woman," which got him an even bigger following.

By 1959, with the release of "What'd I Say," Ray Charles had become an international pop star. At the time few African American artists had been able to "cross over," or have success with white audiences. But everyone, regardless of color, wanted to hear Ray's music.

As the years went by Ray traveled less but recorded more. His 1962 album *More Sounds in Country and Western Music* sold more than one milion copies. In 1986 Ray Charles was inducted into the Rock and Roll Hall of Fame. He was presented with the National Medal of Arts in 1992 for his achievements in popular music. Ray Charles died on June 10, 2004.

Ma Rainey's music often dealt with problems facing African Americans. Her song "Slave to the Blues" makes references to slavery. Ma Rainey's songs also made references to the Jim Crow laws that Southern states enforced at the time. These laws took away many of the freedoms that African Americans thought they would gain when slavery ended.

Ma Rainey's music contained a powerful message. She sang about things that her African American audience could relate to. With her strong voice and passionate lyrics, Ma Rainey helped the blues become more popular.

Phonograph players became less popular during the 1980s, as people began listening to music recorded on cassette tapes (left) and compact discs (upper left).

Bessie Smith: Empress of the Blues

Bessie Smith was born in Chattanooga, Tennessee, sometime around 1894. Her childhood was a hard one. Smith's parents died when she was very young. Bessie and her brothers and sisters were poor and had to depend on each other. Her older sister Viola raised her, and her brother Clarence taught her to sing and dance.

Around 1912 Clarence got Bessie an audition as a dancer with Moses Stokes' traveling show. Bessie won the job and began performing on the road. While traveling she met Ma Rainey, who would have a great influence on her career.

Bessie Smith (left) was influenced by Ma Rainey's singing and style of music.

Ray's family moved to Florida when he was an infant. There Ray attended a special school called the St. Augustine School for the Deaf and Blind. While at school in Saint Augustine, Ray continued to play the piano. He also learned to play the saxophone and clarinet. Early on, Ray's teachers noticed that he had a gift for music. They also saw that he compensated for his lack of sight by learning how to listen with great care, a skill that helped him greatly to understand the music that he heard.

Ray left school at age fifteen to begin a career as a

professional musician. Almost immediately he began developing a unique style of music. Ray spent the late 1940s performing around the country with different blues bands. During the 1950s he continued to perform throughout the United States.

Ray Charles learned how to play many instruments, but he is most remembered as a piano player.

Ray Charles: The Father of Soul

Ray Charles, "The Father of Soul," was born Ray Charles Robinson in Albany, Georgia, on September 23, 1930. He began playing the piano as a very young child, giving his first public performance in a Florida café at the age of five.

Ray had a difficult childhood. He grew up during the worst of the Great Depression, and his family had very little money. At the age of six, Ray began losing his sight and became completely blind by age seven.

On top of this, Ray, like Bessie Smith, had to deal with the early deaths of his parents. Ray's father died when Ray was only ten. His mother died when he was just fifteen. Somehow Ray found a way to overcome these hardships and developed into a great blues artist.

Ma Rainey took Bessie, who was still very young at the time, under her wing. She became Bessie's mentor, sharing what she knew about singing and the blues.

Smith's singing career took off while she was under Ma Rainey's guidance. She added many of Ma Rainey's techniques to her music, while at the same time developing her own unique style of singing.

With training and practice, Smith became a great blues singer. Throughout the 1920s she traveled the South and sang to sold-out crowds. She earned over a thousand dollars a week for her performances, which easily would have made her a millionaire in today's money.

Bessie Smith, who started as a dancer, would eventually find fame as a blues singer.

Bessie Smith enjoyed great success during 1920s, only to experience a decline in the 1930s as swing music became more popular.

In 1923, the same year that Ma Rainey put out her first phonograph recordings, Bessie Smith also began making records. One of her first, called "Downhearted Blues," sold more than 700,000 copies in only six months! Bessie recorded 160 songs in ten years and became known as the "Empress of the Blues." Both city and country listeners enjoyed Smith's music, which blended Ma Rainey's far more country-music singing style with lyrics and a sound that city audiences found appealing.

Sadly, Bessie's career went into decline during the 1930s. Much of this was due to the Great Depression. The Great Depression caused millions of Americans to lose their jobs. People wanted their music to be more upbeat during this grim time, so swing music, which was more optimistic than the blues, became more popular. People also had far less money to spend on records and concert tickets, which also hurt Bessie's career.

Despite these problems, Bessie Smith performed throughout the 1930s until her death in 1937. She is remembered today as one of the most successful blues singers of the 1920s.

Social Studies

Social Studies

Very Special Effects: Computers in Filmmaking

by Stephanie Wilder

Genre	Comprehension Skill and Strategy	Text Features
Nonfiction	• Graphic Sources • Prior Knowledge	• Captions • Labels • Chart • Glossary

Scott Foresman Reading Street 5.3.5

PEARSON

Scott Foresman

scottforesman.com

ISBN 0-328-13545-3

90000

9 780328 135455

Reader Response

1. Outline the steps in the process of creating a computer-generated character from production to the final image.

2. What knowledge did you have of computer-based moviemaking before you read this book? What did you learn about it from reading this book? What would you still like to learn about it? Use a graphic organizer like the one below to help write your answer.

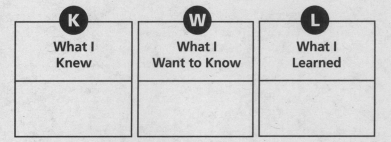

K What I Knew	**W** What I Want to Know	**L** What I Learned

3. Two of the vocabulary words in the glossary contain prefixes. Which words are they? Tell what the prefixes mean, and write five other words with these prefixes.

4. This book contains many images of people involved in making movies. Which image or images did you find the most helpful? Why?

Glossary

background *n.* in a movie, the images that show up behind the actors and other objects in the foreground.

explosions *n.* noisy bursts, usually creating lots of smoke and fire.

landscape *n.* the look and quality of the land when viewed from far away.

miniature *adj.* when something has been done or made on a very small or tiny scale.

prehistoric *adj.* from or of a time long before people began writing and keeping records and histories.

reassembled *v.* brought things back together again.

Very Special Effects: Computers in Filmmaking

01010111010100100100101010100101101
01010001010101101010010110101010101011000

by Stephanie Wilder

PEARSON
Scott
Foresman

Editorial Offices: Glenview, Illinois • Parsippany, New Jersey • New York, New York
Sales Offices: Needham, Massachusetts • Duluth, Georgia • Glenview, Illinois
Coppell, Texas • Ontario, California • Mesa, Arizona

Currently there are few theaters that can show computer-based movies.

For now, movies made using regular film still outnumber the few movies that are made using just computers. Regular film has worked well for over one hundred years. It has a look that movie audiences have grown to love and enjoy.

Right now, the biggest concern in the movie industry is that movies watched on a computer screen, using files downloaded from the Internet, will keep people from going to the theaters. It's hard to believe that people will stop going to movie theaters. But what *is* certain is that computers will continue to play a huge role in moviemaking. Special effects now rely almost completely on computers. And who knows? Perhaps some day the movies you see at theaters will be computer based!

23

Getting Used to Digital

Directors can make and edit computer-based movies for a lot less money than with regular film. But a regular film has a certain look that computer-based movies still can't quite copy. Many times, images made by computers look almost *too* perfect when they're played on a big screen. Regular film can portray shadows and characters' movements in a way that computer-based movies are still unable to show.

Part of the reason for this is that we're used to the look of movies made on regular film. When shown using the proper technology, computer-based movies have more accurate-looking images. But our minds have difficulty accepting them, since we've seen so many images made with regular film! Computer-based movies are getting better every day. Because of this, most moviemakers think that computer-based movies will soon become far more popular than regular films.

The New Way of Filmmaking

For almost one hundred years, special effects in filmmaking changed very slowly. Movies were made using regular film. Special effects were created using camera tricks, clay models, and similar techniques.

Over the last three decades, however, special effects have changed dramatically. The introduction of computer technology has had a major impact on modern films, and it has completely changed the way many movies are made.

Most movies are still shot on regular film rather than videotape, and most moviemakers still use film cameras like the one below. But every year more and more computers are used to create special effects. In some cases, computer-based digital cameras are being used instead of film cameras.

A growing number of movies are being made with computers instead of film cameras.

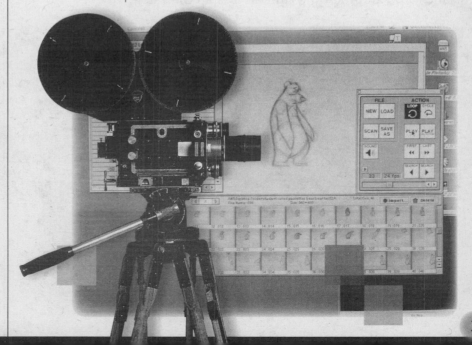

Computers: Making the Impossible Possible

In the late 1970s, filmmakers started using computers to create movie effects. First they filmed their actors on a stage. Later they added backdrops designed by computers. This process was slow and expensive, and wasn't capable of making realistic special effects.

In the past decade, computer technology has gotten much better. It can now create movie images that look amazingly lifelike. This is done through the use of computer pixels. Pixels are the miniature dots of color that make up the images on your computer screen.

Computer pixels have made the moviemaking process much easier. For example, imagine that you are a director. You want to make a movie set in a prehistoric landscape filled with many different dinosaurs. Nowadays, all you need to "create" that prehistoric landscape and the dinosaurs in it is a computer.

Older movies used clay models for special effects.

The CONS of Computer-Based Movies

> Computer-based movies can look grainy on a big screen. That's because they're designed to look best when played on a computer screen.

> Computer-based movies use a lot of computer memory. They take up a lot of space as computer files. A special digital projector is needed to show them in movie theaters.

> People can make copies of computer-based movies easily, and can send them over the Internet. Moviemakers are worried that people will not pay to see their movies anymore because of how easy it would be to copy and distribute the files of computer-based movies.

> It would be expensive for movie theater owners to change over from regular film projectors to digital projectors. Theater owners might have to raise ticket prices to cover the cost of the new projectors.

The PROS of Computer-Based Movies

> Computer-based movies cost less to make. Regular film is expensive. It requires trucks and planes for distribution. With computer-based movies, the files can be sent directly to the movie theater over the Internet.

> Computer-based movies don't take up a lot of space. The only space they require is a computer hard drive!

> It's easy to make copies of computer-based movies.

> The editing of computer-based movies is easy and flexible. Changes can be made at any stage of the postproduction process.

> Computer-based movies don't require any film to be developed.

> Moviemakers can immediately see what they made. They don't need to wait for any film to be developed to see the day's work.

But consider what you would have needed in the past to film such a scene. You would have had to build either a huge stage or a scale model to recreate the dinosaurs' landscape. You also would have had to make dinosaur models out of clay, rubber, or other materials. All of this would have cost a lot of money and taken a lot of time.

Obviously, computer technology is a big help for recreating past worlds! But computers can be used to accomplish many other things in moviemaking. They can be used to cover up background objects. Or they can be used to add background that is too expensive to build.

Now, almost all movies have some kind of computer-based special effects. Have you seen a movie recently that you're convinced was made using only regular film? Watch it again. Chances are you'll spot something that was made using a computer-based process!

Newer movies rely more on computer-based special effects.

These three squirrel pictures are examples of hand-drawn animation.

Computer-Generated Characters

Perhaps the most common type of special effect is a computer-generated character. Computer-generated characters are created for movies that have creatures that do not exist in real life.

Early special effects used hand-drawn animation, clay models, or puppets to make fantasy characters come to life. But today computers are used to create these creatures. They look far more realistic than anything that is hand drawn. They can be made to look three-dimensional and can be given features like fur and scales that look very lifelike. They can even blend in with the actors in the movie in a way that looks realistic.

Computer-based digital movies can be edited, or made ready for production, quickly through the use of a computer. And changes can be made to any part of the movie. The computer's code can simply be rearranged to change either the order of a movie's images or the images themselves.

With regular film, the editing process requires more time and effort. The editor can only make changes by cutting out portions of the film. Then the film needs to be taped together to get it back into the right order.

So far, only a few Hollywood movies have been completely computer-based. This is because most movie theaters can only show movies that have been shot using regular film. At this time theater owners don't want to buy new computer-based projectors. They feel it's not worth the cost.

The following pages explore the benefits and drawbacks of computer-based movies. After you read the two charts, see if you can come up with other advantages and disadvantages.

The man in the top photo is editing regular film. The man to the left is editing a computer-based movie.

Can you spot any differences between these computer-generated fish and the squirrel?

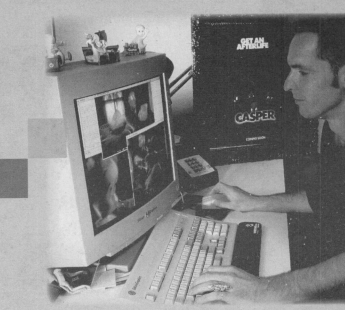

How It's Done with Computers: Preproduction

Imagine you are a computer artist. You're working on a movie that calls for a computer-generated character. What steps do you take to bring the character to life?

First comes preproduction. In preproduction you sculpt a clay model of the character, from which you then create a computer model. The computer model allows you to see how the character will look during its scenes. (You'll read more about this on the next page.)

Next, using regular film, you shoot everything in the character's scenes that can't be done using a computer. You scan that film into a computer. When you scan film into a computer, it gets reassembled into a digital format. Once you have scanned the film and converted it into a digital format, you are ready for postproduction.

A computer artist uses a clay model to create a computer-based model of a dog.

Comparing the Processes

Computer-generated characters such as the one you just read about get most of the attention. But computer artists have created all sorts of different special effects, ranging from different backgrounds and explosions to moving vehicles and even different kinds of weather.

The process for adding computer-based special effects is always the same, at least when it comes to making movies that combine regular film with computer-based special effects. However, some movies are now made using nothing but computers. Such movies, which don't require regular film during production, can be put together using a totally different process.

The next section discusses how computer-based movies are edited. You'll learn that people edit computer-based movies in a way that is totally different from how they edit regular films. Keep reading to find out more!

This digital camera can also be used to make movies.

Anyone with good skills and the right computer can put together a computer-based movie!

Cell phones are now so advanced that you can make movies with them.

A computer artist takes notes while working on three-dimensional camera tracking.

Starting Postproduction

Postproduction is when you create all of your computer effects. The first step in postproduction is to set up three-dimensional camera tracking.

Three-dimensional camera tracking is very important. If it's not done correctly, the character won't look like it fits in the scene. Remember the computer model of the character from page 8? During three-dimensional camera tracking you use that model to track the camera movements that were made while the regular filming was being done. This process ensures that the computer model of the character moves correctly with the cameras. It also ensures that the character moves in a way that works well with the human actors' own movements.

Rotoscoping

The next step is rotoscoping. During rotoscoping, you outline the area within certain scenes. The area that gets outlined is where the character, or object, will be placed.

As the diagram to the right shows, there are two steps to the rotoscoping process. First you, as the rotoscoper, outline each frame of film in which the character, or in this case the space shuttle, will appear. Twenty-four frames are needed for every second of film. That may not sound like a lot initially. But consider this: for the space shuttle to be onscreen for only one minute, you would need to outline over 1,400 separate areas! Even so, rotoscoping is much faster than any similar process that uses regular film. That's because a computer can repeat many different tasks in a short period of time.

For the second step, you, now working as a computer artist, take each of the areas that have been outlined and blank them out. This leaves an empty space, which the space shuttle is later added into. It sounds like difficult work, and it is. But, in a way, it is similar to any cut and paste job that you have done with scissors and paper.

The digital model is combined with the other layers of film, thereby completing the process.

Compositing

When the painting stage is finished, it is time to begin the two-dimensional compositing. During this stage, you bring together the scene's different parts.

To do this, you create many different layers. You layer the computer-generated character over the background scenes that were shot on film. In other scenes, you add in the character's friends or environment as another layer. You pile each layer on top of the other layers. When you finish piling the layers you get a whole image, complete with the movie's human actors, the computer-generated character, the background, and the special effects.

Finally, you turn the digital file, which contains everything that was done on computer, back into film. The result makes it look like the computer-generated character was filmed alongside the actors. Movies from the past used handmade puppets instead of computer-generated characters. But computer-generated characters look much more lifelike!

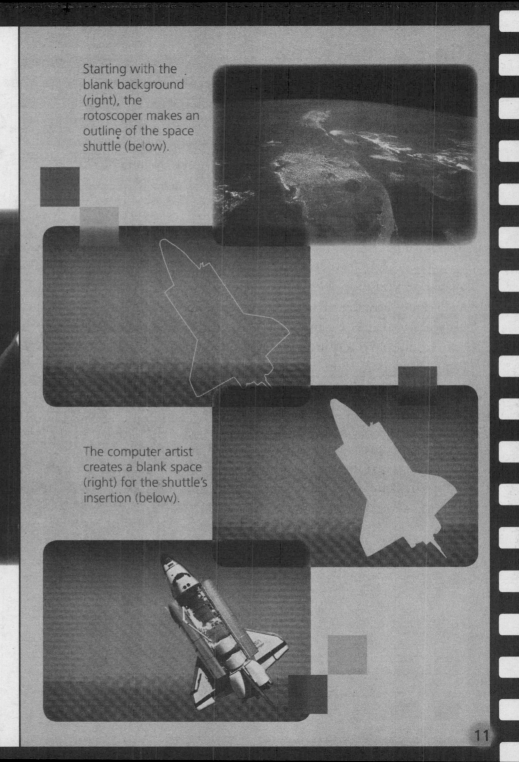

Starting with the blank background (right), the rotoscoper makes an outline of the space shuttle (below).

The computer artist creates a blank space (right) for the shuttle's insertion (below).

The Painting Process

The next stage of postproduction is called painting. Now is when the computer-generated character is actually created!

So how is the character created? First you use a computer to create a digital model of the character, adding different features to create the character's personality. Then you insert the character into the spaces that were created during rotoscoping.

To do this before computers were available, you would have had to create a separate drawing of your character for each frame. For a five-minute scene, that would have required over seven thousand separate drawings! Instead, with computers, the character's digital model is given specific directions. These directions allow the character to be copied into each frame with much less time and effort. Just as with rotoscoping, a computer's ability to rapidly repeat the same task makes the painting process practical.

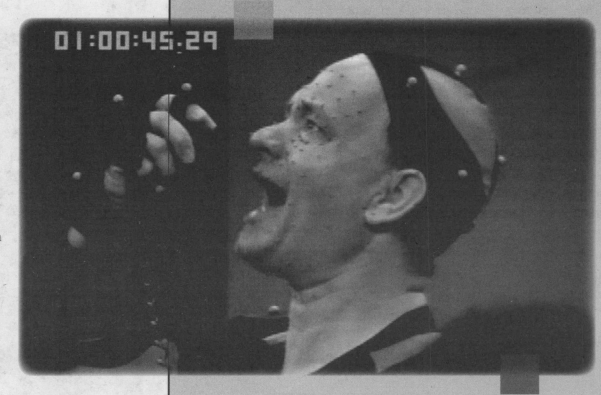

This actor's suit gives information to a computer, from which the computer creates a digital model.

Genre	Comprehension Skill and Strategy
Fiction	• Draw Conclusions • Answer Questions

Scott Foresman Reading Street 5.4.1

PEARSON

Scott
Foresman

scottforesman.com

ADVENTURE
— TO THE —
NEW WORLD

BY GRETCHEN MCBRIDE

ILLUSTRATED BY PHYLLIS POLLEMA-CAHILL

Reader Response

1. Using a graphic organizer like the one below, explain what happened when Jane said "hello" to the Indian girl and why you think it happened. Do you think that the Indian girl knew English? Why or why not?

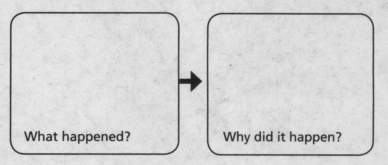

What happened? → Why did it happen?

2. Based on what you read, what do you think happened to the soldiers who were supposed to be at the fort?

3. The word *civilization* comes from the Latin word *civis*, meaning "citizen." How many other words can you think of that come from the word *civis*? Ask your parents or use a dictionary if you need help.

4. If you were Governor White, what would you have done when you saw that the fort had been destroyed and the soldiers were gone?

Roanoke: The Lost Colony

So what happened to the vanished settlers of Roanoke? Some think they joined the Croatoan Indians, who lived near Roanoke on what is now called Hatteras Island. In 1997, archaeologists unearthed copper and brass pieces and parts of lead bullets from the remains of Hatteras Island's main Croatoan village. Then, in 1998, archaeologists digging at the same site found a gold ring, the kind worn by sixteenth-century English noblemen.

In combination with the CROATOAN carving found at Roanoke in 1590 by John White, these discoveries support the theory that there may have been English people living among the Croatoans during the late sixteenth century. But until archaeologists find evidence that proves beyond a doubt what happened to the Roanoke settlers, we can only make educated guesses as to their fate.

ADVENTURE
— TO THE —
NEW WORLD

BY GRETCHEN MCBRIDE
ILLUSTRATED BY PHYLLIS POLLEMA-CAHILL

PEARSON

Scott
Foresman

Editorial Offices: Glenview, Illinois • Parsippany, New Jersey • New York, New York
Sales Offices: Needham, Massachusetts • Duluth, Georgia • Glenview, Illinois
Coppell, Texas • Ontario, California • Mesa, Arizona

No one spoke for several moments after Governor White left the house. Finally, Jane asked her father anxiously, "Are Governor White's words really true? Do you think this colony is failing? If it fails, does that mean we have to sail back to Portsmouth? What will happen?"

Her father shrugged, saying, "Neither I nor your mother can predict what will happen. I hate having to say so, but Governor White's words are true, Jane. There's still a strong chance that this colony will fail. This first winter will be our strongest test. But while it's still summer and the weather is warm, we might as well do everything we can to try and make Roanoke succeed. So why don't we go plant those strawberries? There's still enough time left in the growing season to harvest a small crop of them. Let's go out to your mother's garden and see what we can do."

The family went out into the garden to plant the strawberries. Nobody said a word. Although they were frightened by Governor White's words, they had confidence in their ability to survive through the winter and make Roanoke a success. Jane's family faced an uncertain future. But they refused to give up.

Governor White turned to leave the house. Pausing at the door, he addressed the family. "Before I return to the fort for my official duties, I must remind you all that we live in a time of uncertainty. There is still a chance that this settlement might not survive. We've done well enough through the summer. The crop that we have harvested should last through much of the winter. But it might not be enough. Our hunting parties have had success of late, but I don't know if the meat that they've brought in will be enough to make up the difference before spring arrives and English ships can resupply us."

He continued, "Unfortunately, I will not be able to serve Roanoke much longer, for I have been called back by the Queen. My ship sails next week for England. When I return to our mother country, I will ask for the extra goods and supplies that we need to ensure that Roanoke can live on as a permanent settlement. However, it takes three months to sail across the ocean and another three months to sail back. And that doesn't include the time it will take me to plead our settlement's cause before the Queen and her advisors. So the earliest I will be back is next summer. In the meantime, I am proud of everything that we have accomplished here. This colony has adapted well to the challenges of the New World. So goodbye for now, and good luck."

Author's Note:

The story you are about to read is a piece of historical fiction. Though based on real events, the dialogue and many details have been invented. We know for a fact that three ships and roughly one hundred English settlers set sail from Portsmouth, England, in April of 1587, bound for the settlement at Roanoke Island in what is now the state of Virginia.

Among the settlers was a man named John White, who had been appointed governor of Roanoke. White had to sail home to England soon after the group landed, but he promised to return to Roanoke as soon as possible with more supplies and people. However, a war with Spain erupted, delaying White's return.

Governor White finally returned to Roanoke in the summer of 1590, hoping to find a thriving settlement. Instead, he came across the word CROATOAN, the name of a Native American tribe, carved into a tree. Other than that puzzling clue, nothing of the settlement remained.

To this day, the fate of Roanoke's settlers remains the biggest mystery in the history of England's North American colonies.

Chapter One *Journey's Eve*

It was late April, in the year 1587. Spring had come to the seaport of Portsmouth. For months, Jane's family had been making preparations to leave their life in England behind and start anew in the North American colony of Virginia. Now only a few hours remained until Jane's family and more than one hundred other adventurous English settlers would set sail for the New World.

Jane looked around her small upstairs loft, which she had slept in for as long as she could remember. Her eyes fell upon the yellow curtains that framed the loft's tiny window. She touched them, sending them gently rustling. Jane was pleased with the way the sun shone through the curtains. It bathed the room in a golden glow.

As the evening light faded, Jane tried to imagine leaving her wonderful little loft, her friends and relatives, and everything else that was familiar to her in Portsmouth. She thought of the voyage tomorrow and what life would be like at Roanoke, the island on the coast of the Virginia colony that was the settlers' destination. What did the future hold in store for them?

In a firm but kindly voice, Governor White said, "Jane, I must say that I'm disappointed with you. You disobeyed your parents and forced us to draft a dozen men to go looking for you. Your little escapade has cost our settlement both time and money. And yet . . ." here his tone softened, ". . . and yet we are at a critical juncture with these Indians. Soon I will go conduct peace talks with them. In order to be successful I need all the information I can get regarding these strange and mysterious people. So tell me, Jane, what did you see?"

Jane hesitated. Should she tell him everything? At last, she settled on telling the truth. "I met an Indian girl. She was about my age. The girl said 'hello' when I talked with her, but other than that said nothing. She took me to a place where some strawberries were growing, and we ate some of them together. Then she gave me a strawberry plant to take home for myself. That's it."

Governor White was satisfied that Jane had told the truth. Still, he could not hide the disappointment in his voice. "Well, if that's all that happened, then we'll have to be content with that. I wish the Indian girl had taken you to her village so you could have learned something of how her people live. On the other hand, hearing that you had a friendly encounter with an Indian gives me hope for the future. Perhaps there's yet a chance that we will be able to live in peace with these people."

Just at that moment, Governor White came through the front door, followed by a group of men. Stopping at the sight of Jane, he threw his hands in the air.

"So the girl is safe and sound at home!" Governor White exclaimed. He looked down to address Jane. "Well, Jane, you've certainly given the people of Roanoke a fright. Your father and mother approached me this morning at the fort. They were frantic with worry, saying that you had disappeared into the woods. They told me how curious you were about Indians. They thought you might try to run away and join them!"

Governor White turned to face the group of men. "Well, as you can see gentlemen, the girl is safe. Thank you for helping to search for her. You may now return to your homes," he said, dismissing them with a wave of his arm.

Jane's mother stood at the top of the stairway, watching with a smile as her daughter daydreamed.

"Dear, you need to do your packing tonight for the voyage," she said, speaking quietly. "The ship leaves early, with the morning tide. Your father is having the trunks brought down to the wharf immediately after breakfast. Remember to only bring things that we need; clothes and not much else. I've packed blankets, food, and medicine."

Jane nodded. "Don't worry; I'll have my packing finished before sunset. But I'm scared about journeying to the New World. How do we know that it will be safe for us there? How do we know that we will get there without any problems? I have so many worries. Are you sure that we must go?"

"Yes, dear, I'm afraid we must," Jane's mother gently explained. "Your father and I have already talked about this. Our space on the ship is already reserved, and we have settled all our business here in Portsmouth. We can't turn back now."

Jane's mother saw that her daughter was frightened, and tried to reassure her. "I know how hard it is for you, Jane. I'm finding it as difficult to say goodbye as you are. It won't be easy for us to leave behind the comforts of civilization for an unknown land that promises challenges and hardships."

She went on, "But the opportunities in Virginia are enormous. Queen Elizabeth's plan to settle this Virginia colony and make it grow is positively inspired. Right now it may seem like we are fleeing Portsmouth for an uncertain future. But I assure you, Jane, we'll be the envy of England when they hear of how well we are doing in the New World. Soon all of our friends and relatives will want to join us!"

"I'm sure you're right, Mother," Jane said. "I promise I'll do my best to not grow sad. From now on, I'll think only of the happy future that awaits us in Virginia!"

"Good," her mother replied. "Now make sure to tuck yourself into bed as soon as you're done packing. You need to get a good night's sleep. Tomorrow will be a long day."

As soon as Jane stepped inside her house, she knew she was in trouble. Her father grabbed her arm and demanded to know where she had been.

Jane sucked in her breath. In a low, sobbing voice, she said, "Oh, Father, I know you and Mother are upset with me. But I had to go see for myself what these Indians were like. This morning I snuck off to a place in the woods where I know an Indian village is. There I met a nice Indian girl—and look, she gave me these delicious strawberries to plant in the garden. See, Father, we just might be able to become friends with these Indians!"

Jane's father relaxed his grip on her arm. "You're right, Jane—I am upset with you," he said. "I am upset with you for your foolish venture to the far edge of the settlement. And I am especially upset because you disobeyed my order. I told you that you are not allowed to go beyond our village!"

Jane looked as if she was about to cry. Sighing, her father gave her a hug, saying, "And yet here you are, back safe and sound. Still, you must be punished for your reckless actions. Every night for a month, you are to go to bed immediately after dinner. When you wake up in the morning, you will come to Mother and me before doing anything else. That way we'll know that you're safe. But I do forgive you, Jane. And I'm glad you're home!"

Jane and the Indian girl stood for several moments, smiling and eating the strawberries. Then the Indian girl pulled a clump of them from the ground, with the roots still attached. Holding them up for Jane to see, she made a digging motion, and placed her hand at knee level, showing how high they could grow. Smiling, the Indian girl gave the clump to Jane.

Jane beamed with delight. "Thank you, these look wonderful!" She took the Indian girl's hand and shook it. The sudden gesture startled the Indian girl, and at first she didn't know what to do. But then she smiled and shook back. They had become friends!

From out of the corner of her eye, Jane saw the sun climbing steadily above the treetops. She realized that she had been gone for hours. "It's getting late!" Jane exclaimed in panicked voice. "I must go, but thank you for the strawberries. I'll plant them in my mother's garden!" With the strawberry plant in one hand, she raced back home.

Jane's mother started down the stairs. "Good night, Jane," she called out, the sound of her footsteps echoing behind her.

"Good night, Mother," Jane answered. As soon as her mother left, Jane finished selecting the things that she would need for the voyage and for Roanoke. Paying heed to her mother's advice, she gathered only the most essential items—candles, clothing, scissors, and her small loom and sewing kit. Jane took one last look around her loft, then blew out the candle and climbed into bed.

Jane dreamt that night that she had been brought before Queen Elizabeth at the English royal court. Wearing her finest clothing, she stood before the Queen and the royal advisors. The Queen glittered in her crown and jewelry. Her advisors, serious and formal in their official uniforms, scowled and looked menacing. Jane was explaining to the Queen that she would do everything she could to make Roanoke a successful colony, but the advisors were shaking their heads and whispering in the Queen's ear. Jane was about to plead with the advisors when the sunrise burst into her room, waking her from her dream.

"Jane, wake up!" her mother called from downstairs. The morning was chilly. Jane dressed in her wool stockings, skirt, and cloak, bundled up her things for the voyage, and raced down to the first floor. There she found her father sitting at the small table next to the fireplace, packing and checking the trunks while Jane's mother cooked.

"Good morning, Jane. Ready for our voyage to Virginia?" he called out cheerfully.

"As ready as I'll ever be," Jane answered. "Here are my things for the trip. Is there anything you need me to do?"

"Nothing, other than eat!" her father answered. "Your mother has some porridge ready. Once we're done eating, your mother and I will check the house one more time. Then I'll have the trunks taken to the wharf, and we'll walk down to our ship!"

"But what happens to the house, father?" Jane asked.

"Well, the landlord said that the new tenants will arrive as soon as we leave. So it's no longer ours. But you know what? In Virginia, we won't have to rent anymore. There, we'll able to build a house for ourselves, and we'll have plenty of land on which to grow our crops. No more dirty, cold, crowded Portsmouth!"

"I'll eat to that!" Jane responded, feeling her father's excitement.

The Indian girl still looked confused. But her look quickly changed, as if she had suddenly had an idea. She pointed to a spot deep into the woods, grabbed Jane's hand, and broke into a brisk walk.

I guess she wants to show me something. I better follow! Jane thought, having no idea where she was being led.

The Indian girl led Jane along a faint, densely overgrown path. Jane could still see the clearing where the Indian village lay. But their current path was taking them far from where they had met.

They stopped in a small grove of bushes. Taking Jane's hand for a moment, the Indian girl made Jane pluck one of the ripe red fruits from a nearby patch of low plants. It was a juicy, fresh strawberry!

The Indian girl made a motion for Jane to eat the strawberry, while she herself plucked a few from some nearby patches. Jane hesitated. She knew about strawberries but had never eaten one. Back in Portsmouth they had been too expensive for her family to buy. Jane then saw the Indian girl eat one of the strawberries. Relaxing a bit, Jane took a bite. It was delicious!

Chapter Eight *The Encounter*

. . . *Smack!* Right at that moment, Jane bumped into a young Indian girl. The force of the blow left them momentarily stunned. Rubbing their foreheads in pain, they looked up to see what they had run into.

It was the opportunity that Jane had been waiting for. At last she would be able to find out about these Indians! Summoning her courage, she stammered, "H-h . . . hello."

The native girl, still wincing in pain, looked at Jane directly but did not speak. She looked terrified.

"Hello," Jane tried again, this time with a smile.

"Hello," repeated the native girl.

"You speak English!" Jane exclaimed in wonder.

The native girl again said, "Hello." This time, however, she met Jane's smile with one of her own.

"I was just out for a walk. I have been wanting to meet your people for some time," Jane explained. "Would you show me back to your village?"

The Indian girl had a confused look on her face.

Jane, not understanding that the Indian girl (who in truth knew not a word of English) was only mimicking her, said, "Perhaps you don't speak English as I do. But you still knew the word 'hello,' so you must have known some English people. Oh, I must tell my parents and Governor White!"

Jane and her family finished eating. Jane's father paid some laborers to move the trunks, and the family walked down to the wharf, giving one final glance to their home.

The scene at the wharf was chaotic. People were shouting, laughing, bumping into each other, and bustling about in frantic preparation. A sense of excitement filled the air as everyone thought ahead to the ocean crossing and the new lives that they would make for themselves in the Virginia colony.

The ship's sailors called for everyone to step on board, and Jane's family pushed their way on, jostling for space with the other passengers. One of the sailors was helping passengers place their trunks deep in the ship's hold. As Jane's parents worked with the sailor to move their trunks, Jane stared up at the complex web of spars, lines, and masts that made up the ship's rigging. *It's all so complicated*, she thought to herself. *How does it make the ship sail?*

Jane continued to watch, fascinated, as the sailors scrambled across the decks and prepared the ship. After several moments of intense work, they cast off from the wharf, and raised the sails. The ship plunged forward in the morning breeze. They were off!

Jane waved to the crowd of friends and relatives that had gathered at the end of the wharf to say goodbye. As their ship moved out of the harbor, Jane noticed that there were two other ships traveling with them.

The next couple of days went by slowly as the ships struggled to claw their way west. It was difficult sailing, for they had to fight against the winds and waves that funneled through the narrow English Channel. Jane felt sorry for the sailors, who had to constantly scramble up and down the ship's rigging in order to take down and put up sails. It looked like a hard life!

At last, after stopping briefly at the port of Plymouth to take on more supplies, the ships broke out into the open waters of the Atlantic, just past the westernmost edge of the English coast. Immediately they turned south, to catch the trade winds that would take them into milder weather and warmer water. A full three months of sailing lay ahead.

Jane had had enough. *The adults are frightened for no reason!* she thought. Although Jane had never told her parents about the incident, she remembered the time when she had come across the Indian village while out in the woods picking berries. Jane had been too afraid to do anything other than peek at the village from behind a thick growth of trees. Still, she knew how to get back to it. Jane decided that she would sneak out to meet one of the Indians. She would prove that they were friendly!

As quietly as she could, Jane put on her clothes and snuck out of the house. She tiptoed her way to the edge of the forest and picked up the main hunting trail, only to veer off after a couple hundred yards. Passing a stream, Jane crept towards a small clearing. There she could see some scattered campfires, a small plot of corn, and . . .

"Hmmph," Jane replied, getting up from the table. Upset by her father's order but not wanting to anger him any further, she marched off to sleep on her simple straw bed.

Jane woke up early the next day. As she lay in bed, she could hear her parents in their bed, talking about the settlement's problems. The people of Roanoke were under a lot of stress. The Queen and her advisors had demanded that Governor White find a way to make the colony profitable. Powerful people in England had spent large amounts of money to outfit the settlers' ships for the voyage across the Atlantic, and those investors wanted a return on their investment.

The people back home were especially anxious to make money because of the previous failures to make Roanoke work. Jane's parents and other settlers knew that the Queen and her advisors would be angry with them if they failed to grow abundant crops and find gold and silver. But the settlers knew that the only way they could grow better crops and find gold and silver was if they asked the Indians for advice!

Jane heard her father say, "I don't care what the Queen's advisors are demanding from us. The Indians are many and we are few. Until they send more soldiers and weapons, it is foolish for us to seek contact with the Indians."

Chapter Three *Across the Atlantic*

While the little fleet was at sea, there was little for the passengers to do other than think of the future. They knew that they would face unknown dangers in the New World. Jane and her family took heart, however, in stories that the sailors told them about previous voyages of exploration along the Virginia coast. The sailors spoke of a country where the winters were short and mild and the summers were warm and comfortable. From what they had seen of the lush forests, many rivers, and green fields, it looked as if the land in the New World could grow anything. For a group of settlers that knew little about what that lay ahead of them, such stories were reassuring. Jane listened to the sailors talk and dreamed of a pleasant life at Roanoke.

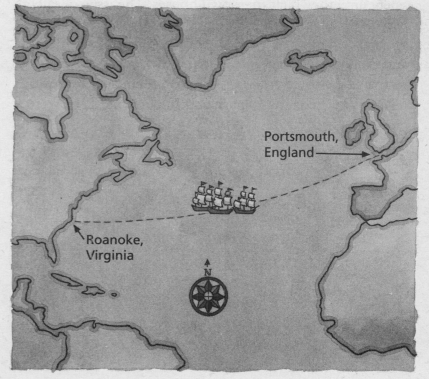

Portsmouth, England

Roanoke, Virginia

N

Jane and the other passengers also took comfort from the fact that they would be greeted by a small group of English soldiers when they arrived at Roanoke. During the previous year, a large group of colonists had left Roanoke and returned to England after running low on supplies and encountering difficulties with the local Indians. The leaders of Roanoke wouldn't allow the island to be totally abandoned, so they had a dozen soldiers sent over from England to guard the settlement until Jane's family and everyone else arrived.

There was other good news as well. The soldiers at Roanoke had built a strong fort from the towering oak trees that grew all over the island. Jane and her family hoped that the soldiers had kept the fort in good repair, since they would have to depend upon it for shelter and safety until they built their own houses. The issue of safety preyed on the settler's minds, now that they knew that the previous colonists had had trouble with the Indians of the area. Jane herself was curious about the Indians. She felt sure that she could make friends with them and improve relations between the English and the Indians, if she were given the chance.

Jane was bored by all of her father's talk. In fact, when she thought about it, she was pretty much bored with everything. It seemed as if all she ever did anymore was help weed the garden with her mother, thatch the roof with her father, and tend to any number of the dozens of daily chores that needed to be done. Her frustration with life at Roanoke came bursting out all of sudden.

"So what if we're learning and adapting? It's still taking too long!" she said defiantly. "I'm curious about these Indians. I want to know what they know. Maybe there are Indian girls my age that I could play with. This village of theirs sounds interesting, and I'm going to go find it!"

Jane's father looked at her sternly. "Jane, you are not allowed to talk to us that way," he said in a very serious voice. "I know that you miss your friends at home and that there aren't as many children to play with here. But we still don't know what happened to the soldiers who were guarding the fort. We don't know if what happened to them involves the nearby Indians, and no one is allowed to visit the Indians unless they have permission from Governor White. You will *not* go looking for their village!"

"They just might have," said Jane's father. "For one thing, as strange and different as these Indians are, there are rumors that they live better than we do. I've heard stories from some of the men who have stumbled onto one of their villages. They said that the Indian's houses were better built than ours. They also said that they have more animal skins drying out in the sun. That means they're better hunters. Also, the Indians' crops were growing much higher than ours. So they're also better farmers, I suppose."

"You really think they're better than we are?" Jane asked.

"It's not that they're better than we are," her father replied. "After all, we have many things—guns, iron tools, and glass—that they don't have. But our ignorance of this land has caused us to make many blunders."

Jane's father then ticked off a list of failures that the settlers had experienced because of their lack of knowledge. "We tried growing crops from seeds we brought from England, only to learn that some of those crops only grow back home. We tried using certain trees to build houses, only to find out that the timber here can't be used in the same way as the timber back in England. We tried eating some of the nuts and berries of the forest, only to find out that some of them make people sick. It's all right, though, because we're learning. We're learning, and we're adapting."

The months at sea passed. One day Jane's father took her up on deck to see if they could spot land. As they gazed, he talked about the history of the English colonies.

"The story of our colonies is the story of a friendship," Jane's father explained. "For years, Queen Elizabeth and the great Sir Walter Raleigh have been close friends. A few years ago, they met to form a strategy for England's future. They knew that Spain, our greatest enemy, had grown rich off of her colonies, and were convinced that she would someday use those riches to try and defeat us. So Raleigh and the Queen decided to start planting colonies of our own. Hopefully, they will provide the resources we need to help us defeat Spain!"

A worried look crept across Jane's face. Her father reassured her, "Oh, don't worry, Jane. The Spanish won't threaten us in Roanoke. Their colonies are way to the south and Roanoke has no value to them. But it is very valuable to us, being our first colony in the New World!"

At that moment, the ship's lookout sang out "Land Ho! It's Roanoke!" Everyone gave a shout of joy. They had made it! The little fleet's captains had been able to steer the ships directly to Roanoke, without being blown off course by currents or bad weather.

Chapter Four *Is This Roanoke?*

It was now July 22. Roanoke had been sighted late in the afternoon, so the captain of Jane's ship decided to anchor right off the beach for the evening. Throughout the night, Jane, her family, and the other colonists busied themselves with preparations for stepping onshore in the morning. After three months at sea, the passengers were tired. But they were eager to see Roanoke for the first time, and to greet the other English settlers.

Jane's family and the other settlers rowed ashore the following morning, landing on a white, sandy beach. Among them was a man named John White, who had been appointed Governor of Roanoke. White guided them up from the beach and through a dense forest to a small clearing where Roanoke's fort and settlement lay.

However, when they got there, they were greeted by a nasty shock.

Jane's father frowned, then answered, "A storm like a hurricane certainly might have threatened the houses. But if that was the case, then what happened to the fort? No, it couldn't have been a storm. Clearly it was a fire that destroyed the fort and caused the soldiers to abandon the settlement entirely. But who set it? And for what reason?"

The family thought in silence until Jane, seeing the serious expressions on her parents' faces as they thought about the previous settlers' fates, changed the subject. "One day, while I was playing outside the fort with the other girls, I heard Governor White talking with some of the men about needing to 'establish relations' with the nearby Indians. Everyone says they're bound to cause us trouble. What are they really like?"

Jane's father sighed. "Nobody really knows anything about the Indians. There has been talk that the soldiers may have mistreated them, and because of that the Indians might have fought back. On the other hand, some people say that the Indians might have been so nice to the soldiers that the soldiers decided to go live among them!"

"Oh, my," Jane's mother exclaimed, putting down her fork. "Would English people really do that?"

Chapter Six *What about the Indians?*

One night in mid-August, while eating dinner with her family, Jane realized how much her family had accomplished in Roanoke. Her father, using an ax, chisel, hammer, and nails, had built tables and chairs. Jane and her mother, using pig's fat, had made tallow candles. From sheep's wool they had woven rugs, blankets, and coverings for the doors and windows. Everything they had, they had made with their own hands!

As they sat eating, the family's thoughts turned from the frantic work of the past weeks towards larger concerns. Jane brought up the mystery of the previous settlers' fate.

"Is it possible that they left because of bad weather, such as a storm?" she asked.

There was almost nothing left of the original settlement! The fort which had promised the settlers shelter and safety had been burned to the ground. Scattered about were a few log houses that had obviously been abandoned long since. Deer grazed around the forest's edge, quite unconcerned by the sudden appearance of Governor White and the other colonists. Other than the sound of a passing breeze, there was only silence.

The colonists turned to face Governor White, looking afraid and concerned. Jane's father spoke up first, his voice loud and demanding.

"I don't understand, Governor White. We were told that there would be soldiers and a fort here. The soldiers have vanished and the fort is ruined. What has happened here?"

Governor White looked around uneasily, trying to come up with an answer that would satisfy both the settlers and himself. But all he could do was shrug his shoulders.

"I don't know," he admitted. "Perhaps they ran into trouble with the Indians. Or maybe they had to move away in order to find food and water. But all is not lost. If we get to work now on building shelters and planting crops, then there's a good chance we'll survive the winter. The harder we work to rebuild this colony, the safer we will be!"

Inspired by Governor White's passionate speech, the colonists began work that day to rebuild the Roanoke settlement. The men took some axes into the forests to cut down trees. Using chisels, hammers, and nails, they assembled the logs into a frame for the new fort. Then they patched up the gaps between the logs with tree sap. For a roof, the women pulled up tall grasses from a nearby field and wove them together into a tight mesh.

Working together, the settlers completed the fort by the end of the day. The fort still needed much work, and became terribly hot at night with everyone packed inside it to sleep. But at least it provided a temporary shelter. Each settler family soon built their own shelter, making the situation at the fort far more bearable. Within a couple of weeks the settlement was dotted with tiny but neat little houses. Then the real work began.

The next task was to get some crops planted before the planting season ended. The men began by chopping down swaths of trees to make clearings. They then built wooden plows and hitched them to horses that they had brought over on the ship. Taking turns with the horses, they furrowed acre after acre of land.

The women followed behind the men, casting onto the furrowed fields the seeds of wheat and other grains that they had brought with them from England. The seeds, nourished by Virginia's warm rain, grew rapidly, promising a healthy harvest.

While waiting for the harvest to ripen, the settlers lived off of the domestic animals they had brought along. From the pigs they made ham and bacon, from the goats they drew milk, from the sheep they spun wool for clothing, and from the chickens they gathered eggs.

The settlers also took advantage of the forest's bounty, gathering walnuts and chestnuts from the vast woods that surrounded Roanoke. When there was time they went hunting for deer, using the guns they had brought from England. When they were lucky they would come back with enough meat to throw a feast for the entire settlement!

Social Studies

Social Studies

Everybody Wins!

The Story of Special Olympics

Genre	Comprehension Skill and Strategy	Text Features
Nonfiction	• Generalize • Predict	• Captions • Maps • Subheads

Scott Foresman Reading Street 5.4.2

PEARSON
Scott
Foresman

scottforesman.com

ISBN 0-328-13551-8

90000

9 780328 135516

by Cynthia Swain

Reader Response

1. Look at the graph on page 8. In your own words, explain how the number of athletes in Special Olympics World Summer Games has changed over time.

2. At the beginning of page 12, as you read about Afghanistan's Special Olympics team, what did you predict would happen? What words made you think as you do?

3. On page 17, find the sentence "Cheering from the audience encouraged a hesitant Gary to pick up a yellow bean bag and toss it into the basket." Read the paragraph and decide what the word *hesitant* means. Does it mean happy? Does it mean Gary is angry?

4. You've read about several athletes who compete in Special Olympics. In general, how do they feel about participating? What does an athlete get out of competing in the Games?

Glossary

abdomen *n.* the part of the body between the thorax and the pelvis, roughly corresponding to the stomach area

artificial *adj.* man-made

gait *n.* manner of walking

handicapped *n.* person or persons having a physical or intellectual disability that substantially limits activity

therapist *n.* a person trained in methods of treatment and rehabilitation that do not use drugs or surgery

wheelchair *n.* a chair mounted on wheels for the use of disabled people

Everybody Wins!
The Story of Special Olympics

by Cynthia Swain

PEARSON

Scott Foresman

Editorial Offices: Glenview, Illinois • Parsippany, New Jersey • New York, New York
Sales Offices: Needham, Massachusetts • Duluth, Georgia • Glenview, Illinois
Coppell, Texas • Ontario, California • Mesa, Arizona

What's Next?

Today, over 1.4 million people who are developmentally challenged compete in Special Olympics training programs, clubs, or events. Special Olympics have come a long way since they started in 1963!

In 2007, Special Olympics World Summer Games will be held in Shanghai, China. Fans will be wowed by amazing athletic feats. Athletes will walk to the medals podium proudly to honor their home countries. Best of all, people who who are developmentally challenged will have the opportunity to play fair, compete, and win.

Joining In

Most people love playing sports. That includes people who are developmentally challenged. This disability is caused by the brain's inability to develop properly before birth.

For a long time, people with who were developmentally challenged weren't included in many activities that are part of daily life. Kids with intellectual disabilities often didn't go to school and were left out of sports. Many people didn't accept them.

Today, that's all changed. People who are developmentally challenged can join in activities at school and in life. In sports, they can compete with other special athletes from around the world—in Special Olympics!

Eunice Shriver: Special Olympics Founder

Eunice Kennedy Shriver started Special Olympics. As a young woman, she saw up close how people with disabilities were treated. That's because her own sister, Rosemary Kennedy, had an intellectual disability. The Kennedy family was involved in politics. They were embarrassed by Rosemary's disability and kept it a secret.

Eunice wasn't embarrassed by her sister at all. When her brother, John F. Kennedy, was elected the 35th President of the United States in 1961, Eunice knew it was time to act.

Eunice convinced her family to admit to the public that their beloved sister and daughter had an intellectual disability. This was big news. It encouraged people all over the country to accept the intellectually **handicapped** in their own families and communities.

Eunice Kennedy Shriver (second from right) with her family.

Many people volunteer during the World Games. There are over 500,000 Special Olympics volunteers from all over. They include adults and kids, amateur and professional athletes, teachers, coaches, and retirees. Even companies get involved.

There's also a program just for students, called The Global Youth Summit, which includes people with and without disabilities. At the 2003 Games, they met to discuss discrimination against people who are developmentally challenged. The group was highlighted on TV shows and in newspapers all around the world. One Summit member, 13-year old Kamna Prem from New Dehli, India, voiced the group's goal: "At the end, attitudes will change toward people with mental challenges."

Join in the Fun!

Do Special Olympics sound like fun? They aren't *just* for people who are developmentally challenged. In fact, there are many ways for athletes without intellectual disabilities and others to join in.

Unified Sports are sports that team up athletes with and without disabilities. These teams also compete in Special Olympics.

Michael Kennet is the Unified Sports partner of Nic Jones. They are both from Great Britain and compete in sailing. Michael has an intellectual disability, and having a friend like Nic helps him compete at his best. Michael and Nic have known each other for four years. It's been a rewarding friendship for both of them.

In the 1960s, Eunice and her husband started summer day camps across the country for children and adults with intellectual disabilities. When Eunice saw the campers playing outside, she realized that many of them were excellent athletes! She encouraged camp leaders to organize sports for the campers.

Then, the Chicago Park District came to Eunice with an idea. They asked if she would help them organize a citywide sports event for people with intellectual disabilities. They wanted to model the event on the Olympics.

Chicago

Special Olympics Get Started

The First International Special Olympics Summer Games were held in Chicago in July 1968. One thousand people who are developmentally challenged came to compete. This was the start of something big.

Two years later, another Special Olympics in Chicago attracted more than twice as many athletes.

Then, in 1977, the First International Special Olympics Winter Games were held. Over 500 athletes competed in skiing and skating events.

Finally, in 1993, Special Olympics went worldwide when the Winter Games were held in Austria. More than 1,600 athletes from more than 50 countries participated.

Today, Special Olympics World Summer Games are held every four years. The Winter Games are held every four years as well.

Fair play also counts. That's why athletes are placed in different divisions, based on their ability. All are given a fair chance to compete and win.

Athletes also get a chance to meet famous and respected people. Former South African president Nelson Mandela spoke at the Special Olympics World Games in Dublin. The President of Poland helped award medals.

Everybody Wins

For Special Olympics athletes, it is the spirit—not the score—that is important. Runner Loretta Claiborne says, "What's important is that you throw a softball when before you couldn't throw a softball. You do better than the last time. That's what counts." Gold, silver, and bronze medals are awarded at Special Olympics events, but all athletes receive a ribbon or medal for participating.

Special Olympics give the developmentally challenged a chance to play their favorite sports and celebrate their victories.

Special Olympics Hit the Big Time

Today, Special Olympics is huge. In 2003, more than 6,500 athletes competed in Special Olympics World Summer Games in Ireland. It was the first time that the Summer Games were held outside the U.S.

Check out the graph below to see how the Summer Games have grown over the years.

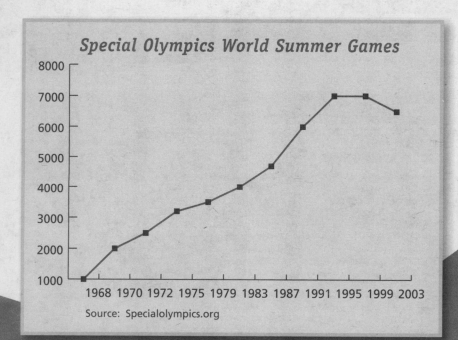

Special Olympics World Summer Games

Source: Specialolympics.org

MATP events may seem easy to you, but for the athletes who participate in them, they require as much practice and determination as any Olympic event. At the 2003 Special Olympics World Summer Games in Ireland, the MATP events were the bean bag lift, ball kick, wide beam and bench, ball lift (small), ball lift (large), ball push, and log roll.

One of the participants in the bean bag lift at the 2003 Games was Gary Durcan, age 14. Cheering from the audience encouraged a hesitant Gary to pick up a yellow bean bag and toss it into the basket. "Gary can't communicate, but we can see the excitement in his eyes," said his father.

The Biggest Challenge

People who have intellectual disabilities sometimes have physical disabilities as well. They might need a **wheelchair** to get around. Some might use **artificial** limbs, like legs and arms. Because of this, physical educators, physical **therapists**, and recreational therapists developed the Special Olympics Motor Activities Training Program (MATP). MATP gives *all* athletes a chance to shine.

All Special Olympics athletes train hard. This is especially true for MATP atheletes. They work to strengthen their arms and shoulders, back and **abdomen**, and feet and legs.

More than 160 countries participated in the 2003 Summer Games. The torch run started on June 4, in Athens, Greece. Dozens of law enforcement officers and 10 Special Olympics athletes joined in on the 9,000-mile, eight-day run. There were three routes across European cities which came together in Brussels. From there, the torch runners carried the flame to Dublin, Ireland.

The torch and runners got warm welcomes all across Europe. In Milan, Italy, over 15,000 people packed the streets to honor the athletes and the Games.

Loretta's Story

Some of the best athletes in Special Olympics come from the United States. Loretta Claiborne is one of them.

Loretta was born partially blind and developmentally challenged. She was not able to walk or talk until age four. She had surgery for her leg. She was teased at school for her awkward gait, suspended from high school, and fired from a job. Still, Loretta did not give up.

When Loretta learned to run, her life took a turn for the better. She started running marathons. So far, she's run in 25 of them! She finished in the top 100 women in the Boston Marathon—twice. But it was competing in Special Olympics that *really* changed her life.

Liinah Bukenya, a 12-year-old swimmer from Uganda, overcame a pretty impressive obstacle as well. Eleven months before the Summer Games, she didn't even know how to swim!

"I thought maybe I might get a silver, but this morning I said to myself that even if I didn't get anything I would be brave," Liinah said during the Games.

Liinah beat her own expectations. She won the gold medal in the 50-meter backstroke!

Brave Competitors

Today all athletes take the Special Olympics Athlete Oath: "Let me win, but if I cannot win—let me be brave in the attempt."

Luis Canel is an athlete from Guatemala. He competed in the Summer Games in Ireland in 2003. He is brave—and he is a winner.

Getting to the Olympics was tough for Luis. His mother died in 1995. His father abandoned the family. Luis loved his sport, and knew he could do well at the Summer Games, but he couldn't afford a bike.

Luis's friends raised money to buy him a bike. When he got to Ireland, he made them all proud. He won a gold medal for bike racing in the five kilometer time trial, and won two bronzes in the one kilometer and 10 kilometer time trials.

Loretta became involved in Special Olympics as a kid. She won medals in many events, and she currently holds the women's record in her age group for the 5,000 meters at 17 minutes. She has competed in Special Olympics eight times, including the 2003 Games.

This amazing athlete also speaks out all across the world. She gives speeches to students about accepting differences in others. She has even had a movie made about her life, *The Loretta Claiborne Story*.

Newcomers to Special Olympics

Special Olympics athletes come from all over, even from countries that are very poor or at war. In 2003, five young athletes from Afghanistan competed for the first time. They were all orphans.

Before 2001, Afghanistan was controlled by an oppressive government called the Taliban. People with disabilities were treated very poorly, and sometimes even killed.

In 2001, the U.S. overthrew the Taliban. Now, the country is struggling to rebuild. Slowly, attitudes toward people with disabilities are changing.

The Afghani athletes were given their first pair of running shoes shortly before they came to the games. They had only one month to train, but their disadvantages didn't hold them back. One athlete, 11-year-old Amin Amin, won gold medals in the 50-meter and 25-meter relays.

"It's a great opportunity for them to experience this feeling," said their coach, Nasrullah Ibrahimzay.

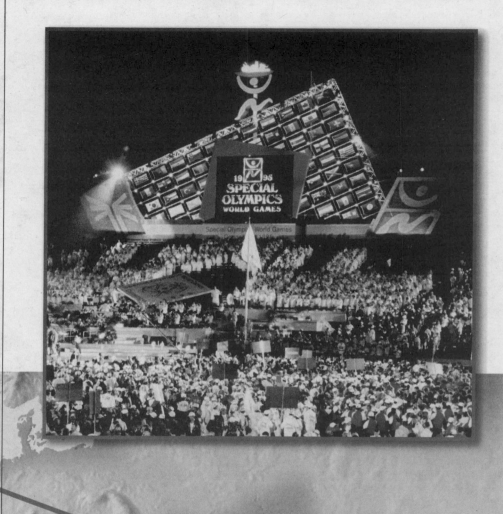

Ireland

Afghanistan

Glossary

critical *adj.* absolutely necessary.

enables *v.* to makes possible.

mucus *n.* a thick liquid that moistens and protects body parts.

scarce *adj.* lacking an amount that is enough to meet demand.

specialize *v.* to put efforts toward a particular activity.

sterile *adj.* free from harmful bacteria.

Changing to Survive: Bird Adaptations

by Lillian Duggan

Editorial Offices: Glenview, Illinois • Parsippany, New Jersey • New York, New York
Sales Offices: Needham, Massachusetts • Duluth, Georgia • Glenview, Illinois
Coppell, Texas • Ontario, California • Mesa, Arizona

These programs bring birds into the zoo where they can mate and have babies. Breeding is **critical**, or absolutely necessary, when a species is endangered.

Scientists who work with birds have special training. They need to understand how to care for young birds. Baby birds must be kept in a **sterile** place that is free from harmful bacteria in order to keep them healthy.

Conservationists have saved a large number of bird species from extinction.

23

Social Studies   Social Studies

Changing to Survive:
Bird Adaptations

Genre	Comprehension Skill and Strategy	Text Features
Nonfiction	• Graphic Sources • Monitor Comprehension/ Seek Help	• Captions • Glossary • Maps • Subheads

Scott Foresman Reading Street 5.4.3

PEARSON
Scott
Foresman

ISBN 0-328-13554-2

90000

9 780328 135547

by Lillian Duggan

Reader Response

1. Look over the illustrations and captions on page 6. How does the author use each one on the pages that follow?

2. How well did you understand the text about penguins and the wandering albatross? Use an organizer like the following to note what you remember.

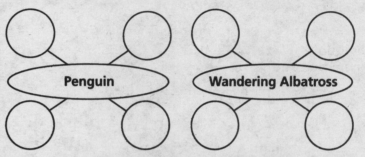

Write a sentence summarizing your findings.

3. What is mucus and how does it help birds eat?

4. This book describes eight different groups of birds. To which group does Pale Male belong?

Bird Conservation

Birds have adapted in many ways to different types of habitats. Unfortunately, growing cities, pollution, and cutting down trees have hurt bird's habitats.

Adaptation takes many years. Many birds have not been able to adapt quickly enough to changes in their habitats. Some of them are now extinct, or no longer exist. Others are still around thanks to the help of conservationists. Conservationists help endangered animals survive.

Sometimes supplies in a bird's habitat become **scarce**, or in short supply. This scarcity happens when a habitat is destroyed. Conservationists help birds by trying to passed laws get that protect their habitat.

When conservationists help animals to breed, they help them to grow. Zoos around the world have breeding programs.

Birds Everywhere

They soar above the clouds like graceful airplanes. Birds can be found nearly everywhere on Earth— from land to sea, desert to tropical rain forest. They are beautiful and diverse. They live all over the world, even ice-covered Antarctica. Some birds spend their lives on the open ocean and move onto land only to nest. Other birds never leave the ground.

There are many kinds of habitats in the world. Some places are hot and dry, while others are cold and wet. Each habitat has challenges for its animal life to overcome. In order to survive in a habitat, an animal must be able to adapt, or change. These changes enable, or make it possible for, an animal to survive in its home.

Birds are one of the most successful animals on Earth. They have adapted to so many different places that they inhabit every type of habitat in the world!

In this book, you'll see how each bird has adapted to survive in its home.

The black-throated sparrow is adapted to life in the desert. It can go without drinking water for days.

From the First Bird to Flying Machines

The first birds were probably relatives of prehistoric reptiles. Scientists have animal fossils with wings and feathers from 150 million years ago. These animals also had reptile features, like teeth, claws, and a long tail. Scientists named this ancient animal *Archaeopteryx.* The wings and feathers of the Archaeopteryx show that it could fly, but scientists don't think it stayed in the air for a very long time.

Over thousands of years, birds have evolved into flying machines. Their bodies are well suited for air travel. Birds are faster and can stay in the air longer than other flying animals, like bats or insects. Certain birds have been known to fly 100 miles per hour and travel over a thousand miles without stopping.

How do birds do this? It helps that birds have wings and bodies that are almost completely covered with feathers.

Archaeopteryx probably descended from a small dinosaur.

A ruby-throated hummingbird can beat its wings fifty-three times a second.

The European bee-eater's long, pointed beak helps it grasp large insects.

Expert Fliers

Some birds are better fliers than others. Many skilled fliers have interesting ways to get food. Hummingbirds, for example, can beat their wings more than fifty times per second, allowing them to hover in mid-air. A hummingbird uses its long beak to drink nectar from flowers.

The ruby-throated hummingbird lives in forests. It migrates to Central America for the winter, flying nonstop across the Gulf of Mexico.

Many expert fliers catch their food straight out of the air. The European bee-eater specializes in eating bees and wasps. It captures its prey in mid-air. The bee-eater rubs the insect on a branch to destroy its stinger before eating it, and then swallows up the non-stinging insects.

Swifts are fast and skilled. Because they have small legs and feet, swifts don't walk much. These birds can do almost everything in the air. They catch insects, eat, and drink while in flight. Nesting is the only activity swifts must do on land. The Eurasian swift spends two to three years in flight without landing!

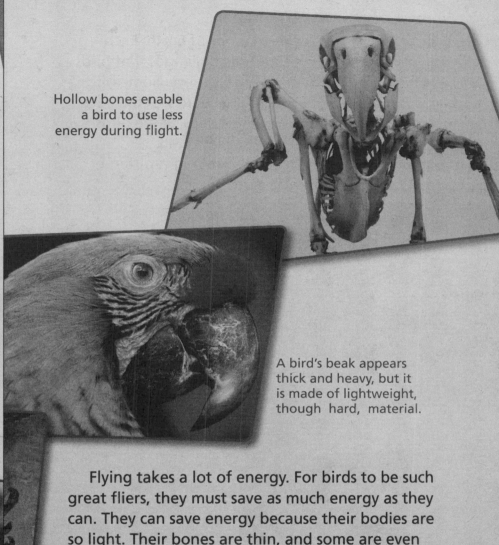

Hollow bones enable a bird to use less energy during flight.

A bird's beak appears thick and heavy, but it is made of lightweight, though hard, material.

Eurasian swifts feed on small airborne insects and spiders.

Flying takes a lot of energy. For birds to be such great fliers, they must save as much energy as they can. They can save energy because their bodies are so light. Their bones are thin, and some are even hollow. Even a bird's beak is thin and lightweight.

To get the energy they need to fly, birds eat a lot. For small creatures, they have big appetites. In fact, birds eat more food than other animals the same size. They also choose foods high in energy, such as seeds, fruits, fish, worms, and insects. Birds digest food quickly so they can use the energy right away.

Homes Around the World

Birds live in nearly every corner of Earth. Each new location had its own set of challenges that birds have had to adapt to in order to survive. Some birds have long beaks; others have short ones. Some have long legs while others need short legs. Some birds fly fast, while others never leave the ground.

In this book, you will read about eight different groups of birds—

Sea Birds

Shore Birds

Water Birds

Land Birds

We usually think of birds as flying animals. Most birds do fly, but there are some that don't. Some land birds have wings that are too small for them to flying. Some land birds can fly, but they only use their wings to make short flights into the trees at night. These birds are known as game birds. They include turkeys, pheasants, and quails.

Some land birds have become fast runners, with tall, strong legs. The fastest of these is the ostrich. The ostrich is the largest and heaviest bird in the world. Ostriches are nearly six feet tall. They weigh between two and three hundred pounds. An ostrich can run forty-three miles per hour, making it able to outrun most of its enemies.

The ostrich is well adapted to its environment. It lives in semi-desert and grassland areas in Africa, where it can walk a long way in search of food. Plant shoots and leaves, flowers, and seeds make up most of its diet.

Ostriches travel in flocks of ten to fifty birds in search of food.

6

Tree Birds

Tree birds are adapted for feeding and nesting in trees. Some, such as pigeons and parrots, eat seeds, nuts, and fruits. Others, such as woodpeckers, eat insects that live on tree trunks and leaves.

Woodpeckers have a unique way of finding food. With its heavy, pointed beak, a woodpecker hammers into tree bark to find insects. When the woodpecker finds an insect, it stretches out its long, sticky tongue and grabs it. Some woodpeckers have prickles or special **mucus**, or thick sticky fluid, on their tongues for snatching up insects. Their tongues make them act a lot like a frog.

A woodpecker's head has also adapted to protect itself. Woodpeckers peck hard and quickly, like a jackhammer. Their brains need protection from this repetitive jarring motion. Woodpecker's skulls are made up of spongy, shock-absorbing bones.

The pileated woodpecker lives clinging to tree trunks in the eastern and northern United States.

Tree Birds

Expert Fliers

Land Birds

You'll see how they had to adapt to survive.

Sea Birds

The ocean is probably the hardest place for birds to survive. There is a bird that spends most of its life in the air above the ocean. This bird is called the wandering albatross. It may look pretty tiring to stay airborne so long, but the albatross has adapted to make flying easy. With nearly an eleven-foot wingspan, this bird uses the flow of ocean air to glide effortlessly.

Penguins are seabirds too. Living in the cold region of Antarctica, penguins may not fly, but they're great swimmers and divers. Instead of wings, they use flippers to push themselves through the water. Webbed feet and a tail help them to steer.

Penguins have also adapted to survive in freezing cold ocean water. Thick layers of waterproof feathers keep them warm and dry. Below the feathers, a layer of fat keeps them warm.

Emperor penguins are the only animals that spend the winter on the ice in Antarctica.

Like the nightingale, the mockingbird is a famous singer. The mockingbird can copy the calls of other bird species. It can also mimic the sounds of other animals and objects, such as saws. Mockingbirds use their songs for protection, and their constant singing tells other birds to stay away.

The North American dipper is a songbird that has adapted to life on the water. Its name comes from the habit of quickly raising and lowering their bodies into the water by bending their legs. It lives in mountain streams and ponds. The dipper has strong feet that can grip slippery rocks in the water. It perches on these rocks and dips its head underwater to search for food. Insects, worms, snails, small fish, and fish eggs make up the dipper's diet. When the dipper spots a tasty meal, it either wades into the water or dives under. Dippers aren't good surface swimmers, but they are fast underwater. They even flap their wings in underwater "flight." They have a thick undercoat of feathers, which keeps them warm. They also have flaps that close their nostrils to keep out water and an extra clear eyelid to protect their eyes.

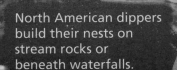

North American dippers build their nests on stream rocks or beneath waterfalls.

Northern mockingbirds spend most of their time running or hopping on the ground.

Songbirds

Some birds are known for singing beautiful melodies. These are called songbirds. Some songbirds simply string a few notes together, while others sing enchanting songs. The songs of the lark and the nightingale are two of the most admired. Songbirds sing to attract mates or to defend their homes. Except for a few species, only males have this talent.

Songbirds are also called perching birds, because they have special feet which help them balance on tree branches. Three of their four toes point forward and one points backward. This enables songbirds, or perching birds, to wrap their toes around a branch or a wire easily.

Songbirds have different types of beaks, depending on what they eat. White-winged crossbills have beaks with crossed tips that specialize at eating pinecone seeds. They use their beaks to pry apart the scales of pinecones. Then their tongues lift out the seed hidden between the scales. Crossbills can eat three thousand seeds in a single day!

The white-winged crossbill's unique beak is adapted for eating pinecone seeds.

The wandering albatross is almost always in flight. It returns to land only to breed.

The pheasant-tailed jacana eats invertebrates, frogs, and fish.

Shore Birds

Shore birds spend so much time in shallow water that they're also called wading birds. Shore birds usually have long, pointy beaks and long, thin legs. They like being close to land. Their pointy beaks help them dig in dirt or sand for worms, insects, crabs, and snails. Long legs keep the rest of their bodies dry above water.

Shore birds, such as sandpipers and plovers, live all around the world. Sandpipers live along shorelines and in marshes. They eat snails and worms in the winter and insects in the summer. Sandpipers, or common snipe, have mastered the art of catching and swallowing their prey with their bills still underground!

Pale Male, a City Hawk

The city is a noisy place with a lot of buildings. Red-tailed hawks love open spaces where they can soar in the sky for hours. It seems unusual that they live in cities. In fact, a particular red-tailed hawk lives in one of the largest cities in the world, New York City. Pale Male, is a real New Yorker. Pale Male got his name because his feathers are lighter in color than those of other red-tailed hawks.

Some red-tailed hawks migrate from Canada to Mexico or Central America in the winter, passing through New York City. In 1991, Pale Male decided to stick around in the Big Apple.

Surprisingly, Pale Male has lived in New York ever since. Living near the city's largest park, Central Park, he can easily find food. He can swoop down from his lookout spot and snatch up prey in seconds. He has had several mates and produced many offspring. Pale Male and a recent mate raised their young in a nest on the ledge of an apartment building overlooking Central Park.

Pale Male has lived in New York City since 1991.

Farmers used to rely on barn owls to keep their grain safe from hungry rodents.

This common snipe is enjoying an underground meal.

Birds of Prey

Birds of prey are hunters. Eagles, hawks, and buzzards are all birds of prey. They have powerful eyesight that allows them to find their prey, or food easily. They have sharp claws for catching animals and hooked beaks for tearing their food.

Owls are nocturnal, which means they hunt at night. Owls are known for their huge eyes in the front of their faces. They can hunt well in the dark because of their powerful eyes and ears. They can also rotate their heads almost all the way around to search for prey. Unlike most birds, owls have feathers with soft edges, making it easy for them to sneak up on their prey quietly.

Barn owls spend their days resting inside tree holes or barns. They eat mostly mice and other rodents. They can catch these rodents in total darkness because of their powerful hearing.

Unlike many other shore birds, plovers have short beaks and short legs. They don't need long beaks because they eat above the water. With their short legs, plovers spend less time in the water than sandpipers.

One plover, the wrybill, has a beak that bends to the right. It looks funny, but it's useful. As it moves, the wrybill sweeps the tip of its bill over the mud like a pair of scissors, picking up insects. The New Zealand wrybill walks in circles while it hunts for food.

Another short-beaked shore bird, the jacana, is known for its unique feet. The jacana's toes and claws are long and spread out. These special feet enable it to walk on wobbly surfaces like floating lily pads. The jacana lives in lakes, marshes, and ponds in India, China, and Southeast Asia.

14

11

Water Birds

Water birds live near lakes, rivers, ponds, and marshes. These are great nesting spots. They are surrounded by tall plants that keep the birds safe and hidden.

Flamingos may be the most beautiful and unusual water birds. They are large with long legs and necks. The flamingo is perhaps one of the most popular birds in the world. Who can help but admire its long, curvy neck and pretty pink color? Flamingos have an unusual downward-pointing beak. They stick their heads in the water upside-down to find food, using their beaks like scoops. The flamingo's muscular tongue pumps water into its beak. Then, the water is strained out, leaving tiny plants and animals behind.

Geese, ducks, and swans live on ponds and lakes from big cities to the remote tundra. These birds are built for swimming. They have webbed feet, which they use like paddles to push themselves through the water. They not only swim well, but they are good fliers. They migrate great distances each winter to warmer areas in the south.

Mallard ducks are beautiful and colorful. Like other ducks, mallards get food from the water's surface. The sides of their bills are lined with filters that strain food from the water. They are also very resourceful. They are willing to get food in many ways, such as taking scraps from people's hands.

Like the flamingo, the pelican is an unusual-looking water bird. They have the longest bills of any bird. Pelicans use a pouch on their bills to catch fish. When the pelican plunges its bill below the surface of the water, its pouch opens up. The water drains out of the pouch, and then the pelican enjoys its meal. Like ducks, pelicans have webbed feet to help them steer in water. They're also good fliers, and many migrate over long distances. The great white pelican lives in parts of Africa, Europe, and Asia.

Sometimes mallards dive into shallow water to feed from the bottom.

Great white pelicans feed in groups, herding fish together.

Flamingos' feathers turn pink because of pigments in the foods they eat.

The New Kid at School

by Lisa Oram

Genre	Comprehension Skill and Strategy	Text Features
Nonfiction	• Generalize • Graphic Organizers	• Glossary • Headings • Photos

Scott Foresman Reading Street 5.4.4

PEARSON

Scott
Foresman

scottforesman.com

Reader Response

1. This book explores the experience of being the new kid at school by hearing what it was like for a boy named Marcus. Describe in a general way what it's like to go to a new school.

2. Kids in a school can welcome new students in many different ways. The new kid can also help him/herself feel more comfortable in the new school. Draw two webs, like the ones below, to map ideas of how each side can make the change easier.

3. Identify four words in this book that are unfamiliar. List each word on a separate sheet of paper and write a guess at its meaning. Then look up each word in this book's glossary or in a dictionary and write its definition next to your guess. How close did you come?

4. Look back through this book at the headings. What do the first four headings have in common? What do the second four headings have in common?

Glossary

cavities *n.* pitted areas in teeth that are caused by decay and often filled in by a dentist.

combination *n.* the joining of two or more separate things.

demonstrates *v.* shows clearly.

episode *n.* one part in a series of related parts; often refers to dramatic performances such as television shows.

profile *n.* a description of a person that includes his or her most important or noteworthy characteristics.

strict *adj.* having a strong style or approach in handling discipline.

The New Kid at School

by Lisa Oram

Editorial Offices: Glenview, Illinois • Parsippany, New Jersey • New York, New York
Sales Offices: Needham, Massachusetts • Duluth, Georgia • Glenview, Illinois
Coppell, Texas • Ontario, California • Mesa, Arizona

So, back to those sneakers from the beginning of this book. When a new student arrives at your school, try walking for a few minutes in his or her shoes. Step in and step up. You can show the new kid that your class is a great place to be. And you will have a new friend that might become your best one yet!

If you're the new kid, take a deep breath and start asking questions. Give yourself time. It's a little like getting new shoes. You need to break them in, but soon you will be able to hit your stride in them. Just as soon, you will have become used to the new school.

No matter how prepared you try to be for all these changes, there are bound to be days when nothing feels right. Life was probably a little up and down before changing schools, and it won't be any different afterward. It helps to expect the ups and downs rather than imagining that everything is going to be perfect if you just... find a best friend, or ace the first test, or whatever.

No single thing is going to make everything at your new school great, and no single thing will make it all bad either. Realistic expectations will help you get through a process that takes time.

Do you remember a time when you got a new pair of sneakers? Were you really excited? Had you wanted them for a long time? What was it like on the first day you wore them to school?

New shoes often mark the beginning of a new school year or the start of a sports season. If the shoes are a birthday present, you are beginning a new year in your life. If you have outgrown your old shoes, your body is different than it used to be. Shoes are just shoes, of course, but it seems that when they change, life is changing too.

Everybody experiences change—sometimes big changes and sometimes simple ones. Any change can bring with it a combination of opposite feelings.

You might be excited about the new thing, and you might also be nervous. You might be sad about something you are leaving or losing, while at the same time, you welcome a fresh start. You can toss your ratty old red sneakers and love your new green ones, but you'll probably never forget wearing that old pair when you broke the record for the 50-yard dash or on your first day at a new school.

Going to a new school is one of the biggest new beginnings there is. Whether it's moving from elementary school to middle school with all your friends, or moving to a new neighborhood in the middle of the school year, it's a big change.

In this book, you will explore the experience of going to a new school. If you are the kid who is new, there are things you can do to help yourself with the changes. If you are the kid who's been around for a while, there are things you can do to help a new kid feel welcome.

Expect Ups and Downs

Fifth grade can be a year of many changes even without going to a new school. Becoming ten years old and moving into the double-digit period of life feels to many kids like the beginning of being a teenager. You want to be more independent. You want to experiment with different ways of acting around your peers, your parents, and your teachers. As the new kid, you have two sets of changes at the same time—the new place and new people on the outside, and your changing feelings on the inside.

In many schools, fifth graders are the oldest kids around, the ones with the most experience, but this profile changes quickly when they go off to middle school and become the youngest ones again. Knowing that they are soon to lose their status, some fifth graders want to make the most of their position while they can. Sometimes that means being bossy or excluding anyone who doesn't match their personal level of "cool."

NO SCHOOL 80

This is Marcus. He moved from a small town to a big city when he was in fifth grade because his father got a new job. He didn't want to move and was mad at his parents for a long time, but now he says it's better. He still misses his old school, but his new one feels okay. We are going to learn from him what it was like to be the new kid, how others helped him, and how he helped himself.

About his first day, Marcus says, "I was worried about a lot of things. The new school was much bigger than my old one, and I was scared of getting lost. I wondered if my new teacher would be strict or nice. I was afraid I would never make new friends or that other kids might be mean to me."

Knowing that a new student might feel the way that Marcus did, what could you do to help?

Be Yourself

Sometimes moving to a new school feels like an opportunity to reinvent yourself. Nobody knows you are a great singer, so if you don't want to join the chorus, you don't have to. Your new teacher has never given you a zero for not doing homework, and you can make it so he never does.

Marcus says, "I thought maybe I would tell people that my old house had burned down and that was why my family had to move. If the kids felt sorry for me, maybe they'd like me better. Or maybe they would just think it was interesting and want to talk to me."

The bottom line is that a fresh start is a chance to do things better, but you can't be anyone other than your true self. You have to be real and follow your heart. If some kids in your new school say, "Everyone around here cuts class, and it doesn't matter," but you think it's not right, don't be afraid to stand up for yourself. Those kids might not like you, but then ask yourself if those are the kids you really want to be friends with. There will be other kids who respect your courage and honesty. In the end, the only way to be happy is to be true to yourself.

Introduce Yourself

Making friends is probably the biggest concern of someone who starts at a new school, especially if the person has moved from far away and doesn't know anyone at all. Make the first move. If you are sitting next to the person, say hello. At lunch, ask your new classmate to sit with you and your friends. Introduce all the kids around you to the newcomer.

Sometimes kids worry that a new friend will somehow take away the friends they already have. But, really, you can never have too many friends, and the new kid will surely appreciate your efforts.

You might feel shy or embarrassed talking to someone you don't know at all, but remember, the new kid is probably feeling a lot more worried than you.

Start a Conversation

If you don't know a person well, it might feel like you don't know what to talk about. In fact, not knowing someone means there's a lot to talk about. You don't know anything about that person so you can be curious and ask about almost anything.

You can start by finding out what your new friend likes to do. Does she play sports? Does she like to read or go bike riding? Does he like video games? Does he have any collections? Keep asking questions, and pretty soon you're sure to find something you have in common.

Show Off

Find an activity that demonstrates a special side of you or shows off your strongest skills and interests. Probably anything that you liked at your old school will be available at your new school, even if it's not offered in exactly the same form.

If you like playing soccer, ask about a school team. If you were in the photography club, and there isn't one at your new school, ask your teacher if there are other ways to use your skill. Perhaps there's a school newspaper or yearbook that needs photos. Maybe the principal likes to display photos of school events in the office or hallways. When you pursue your favorite activities, you will naturally meet other kids who share your interests and who could become new friends.

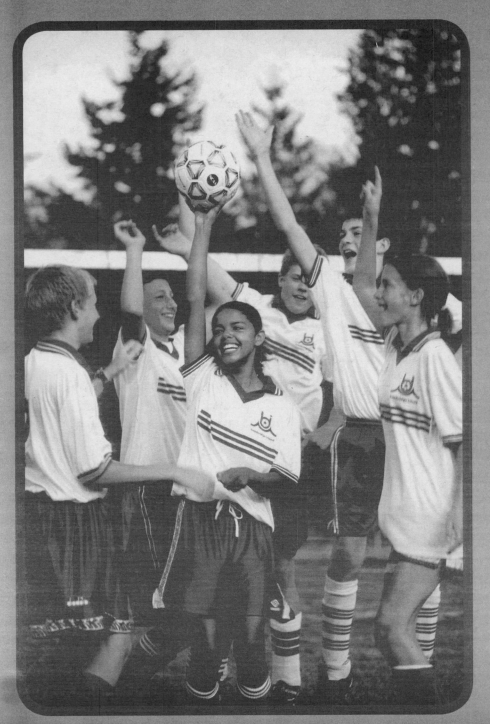

Kids come to a new school for lots of different reasons. The more you talk together, the more you'll find out about each other's lives. Sometimes kids end up in a new school because of difficult home situations. You may hit upon a topic that your new friend doesn't want to talk about.

Eventually, when you know each other better, you both will feel more comfortable talking about personal matters. In the meantime, if you feel awkward, just change the subject to something really silly like, "Wanna see my cavities?"

Be Prepared

One of the worst feelings when starting at a new school is the feeling that the people at the new school don't know what to do with you when you get there.

It's unsettling to see people scrambling around, asking, "Where does the new kid go?" It's embarrassing to arrive at your new classroom and wait around while a bunch of other kids move their seats so there's somewhere to sit. The last thing you want to hear from your new teacher is something like, "He's not supposed to be in my class. I thought he was supposed to go into the other fifth-grade class." If your class and your school do a little advance work, a new student's entry can be a whole lot nicer.

Marcus says, "At my new school, the assistant principal gave me a welcome kit on the first day. It was just a little bag of things, like a notebook, a pen, a map of the school, and a copy of the school newspaper. There was even a dollar in there so I could buy something in the cafeteria. I thought it was really nice."

Your class could also create a welcome gift, like a flower on the new person's desk or a special snack for the class that day.

You could create a book containing one sentence of advice from each student in the class. What other ideas do you have about doing something special to greet a new student in your class?

Saying Good-Bye

Perhaps as important as being able to say hello is being able to say good-bye. As you are preparing for the change, it's tempting to ignore this part. You don't want it to happen, so maybe if you pretend it's not coming up, it will go away.

As much as possible, you need to say good-bye—to your friends, your teachers, your playground, your lunchroom. Sometimes a move comes up quickly, and you're not given much, or any, time to get ready. In that case, you can write and send a good-bye letter after you are gone. The people you have left also wanted to say good-bye, so a letter will help them too.

If you can, take photos or mementos with you to help you remember the place you are leaving. Make plans about how you can communicate after you've left, or when you might visit again. Keeping connections with parts of your past will ultimately make it easier in the long run to make similar connections in your future.

If you are changing schools or moving into a new town, it's not only up to others to help you feel welcome. *You* need to help make the change successful. You may be a kid who's moved a lot, so you have a system. Maybe you lay low at the beginning and then slowly warm up. Maybe you go in wanting to make a strong impression right from the start. There's no right or wrong way. If you're moving to a new school for the first time, you will need to find the way to fit in that best suits your personality.

Remember, though, you were a new kid at least once before, when you started kindergarten. One way to help yourself is to think about that time, even though it may have been a long time ago, and remind yourself that you got through it. Way back then you didn't know anything about school at all. At least this time, you already know the basics.

Be an Expert

Marcus not only had to change schools but he had to live in an apartment instead of a house and get to know a whole new town. His family had to figure out where the grocery store was, where the post office was, and who to choose as a new doctor. Marcus was on the basketball team at his old school, so he needed to find the coach at his new school.

When you're the old kid, you can be an expert. Offer the new kid a tour of your school or of your town. Point out the nurse's office, the library, or the gym as you walk between classes. Even if someone else has already given the tour, there are so many things for the new kid to remember at the beginning that your help will still feel useful. Another word for this kind of expert is *mentor*, someone more experienced than another person, who takes on the role of an advisor and a helper.

When you learn more about what your new classmate likes to do, offer suggestions that relate to his or her interests. If the new kid likes computers, or painting, or dance, but it's a subject that you don't know anything about, steer him or her to someone who does.

You also might have special insider information to share—like your teacher loves to watch reruns of Star Trek and asking about his favorite episode can delay a spelling quiz. Getting the inside scoop takes away the feeling of being an outsider.

If the new kid has changed schools within the same town, the new things to learn will be fewer than they were for Marcus. Still, you know things that the new kid doesn't, so you can lead the way.

Social Studies

Social Studies

Strange Sports with Weird Gear

Genre	Comprehension Skill and Strategy	Text Features
Nonfiction	• Draw Conclusions • Visualize	• Captions • Glossary • Headers • Photos

Scott Foresman Reading Street 5.4.5

PEARSON

Scott Foresman

scottforesman.com

by Benjamin Lazarus

Reader Response

1. Which of the sports you read about demands the most speed? Which one could be played outside on a cold winter's day? Which one has more women competitors than men?

2. Which of the three sports is probably the noisiest, not counting the music or crowd noise? Explain your answer.

3. Which suffix **cannot** be added to the word climb to make another word?

   A. -ed

   B. -er

   C. -est

   D. -ing

4. Divide the word *cooperative* into prefix, root, and suffix.

Glossary

bluish *adj.* blue-like color.

cartwheels *n.* sideways handsprings.

gymnastics *n.* exercises that use strength, agility, and coordination.

hesitation *n.* pause or falter.

limelight *n.* the focus of attention.

skidded *v.* slid.

somersault *n.* rolling over by turning heels over head.

throbbing *v.* vibrating.

wincing *v.* a shrinking gesture.

Strange Sports with Weird Gear

by Benjamin Lazarus

PEARSON
Scott Foresman

**Editorial Offices: Glenview, Illinois • Parsippany, New Jersey • New York, New York
Sales Offices: Needham, Massachusetts • Duluth, Georgia • Glenview, Illinois
Coppell, Texas • Ontario, California • Mesa, Arizona**

Jai Alai Gear

A player uses a wooden basket to catch and throw. Each basket is made to fit a player's hand. It is covered with a leather glove. The ball travels so fast that the players have to wear helmets.

The playing wall has to be strong to withstand such a powerful game. The wall is made of thick granite blocks 18 inches thick.

How Is Jai Alai Played?

There are four players on each team. Each player lines up, one behind the other. The goal is to throw the ball so fast that the other player can't return it after one bounce. Players are not allowed to block the other team from catching or throwing the ball. The ball must be thrown right after it is caught. It is a fast and difficult game.

Strange Sports Gear

Do you have a favorite sport? Most people can name a sport they most like to play, watch, or both. Everyone knows the most familiar sports in the United States—football, basketball, hockey and the game that is called our national pastime, baseball. Each of these athletic activities has millions of fans. Yet there are other popular sports that many Americans don't know much about.

Can you imagine playing a sport on bluish ice using a stone and brooms? What if you had to wear two different kinds of shoes? Have you heard of a sport that uses wooden baskets? These are some examples of real sports gear. In this book, we will learn about the sports that require this type of gear. You will read about curling, rhythmic gymnastics, and jai alai.

Each heavy stone is made of granite.

Curling

Curling is a sport that has been played for at least 500 years. It is played with a heavy polished stone and a specially prepared sheet of ice. The origin of curling is unknown. Some people believe it began in Scotland and others say it started somewhere else in Europe.

Most people think curling has to do with weight-lifting. It's actually a game played on a sheet of ice. It's a little like bowling on ice. Curling describes how the stones naturally curve as they slide across the ice.

© Pearson Education, Inc.

4

Jai Alai

Jai alai is the world's fastest ball game. It's a lot like handball, but much faster. A player serves the ball by hitting it against a wall. The other player must do the same thing when the ball bounces back.

Jai alai is played with a rubber ball covered with goatskin. The ball is a little smaller than a baseball. Balls may reach a speed of 185 miles per hour. This makes the game very exciting to fans.

Curling is played by two teams of four people. Each player slides two stones. After a stone has been cast by one team, the other team takes a turn. Each team tries to get their stone closest to the goal. Players often try to keep the other team from scoring by knocking that team's stone away from the target.

Why Brooms?

Brooms are an important part of curling. The team captain uses the broom to help the slider aim for the goal. The captain holds the broom next to the goal so that the other player can better aim toward the goal.

Brooms also improve the player's aim by smoothing the ice. One or two people on the same team can sweep the ice in front of the sliding stone. The brooms polish the ice, giving the stone a smoother ride. This also helps the stone to go farther and change direction.

Sweepers must be in good shape; sweeping demands a lot of energy. Curlers must be physically fit. Each curler walks an average of two miles during a game.

Rhythmic Gymnastics in the Olympics

Rhythmic gymnastics became an Olympic event in 1984. That year, Canadian Lori Fung won the gold medal. It was her moment to shine in the limelight.

Gymnasts perform on a 40 foot mat. Each movement they make is judged on how difficult it is and how well it is done. The difficulty level of each movement is written down in a rule book. This rule book also tells judges what a movement should look like if it is done perfectly.

A perfect routine is flawless and performed without hesitation. It blends balance and motion. Points are given for grace and flexibility. Each gymnast must keep the gear moving during the whole routine.

Lori Fung won the gold medal in 1984.

Curlers use their brooms to help them aim for the goal.

Different Shoes on the Same Pair of Feet?

Players usually slide on the ice until they let go of the stone. In the early days, it was hard for players to keep their balance. Wearing two different shoes became an important part of the curler's gear. The shoes look like normal sneakers, but there are important differences. One shoe is made to slide easily. The other grips the ice to keep the player from slipping or falling.

Other important rules of the sport are: Each player slides two stones. After a stone has been cast by one of the teams, the other team takes a turn. The player must release the stone 21 feet from his team's end, which is called the hogline. Players may try to keep the other team from scoring by knocking a stone already cast by the other team away from the target.

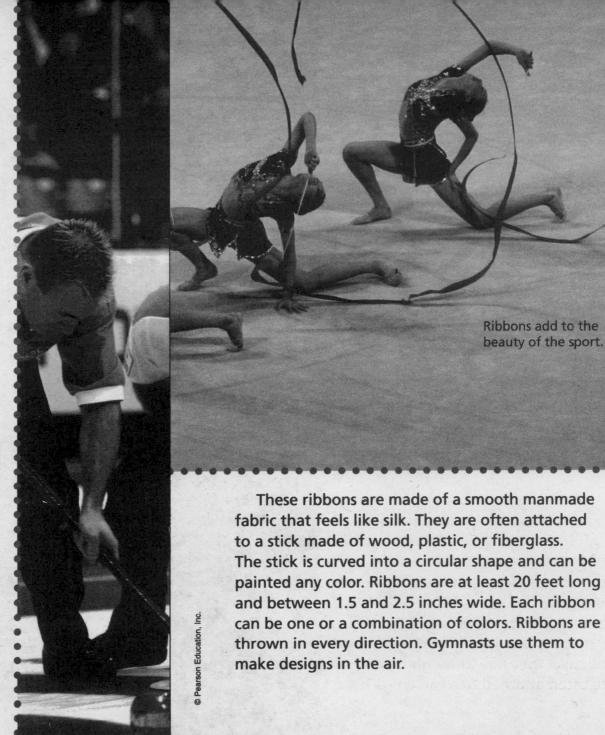

Ribbons add to the beauty of the sport.

Curlers wear special shoes to help them grip the ice.

These ribbons are made of a smooth manmade fabric that feels like silk. They are often attached to a stick made of wood, plastic, or fiberglass. The stick is curved into a circular shape and can be painted any color. Ribbons are at least 20 feet long and between 1.5 and 2.5 inches wide. Each ribbon can be one or a combination of colors. Ribbons are thrown in every direction. Gymnasts use them to make designs in the air.

Clubs are also used in competitions. They are shaped like bottles and are made of wood or plastic. They come in many colors. They weigh at least five ounces and are rolled, twisted and thrown. They are good pieces of equipment for people who can use both hands equally well, because they need to be handled with care and accuracy.

Ribbons used by rhythmic gymnasts are smooth and silky. They flow through the air gracefully. They are often attached to a curved stick.

10

Rhythmic Gymnastics Gear

Here's some information about the equipment used in rhythmic gymnastics. The rope is measured to be the same length as the height of the gymnast. It has a knot at each end, and can be any color. The rope may be loose or tight when it is moved. It often is made to look like a snake attacking the gymnast, appearing to grab and wrap around the gymnast.

Gymnasts use hoops to spin, roll, and walk through. The hoops are made of wood or plastic that doesn't bend. They are less than three feet across and weigh just over half a pound.

The gymnasts use balls to throw and catch. This is a hard to do when a gymnast is always moving! The balls are light and made of rubber or plastic.

Gymnasts often use hoops in their routines.

Curling: Then and Now

Hundreds of years ago, curling stones weighed as much as 130 pounds The stones were called boulders. They were so hard to move around that players skidded them toward the goal with their feet.

Through the years, the stone has been crafted to curve or curl down the sheet of ice for better aim. The stones now have handles for better control. The stones also have hollowed out bottoms, making them much lighter. Today they only weigh 42 pounds.

Curling is a sport that is always changing and improving. The methods used to slide the stone and knock out opponents' stones have recently been changed for the better. The quality of curling equipment and the ice sheet have improved as well.

Early curling stones were much heavier than they are today.

Rhythmic Gymnastics

Rhythmic gymnastics is not like gymnastics you may be used to seeing. It's gymnastics without somersaults or cartwheels. Like regular gymnastics, it tests an athlete's strength, balance, and grace. Gymnasts must train carefully or they may end up wincing from throbbing muscle injuries.

Rhythmic gymnastics combines dancing with gymnastic skills. The routines are performed to music. Athletes add to the beauty of their dancing by using hoops, ropes, balls, ribbons, and clubs.

Rhythmic gymnastics was born in the early 1900s as a combination of exercise programs developed in Europe in the 1800s. A Swedish fitness expert created a kind of gymnastic exercise that concentrated on beautiful movement. At around the same time, an American woman named Catherine Beecher came up with a system of short but physically tough exercises performed to music.

Then, in Switzerland, Emile Dalcroze developed an exercise program for dancers. Finally, George Demeny, a Frenchman, designed exercises performed to music that were meant to improve gracefulness, muscle strength, and posture.

Rhythmic gymnasts are strong and graceful.

Social Studies

Double Play

Genre	Comprehension Skill and Strategy
Fiction	• **Literary Elements: Character & Plot** • **Activate & Usae Prior Knowledge**

Scott Foresman Reading Street 5.5.1

PEARSON

Scott
Foresman

scottforesman.com

by Jesse McDermott

illustrated by Albert Lorenz

Reader Response

1. If Bill and Mr. Jenkins were real people, how would you describe them to your parents?

2. Think about a time you changed your mind about a person. What happened? What made you change your mind?

3. Many words have several meanings. Look up *spectacle* to find at least two meanings. List other words in this book that have multiple meanings.

4. Bill's father liked to say that "a stranger is a friend you haven't met." What does the comment mean? What experiences have you had that suggest that the observation is true?

The United States and Vietnam Today

The United States brought its last troops home from Vietnam in 1973. In 1975, the South Vietnamese army collapsed. North Vietnam united the country under a Communist government.

About fifteen years later, Vietnam reached out to the United States. It needed machinery to bring its factories up to date. It needed places to sell its products overseas.

Many Americans didn't want to help an old enemy. U.S. Senator John McCain disagreed with them. McCain was a Navy pilot during the war. The North Vietnamese shot down his plane in 1967 and kept him in prison until 1973. In the 1990s, he helped convince U.S. leaders like President Bill Clinton that closer ties with Vietnam would be good for both countries.

President Clinton with John McCain who was a fighter pilot during the Vietnam War. Today, he is a U.S. Senator. He believes that trade with the West will encourage Vietnam's Communist government to give its people more freedom.

32

Double Play

by Jesse McDermott

illustrated by Albert Lorenz

PEARSON

Scott Foresman

Editorial Offices: Glenview, Illinois • Parsippany, New Jersey • New York, New York
Sales Offices: Needham, Massachusetts • Duluth, Georgia • Glenview, Illinois
Coppell, Texas • Ontario, California • Mesa, Arizona

"Gee, thanks, Coach," Bill said. "Thanks! That's really great!"

"By the way," the coach added, "you'll be playing with Rob and Craig. They're on the team, too."

"Hey, Dad!" Bill called after he hung up the phone. "I made the team!"

He wanted to tell Mr. Jenkins, too. He knew Mr. Jenkins would be as glad as his father to hear the news. He couldn't wait to see Mr. Jenkins's face when he told him after school. A *double play*, Bill thought. I got an A, and I got on the team. I made a double play!

A phrase passed through Bill's mind as he thought of Mr. Jenkins. *"A stranger is a friend you've never met,"* the phrase went. Bill forgot where he first heard those words, but they certainly fit Mr. Jenkins.

31

On Saturday morning, Bill and his friends walked past Mr. Jenkins's house on their way to the tryouts. Bill held his mitt up and waved to Mr. Jenkins, who was working in his garden. Mr. Jenkins gave him a thumbs-up sign. "Good luck, soldier," he said.

"What were you doing?" Craig whispered when they were a few houses away. "You don't wave to a crazy man."

"He's not crazy," Bill responded. "He's the guy I interviewed for my report. He was a Marine, and he fought in Vietnam, and he's really a nice guy. He knows more about baseball than anyone I've ever met."

"Wow, really?" asked Rob. That changed everything.

"Yes, really," Bill said.

Bill had stopped worrying about the presentation. Thanks to Mr. Jenkins, he felt as prepared to give his report as he did trying out for the Little League majors.

He was right to be confident. On Monday, he gave his report. It was a little long—he wanted to get in all of Mr. Jenkins's stories—but he kept the class interested, and Ms. Cunningham gave him an A.

After dinner that night, the Little League coach called. As usual, he was all business. "Bill," he said, "this is Coach Brown. I've got good news. You're in the majors."

"Great!" Bill blurted into the phone. "That's great! Thanks! Am I a pitcher?"

"You've got real promise as a pitcher," the coach said, "but you're a good catcher right now. The team needs a good catcher right now, so that's what I want you to be."

CONTENTS

Chapter 1

Friday Morning

"Bye, Mom," Bill Harrison called over his shoulder as he was leaving his house. "Bye, Chester," he called to his dog. "See you after school!"

"Bill, wait!" his mother said. "You forgot your lunch!" She handed him the brown bag he had left behind.

"Thanks, Mom!"

Outside, Bill tucked the bag into his backpack and zipped up his jacket. Though May was half over, it felt like March.

In a few minutes he was walking by the park. Bill and his friends played war there a couple of times, crawling on their bellies around the big bushes. That was fun!

Chapter 7

Making a Double Play

Bill spent the afternoon writing down what Mr. Jenkins had told him about Vietnam. On Sunday, the weather had cleared up, and he practiced pitching with his dad. Then Bill had his father pitch to him so that he could practice catching. His Dad was surprised. "What got you thinking about catching again?" he asked.

"Oh, just something Mr. Jenkins told me, I guess," Bill said.

The week passed quickly. Bill's regular homework kept him busy, but he continued to work on his oral report. He wrote down what he wanted to say and learned part of it by heart. He drew a large map of Vietnam and chose pictures from the library book to show the class. And every night before he went to sleep, he read a chapter of *The Land of Oz*.

Then, if he got a chance, he would slide into home plate with one foot in the air. Catchers got out of his way pretty fast when they saw Cobb's cleats coming at them. He scored a lot of runs that way. But good catchers aren't so easy to scare. The quick ones learned how to tag Cobb with the ball without getting their legs cut up. Catching teaches you to be quick and tough."

"Did your grandfather know Ty Cobb?"

"He met him. Cobb was very superstitious. He thought it was bad luck to wear or even carry his baseball shoes into the ballpark. One day my grandfather tried to sneak into a game with some other kids and got caught. Well, who comes along but Ty Cobb. 'Here, kid,' Cobb said. 'Carry my shoes for me.' And so my grandfather got into the game after all, and Cobb stole three bases that day."

"Cool," Bill said.

"I think so, too," Mr. Jenkins said.

Bill wanted to keep talking about baseball, but he figured he ought to ask more questions about Vietnam instead. Mr. Jenkins told him about visiting Vietnam with some other veterans in 1999. "We were shown around by guys who had fought against us 30 years before," he said. "That's when I realized how stupid wars are. It's a lot easier to be someone's friend than it is to be an enemy."

Later, at home, Bill told his father everything he had learned about Mr. Jenkins. "It sounds like he's a baseball nut, just like us," his father said. "Maybe the three of us could go to a game together."

"I'd really like that," Bill replied. "When I take the Oz book back to him, can I ask him?"

"Absolutely," his father said.

It was Friday, and Bill was looking forward to the weekend. With Little League tryouts only a week away, he was going to practice pitching and hitting with his dad. Last year Bill's team won the local championship. But younger players like Bill didn't get on the field very much. This year would be different, he promised himself. He had been practicing with his father since the beginning of spring.

Bill's friend Rob was waiting where he always did, at the stop sign at the busy intersection near his house. Lost in thought, Bill walked right past Rob and the stop sign.

"Hey, Bill!" Rob called to him. "Watch out!"

Bill had one foot on the curb and one in the street. A blue van whipped past him, and he jumped back on the sidewalk.

"Phew, that was close. Thanks, Rob!"

"No problem," Rob replied. "What were you thinking about?"

"Little League tryouts. What else?"

"Right now, there's nothing else," Rob said. "I really want to make the majors this year."

"Me, too. My dad's been practicing with me, so I feel pretty good about it."

Little League had two divisions. Rob and Bill had played in the minors last year. The older boys usually played in the majors, where players were allowed to steal bases. Both boys were 10-and-a-half years old. They would be a little embarrassed if they didn't make the majors this year.

They chatted about batting averages while waiting for their friend Craig to show up. Soon Craig came running into view. He slowed to a walk when he spotted Bill and Rob and was panting when he reached them.

"Hi, guys," he said. "I bet you were early."

"Actually, I was," Rob said. "But it doesn't matter. We're not late."

The ten minute walk to school took the boys along several blocks of tree-lined streets.

Near Mrs. Snippley's yard, the chop-chop-chop of an old-fashioned lawn mower turned their heads. A big, bald man was pushing it. He had a long, gray beard that made him seem out of place in the neighborhood. His lawn mower looked like a giant pencil sharpener on wheels.

"My mom says he's crazy," Rob said as they sneaked through Ms. Snippley's yard.

"Crazy how?" asked Bill.

"Well, like that," Rob said. He nodded toward the man, who was now walking backwards and pushing the lawnmower behind him.

"Sometimes people say hello, and he doesn't even look at them," Craig chimed in. "My dad says it's because he's sick."

He seemed pretty healthy to Bill. In fact, he looked as strong as the Harley motorcycle sitting outside his garage.

The boys slipped through Ms. Snippley's yard and across an apartment building parking lot. They reached school about ten minutes before the bell.

"How long did you spend in the jungle?" Bill asked.

"It depended on the mission. The longest I ever spent there was about a month. Back at the base, we got some rest when the VC weren't lobbing shells at us. We played cards, wrote letters home, and even managed to play a few games of baseball."

Bill's eyes lit up. "You played baseball?"

"Oh, sure. I was a pitcher at my high school, and I was pretty good. We had some good games in 'Nam, some good players."

"I love baseball," said Bill. "Tryouts for Little League are next week."

"No kidding?" Mr. Jenkins said. "What position do you play?"

"Last year I was a catcher, but I'd really like to be a pitcher. I've been practicing with my dad."

Mr. Jenkins smiled. "Don't be too quick to change positions," he said. "Without a good catcher, the pitcher is nothing. And you've got to be tough to be a catcher. It's good training for life."

"What do you mean?" Bill asked.

"Well," Mr. Jenkins replied, "I'll tell you a story about my grandfather. When he was a boy in Detroit, a guy named Ty Cobb played outfield there. Cobb was one of the greatest players ever. Before he retired in 1928, he made 4,191 hits and stole 892 bases. But he played a rough kind of baseball, and many players didn't appreciate that."

"You mean he'd hit people?"

"Not exactly," Mr. Jenkins said. "He liked to make the metal cleats on his shoes as sharp as daggers.

Chapter 2

The Research Paper

Behind the school, some kids were playing soccer without a net, and a few of the sixth graders were tossing a football. Rob joined the soccer game. Bill and Craig walked over to some classmates who were discussing schoolwork. "Ms. Cunningham is going to give out the assignments today," said a red-haired girl named Susan Jones. "My brother did it last year and said it's all about research. Two kids in his class got Fs because they didn't do it right," she added.

"No way," said a boy. "She's too nice for that."

"It's true!" Susan insisted. "If you don't do it right, you don't get promoted to sixth grade."

"What was it like to be there?"

"I bet it sounds really cool, huh? Using real guns, the tanks, and helicopters and all?"

"Yeah, kind of."

"Well, the truth is, there's nothing worse than being in a real war. A real war means walking, walking, and more walking. We trudged through swamps and jungles, for weeks at a time. Jungles look real pretty from up above, but when you're down in them, sweating and swatting at bugs and sleeping in mud, things are very different."

Mr. Jenkins cleared his throat. "We moved slowly, because we had to watch every step. The North Vietnamese put traps and land mines everywhere, and you didn't want to step on one of those. We knew the enemy had the edge. It was their country, after all. They knew the jungle, how to blend in, where to find the best spot for an ambush."

"At night," Mr. Jenkins continued, "we dug trenches to sleep in. That's when the bugs became our biggest enemies. Bugs in Vietnam were like mosquitoes, only bigger and meaner. Severe rainstorms would make the ground so muddy you could sink in up to your shoulders, or worse. I'm not kidding."

"Yuck," Bill said, looking out the window at the falling sheets of rain.

"It wasn't a walk in the park, that's for sure, but I had my buddies with me, fellow Marines," Mr. Jenkins said. "When you're thrown into that, you become real close with the people around you. You depend on one another. You help one another get through it all. I made friends in 'Nam I'm still in touch with."

Chapter 6
Walking in 'Nam

"Why do you call it 'Nam?" Bill asked.

"That's soldier-talk. Soldiers have their own names for things. We said 'VC' for Viet Cong, people in South Vietnam who fought for the Communists. The VC were farmers during the day and fighters at night. It was real hard to tell the good guys from the bad guys."

"When were you in Vietnam?"

"My first tour of duty was in 1968. Each tour lasted a year. I didn't stay in Vietnam for the whole tour, though. I got shot in the leg and landed in a hospital. When I got out, I signed up for a second tour."

"Why?"

"To get back at the guy who shot me, I guess. I was really mad."

Susan was the class worrier, and she was good at making others worry along with her. Bill didn't believe Ms. Cunningham would actually give anyone who worked hard an F in anything. She had a way of making sure everyone did his or her best. But her end-of-the-year assignment was famous for being really hard, and Bill had been dreading it all year.

A loud bell rang twice, and the students lined up by class at one end of the playground. A couple of Bill's classmates were still whispering about the up coming assignment as they filed into the school. Bill was really nervous now. He wasn't a straight-A student, but he had never flunked anything. He didn't want to start now.

He made his way to Room 12 with the other fifth graders. Colorful posters lined the walls, and the windows looked out onto the playground. There were 25 desks set neatly in rows of five, each with a chair placed upside down on top.

Where was Ms. Cunningham?

She was always the first one there. The students put their chairs in place, sat down, and began talking. They talked quietly at first, then loud enough to fill the room with a dull roar. A paper airplane flew by Bill's seat in the third row and hit Susan in the back of the head.

Just then, the door flew open, and Ms. Cunningham raced into the room. "I'm sorry to keep you all waiting," she said as she plopped down a large canvas tote bag. "My car had trouble starting this morning."

Ms. Cunningham quickly hung her jacket on the back of her chair and walked around to the front of her desk. "Looks like everyone is here on time today except me," she said. "So there's no need to take attendance. Let's start right out with the research paper."

The class groaned, and Ms. Cunningham smiled. "People," she said, "you've got nine days to do this, and it's going to be fun because you're going to make it fun."

The students looked back at her, waiting to be convinced.

"Here's how it's going to work," Ms. Cunningham said. "A week from this coming Monday, each of you will give an oral report about an event in American history. I've chosen the topics and written each one on a slip of paper. The slips are in this bag," she said, holding up a small grocery bag. "Now, after lunch

"What was the last book you read?"

"*The Wizard of Oz.* The book is sure better than the movie."

"Oh, I loved the Oz books," said Mr. Jenkins.

"You mean there are more?"

"There sure are. Twelve or 13 more. In fact, I think I still have them on one of these shelves. . . ." Mr. Jenkins got up and walked over to a bookcase. "Ah-ha!" he said, pulling out a beaten-up paperback. He brought it over to Bill.

"Here you go. You can borrow this if you want to read it. I have the rest of the series here, too."

Bill read the title, "*The Land of Oz.* Cool! Thank you, Mr. Jenkins!"

"You're welcome, Bill. But I don't think you came here because of all my books, did you?"

"No, sir, I didn't. I have to give this presentation in school about what it was like to be in Vietnam during the war. I have to interview someone who was there, and, well, you're it, and. . . ."

"Go ahead," Mr. Jenkins said, opening his eyes. "You can ask me anything you want to about 'Nam."

"We used that word when we studied Roman history," Bill said. "The Roman emperors used to put on spectacles like circuses to keep the people happy."

"Well, yes," Mr. Jenkins said. "That's another kind of spectacle. A lot of them were pretty bloody. Like Vietnam, in fact."

Mr. Jenkins located his glasses and slipped them into his shirt pocket. "Now, then," he said, sitting down. Bill had just noticed that the walls were lined with books. "Have you read all these books?" Bill asked.

Mr. Jenkins chuckled. "Most of them, yes. You see, I'm a writer. And if I don't read, I don't have anything to write about."

"Do you write books?" Bill asked.

"I used to when I taught at the university," Mr. Jenkins said. "You wouldn't have liked them. I wrote them for other college teachers, and I'm sure many of those teachers didn't like the books, either." He smiled.

"Don't you teach anymore?" Bill asked.

"No," Mr. Jenkins replied. "My wife died, and . . . Well, that's another story. Do you like to read?"

"Sometimes," Bill said. "I mean, I like reading about exciting stuff. Harry Potter, for instance, or fighter planes."

today, we'll go to the library so you can find a book or two about your topic. That should be easy for you now, since we've just learned how to use the library for research, right?" The children nodded their heads.

Rob raised his hand. "Can we use the Internet?" he asked.

"Not this time," she answered. "I want you to learn how to research topics in books first. Books can't tell you everything, though, so I want each of you to ask your parents if they know anyone who experienced the event. That person can be a relative, a neighbor, or someone else you know. I want you to interview that person to get a first-hand report on the event—what it was like to be part of it."

"I want you to present your research in two parts. In the first part, you will tell us what you learned from books. In the second part, you will tell us what it was really like to be there."

A girl in the front row raised her hand.

"Yes, Rachael?"

"What if we can't find anyone who was there?" asked Rachael.

"Don't worry," Ms. Cunningham smiled. "Come to me. I'll help. Anything else? No? Okay, then, let's pick our topics."

One by one, the students went to the front of the class and drew a slip of paper from the grocery bag. When Bill's turn came, he plunged his hand to the bottom of the bag. There were several slips left. He settled on one and pulled it out. "The Vietnam War," he read aloud. "When was that?"

"Not so long ago, Bill," Ms. Cunningham said. "You shouldn't have any trouble finding someone to interview about that."

Chapter 3

Getting interested in Vietnam

The class reviewed decimals for the next hour and spent another hour discussing a lesson on World War II. In that war, the United States helped defeat Germany, Italy, and Japan. *Who were U.S. troops fighting in Vietnam?* Bill wondered. *Why were they there?* He looked ahead to a chapter called "Conflict in Southeast Asia." The pictures of airplanes and soldiers looked interesting. *Maybe this won't be so bad after all,* he thought.

During the hour before lunch, the students discussed their assignments. Ms. Cunningham explained what she meant by interviews and how to make a list of questions to prepare for them. The more she talked, the more eager Bill was to get started on the assignment. The Vietnam War sure sounded a lot more interesting than some of the other topics.

© Pearson Education, Inc.

"This must be Bill," Mr. Jenkins's voice boomed as he opened the door. Bill had forgotten how big he was. Mr. Jenkins towered over him.

"Hi, Dan," Bill's father said. "Yup, this is the young historian himself."

"He-hello," Bill stammered.

"Hello, there," Mr. Jenkins said. "Come on in out of the rain." He stepped aside to let Bill enter. "Bob, I've got some coffee on," he said.

"Thanks, Dan," said Bill's father. "But I've got a leaky faucet to fix." He handed the umbrella to Bill. "Bill, I'll see you at home. Dan, thanks a lot for taking the time to do this."

"I'm going to enjoy it," Mr. Jenkins said. "It's not every day that someone treats you like an expert."

"Why don't we sit in my study?" Mr. Jenkins said. He led the way to a large room. A desk sat in front of a picture window that opened onto the backyard. It was covered with papers, books, and a laptop computer and a printer. On the corner of the desk, a small glass vase held a few withered flowers.

"Have a seat at the desk, Bill," said Mr. Jenkins. "You may want to take some notes." He moved a wooden armchair close to the desk, but did not sit down right away.

"Just give me a moment to find my spectacles," he said.

"Your what?" asked Bill.

"My spectacles. Eyeglasses, to help me see."

The lunch bell rang, and the children lined up and walked quietly to the cafeteria. Bill sat with Rob and Craig and a few other friends.

"So, do you guys know anything about your topics?" asked Rob.

"Nope," said Craig.

"Nothing," replied Bill. "But I think the Vietnam War will be kind of neat. I mean, studying a real war sure beats playing war, and I get to talk to someone who's actually been in a real one."

"Yeah, you have a good topic," said Rob. "Want to trade?"

"What have you got?" Bill asked.

"A march that Martin Luther King led in Washington."

"Well, I'd like to know more about Martin Luther King," Bill said. "But I think I'll stay with the Vietnam War."

The boys passed the rest of lunch talking about other things, especially the coming Little League tryouts. When they got back to Room 12, Ms. Cunningham said, "Don't sit down. Just pick up a notebook and a pencil and follow me."

The students were soon leafing through the library's card catalog. Ms. Cunningham helped them find books and encyclopedias on their topics.

Bill found a book showing a helicopter flying over a jungle. *Cool,* he thought. Jets and helicopters fascinated him, so he began reading.

For the rest of the school day, Bill read about the war in Vietnam. He learned that Vietnam was divided into two parts in 1954. The Communists who ran North Vietnam wanted to rule all of Vietnam. The United States didn't want them to succeed. In 1961, President John F. Kennedy sent a few hundred U.S. troops to train soldiers in South Vietnam. The South Vietnamese couldn't defeat the Communist forces all alone. So in 1965, President Lyndon Johnson sent thousands of U.S. soldiers to back them up. Soon the United States was in an ugly war.

Bill read about some weapons that were used and some of the biggest battles. He learned that more than 50,000 Americans lost their lives in Vietnam.

Bill checked out the book and took it home. He finished it just before his mother called him to supper.

© Pearson Education, Inc.

Chapter 5

Talking to the Expert

When Bill woke up on Saturday morning, he glanced out the window. A mist was creeping over the front yard, and it was raining. The whole scene was eerie, like something out of a scary movie.

He fixed a bowl of cereal and flipped on the TV, changing channels until he found a weather report. When his parents awoke a little later, he knew the rain was going to last all day.

"We can't play ball in the rain," said his father. "Why don't you visit Dan Jenkins today?"

"Well, maybe." The prospect of learning more about the Vietnam War was attractive to Bill. But the prospect of spending time with Mr. Jenkins made him uneasy.

"Mr. Jenkins is a really nice man," said Bill's father. "C'mon, I'll call and see if he's free. If he is, I'll drive you over so you don't get soaked."

Mr. Jenkins was free, and around 11 o'clock, Bill and his father pulled up outside his house. Bill's dad walked with him up to the door, holding an umbrella over both of them.

"He was walking backwards and pushing this old-fashioned lawnmower behind him."

"It would be a pretty boring world if everybody did everything the same way," said his father.

"Well, Rob's mom thinks he's crazy. Craig's mom said he was sick."

"Sick?" said his father. "He looked pretty healthy when we met him at the party."

"Many soldiers came home with nightmares that haunted them day and night," his mother said. "Maybe that's what Rob's mother meant by 'sick.'"

"Oh, I see," said Bill, but he was still a little worried.

"We should really call Mr. Jenkins and ask if Bill can interview him," said his mother. "A lot of veterans don't like to talk about Vietnam."

After dinner, Bill's father called Mr. Jenkins. "He said you can visit him anytime this weekend," he told Bill afterward. "Just call first to let him know you're coming."

Vietnam was divided in two in 1954. Hanoi became the capital of North Vietnam. Saigon (now Ho Chi Minh City) became the capital of South Vietnam. After years of fierce fighting, the Communist government of North Vietnam got what it wanted in 1975. It defeated the South and brought both parts of the country under its control. The war took the lives of more than 2 million Vietnamese.

Chapter 4

Finding Out about Mr. Jenkins

Dinner in Bill's house always went the same. His parents would talk about their day, and then Bill would talk about his. But this time Bill was so excited about the assignment that he started talking as soon as he sat down.

"What have you learned about the war so far?" his father asked.

"A lot," Bill answered. "But I need to find out what it was really like to be there. Ms. Cunningham wants us to interview someone."

"That's interesting," his mother said. "Bob," she asked her husband, "do we know any Vietnam veterans?"

He pondered the question for a moment.

"What about Dan Jenkins? He's a veteran, and I think he was wounded there."

"That's right," Bill's mother said. "He's a very nice person."

"Who is he?" Bill asked. "Do I know him?"

"You probably pass his house on the way to school," his mother said. "He's got the best-kept yard on his block."

"And the best-kept beard, too," his father said. "We met him at the Davis's Fourth of July party last year. He had some hair on his head then, but last time I saw him he had shaved it all off."

"That guy?" Bill said. "I saw him today. . . . He seems kind of . . . well, weird."

"What makes you say that?" his mother asked.

Suggested levels for Guided Reading, DRA™, Lexile® and Reading Recovery™ are provided in the Pearson Scott Foresman Leveling Guide.

Physical Science

Science

Science

EXPLORING WITH SCIENCE

BY DONNA LONGO

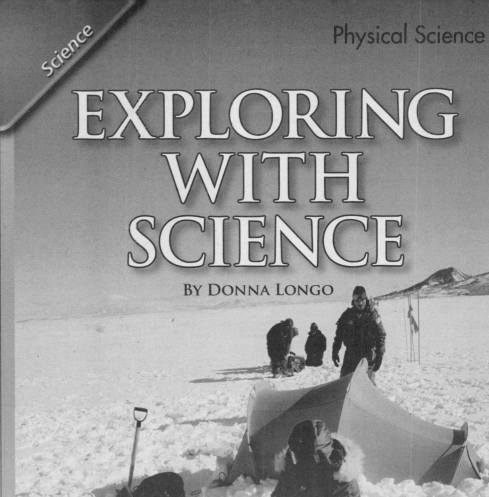

Genre	Comprehension Skill and Strategy	Text Features
Nonfiction	• Ask Questions • Graphic Sources	• Captions • Charts • Labels • Photos

Scott Foresman Reading Street 5.5.2

PEARSON

Scott Foresman

scottforesman.com

ISBN 0-328-13566-6

90000

9 780328 135660

Reader Response

1. Reread the fourth paragraph on page 4. What details support the main idea that Mount Everest is a challenging mountain to climb?

2. The writer didn't tell us much about how Hillary and Norgay felt when they reached the top of Mount Everest. What questions would you like to have asked them about their trip to the top?

3. If you do not know a word's meaning, you can find it in a dictionary. Find an unfamiliar word in this book. Look it up in a dictionary and write its meaning.

4. Look at the diagram on page 5. What is the second tallest mountain? What is the shortest mountain?

Glossary

cramped *n.* tightly crowded and close together.

debris *n.* pieces of broken materials, scattered over an area.

interior *n.* the most remote, inner area.

ooze *n.* very soft and slimy mud.

robotic *adj.* a robot-controlled device, such as an arm.

sediment *n.* dirt, rocks, and sand that have been moved and dropped by wind, water, or ice.

sonar *n.* a system that uses sound waves to locate objects underwater or to determine how deep water is.

EXPLORING WITH SCIENCE

BY DONNA LONGO

PEARSON

Scott Foresman

Editorial Offices: Glenview, Illinois • Parsippany, New Jersey • New York, New York
Sales Offices: Needham, Massachusetts • Duluth, Georgia • Glenview, Illinois
Coppell, Texas • Ontario, California • Mesa, Arizona

The Team

First, the head scientist posts announcements to find the right team members, including meteorologists, geologists, and physicists. They must meet these qualifications:

- understand world exploration charts
- know radar topography for showing mountains, valleys, rivers, forests of Earth's surface
- experienced at mountaineering

The Clothing

At McMurdo Station in Antarctica, team members will need extreme weather gear (EWG) including:

- fleece jackets
- a cap called a "yazoo" that has a warm inner layer
- a gaiter for the neck (very important)
- bibbed polar pants

The Technology

Some of the tools used in satellite work are:

- 3-D maps for Earth observation
- weather satellites for measuring cloud patterns or air pollution
- TV and telephone signals, radio relays for communication
- navigation tools

After the plans are made, and the tents are set up, the real work begins: observing Earth!

Planning a Satellite Launch

Suppose you were looking over the shoulder of a scientist who is gathering a team to launch a new satellite. You see the group has chosen Antarctica as the launch site. The goal is to measure heat radiation on Earth's surface. Before setting out for Antarctica, the scientists need to make some plans.

At the Summit

You are on top of the world! Standing at the summit of Mount Everest, you are standing on the world's tallest mountain. Your climb has been tough. You carried on through snow blindness, little oxygen, and extreme tiredness. You push aside your oxygen mask and smile at your victory.

Due to the lack of oxygen, climbers use oxygen tanks to breathe at high altitudes .

THE WORLD'S HIGHEST MOUNTAIN

Mount Everest was named in honor of Sir George Everest. He created maps of India and the Himalaya Mountains, where Mount Everest stands.

In 1953, Sir Edmund Hillary and Tenzing Norgay became the first people to reach the top of Mount Everest. Since that time, over 1,300 climbers have made it to the top. In 1956, scientists measured the mountain for the first time. They estimate its height at 29,028 (8,847 meters) feet high.

There are many reasons why climbing Mount Everest is challenging. First, there is little oxygen at such a great height. The mountain is also very steep and has several deep, dangerous cracks. Avalanches are another great danger. They are unexpected and overpowering, and their heavy debris can be fatal.

Then there's the weather. Fierce winds and bitterly cold temperatures mean a chance of frostbite. Temperatures can fall to -50° Fahrenheit. Winds can whip at 120 miles per hour.

Radio Transmitters

Biologists are studying the emperor penguins of Antarctica. They want to learn more about the places where penguins feed at sea. They track their movements with radio transmitters, which they attach to penguins. The transmitters send out radio waves. Using an antenna, headphones, and a receiver, a scientist can listen to the signals from the transmitters.

Time to Head Home

You've been on top of the world at Mount Everest and on the bottom in Antarctica. Now it's time to head for home. All the technology you have seen has encouraged you to keep working on a robotic auger you're building to take back to Antarctica on your next visit!

Sea stars and sea urchins

Science in Water and on the Ice

Marine biologists in Antarctica face frosty challenges. To reach the ocean waters, they must drill through six feet of ice. A giant auger digs diving holes into the thick ice.

Underwater, sonar equipment finds objects that divers can't see. By bouncing sound waves off objects, the device measures how far away they are.

Using underwater cameras, marine biologists capture photos of sea stars and sea urchins.

What are scientists studying underwater? As you have seen, some are watching marine life. Others are collecting samples of sediment from the ooze at the bottom of the sea. It is tough work and it involves hauling pails of mud through the water.

Under the ice, these biologists remove samples of plankton to study. These tiny animals and plants supply food for fish and other marine life.

THE WORLD'S HIGHEST MOUNTAINS

The chart below includes the world's ten highest mountains. Each rises higher than 26,248 ft. (8,000 m) above sea level. Look at the summit of Mount Everest. Then compare the heights of the other mountains.

Everest	29,035 ft. (8,850m)	Cho Oyu	26,906 ft. (8,201m)
K2 (Godwin Austen)	28,251 ft. (8,611m)	Dhaulagiri	26,795 ft. (8,167m)
Kangchenjunga	28,497 ft. (8,686m)	Manaslu	26,781 ft. (8,163m)
Lhotse	27,890 ft. (8,501m)	Nanga Parbat	26,795 ft. (8,167m)
Makula	26,781 ft. (8,163m)	Annapurna	26,545 ft. (8,091m)

THEN AND NOW

When Sir Edmund Hillary reached the top of Mount Everest, he did his own measuring. He found it to be 29,000 feet high. Since the first measurements were taken, there have been major advances in science. New measurements were taken in 1999 using this new science. Thanks to satellites orbiting Earth, scientists correctly measured Everest at 8,850 meters (29,035 feet).

How did they do it? Professor Bradford Washburn used radar and global positioning satellites (GPS). The new, high-tech equipment was light—less than forty-two pounds. It was broken down into four pieces, so four people carried its parts to the top of Mount Everest.

Now people use GPS units in their cars. They tell drivers where exactly they are, and they can tell the best way to get somewhere.

Placing a hydrophone in water

New Science in the Water

What tools do scientists use in the Antarctic? It depends whether their work is on land or in the water.

The hand-held GPS used on Mount Everest comes in handy in Antarctica, too. It's not like the sextant that Roald Amundsen used to learn his location. The GPS device communicates with a satellite to find an exact location.

What does a 10-ton killer whale sound like? A hydrophone helps marine biologists find out. The first hydrophones were used to locate submarines and icebergs. A hydrophone works by picking up the sounds that pass through water. It changes them to electromagnetic waves. Now scientists can listen to how marine mammals communicate underwater.

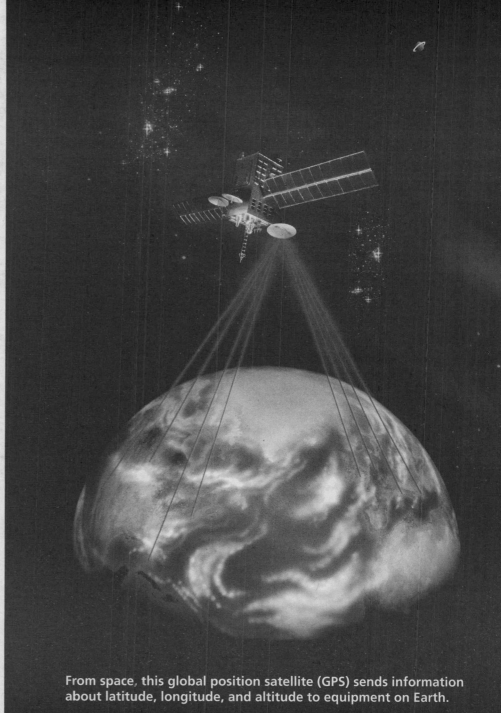

From space, this global position satellite (GPS) sends information about latitude, longitude, and altitude to equipment on Earth.

CALL OR E-MAIL FROM MOUNT EVEREST

When Sir Edmund Hillary and Tenzing Norgay first reached Mount Everest, it took days before their big news reached the rest of the world. Times have changed. Advances in science help people communicate from the top of the world by satellite telephone.

Scientists and climbers depend on satellite phones on Mount Everest. Photographers and journalists use them to help us learn more about the mountain.

What are satellite telephones? They are also called "sat phones," or "satellite terminals." As their name suggests, they use satellite technology. There are several satellites now orbiting Earth. Sat phones send signals to these satellites. They also receive signals from them. Standing at the top of the world, a joyous adventurer can call just about anyone on Earth to share the goods news.

The McMurdo Station is a year-round research center. It is the largest research base in Antarctica.

ON TO ANTARCTICA!

A RESEARCH CONTINENT

In the 1950s, Richard Byrd of the U.S. Navy explored the continent by air. Soon, a flurry of scientists headed for Antarctica. By 1959, twelve nations had signed the Antarctic Treaty. It was an agreement that said the continent would be used for research.

The United States's McMurdo Station is one of thirty stations on the continent and its islands. The United States also uses the Palmers Station on Anvers Island and Ross Island's Amundson-Scott South Pole station.

Scientists live at McMurdo Station throughout the year, even during the sunless winter months of June and July. McMurdo Station is home to most of the people on the continent. It's like a very small village with only two-hundred tough residents. In the summer, however, more than twelve-hundred scientists and researchers live there.

A satellite telephone allows people to make calls from the most remote places.

How would you like to get an e-mail from Mount Everest? Sat phones make that possible too. Explorers and scientists have sent e-mails to co-workers, family, friends, and students waiting eagerly for news. Digital pictures, audio messages, and videos can also be sent using sat phones.

HAND-HELD TECHNOLOGY

You have learned about the satellites in orbit around the Earth. They help us learn about and communicate from Mount Everest. What other tools help those who explore the mountain?

An important part of mountain climbing is knowing where you are. A hand-held GPS device can help. This light and portable device allows climbers to figure out their location on the mountain. Climbers also need to know their altitude as they climb. An altimeter shows height above sea level. This small altimeter is worn like a watch. It includes a barometer to track changes in the weather.

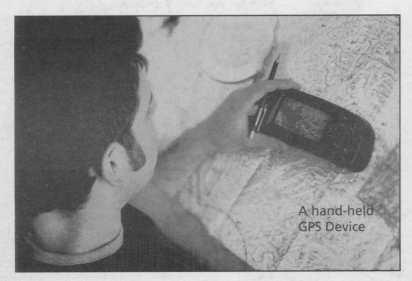

A hand-held GPS Device

Antarctica is one of the coldest places on Earth.

Now that you have conquered Everest, you are off on your next adventure: Antarctica. It has great challenges, too. The weather is its greatest test.

Antarctica has been called a desert of ice, the last frontier, the frozen continent, and the unknown land. With its bone-chilling weather and hurricane-force winds, it may be the planet's most uninviting place. Massive icebergs crowd its waters. Gigantic glaciers move across its lands. Coastal areas have summer temperatures of around 50°F (10°C). The interior of the continent is frigid. It boasts the world's lowest recorded temperature -128.6°F (-89.2°C). That's why it's used mainly for research.

In the 1800s, explorers sailed along the coasts of Antarctica. It was not until 1911 that people explored its interior. In a race to reach the South Pole, Roald Amundsen won on December 14, 1911. He used a tool called a sextant to check his latitude and longitude. That way, he could be sure he had reached the pole.

An altimeter

Braving the Elements

When climbing to extremely high altitudes, people must be careful. They must slowly get used to the lower levels of oxygen. This is called "acclimatization." The change to a new height takes place over several days. In time, the body adjusts to less oxygen. What happens when someone climbs too high too quickly? Acute Mountain Sickness (AMS) can happen.

It can be hard to take care of a sick person in such a remote place as Mount Everest. With new technology, AMS can be treated with a Gamow Bag. This portable pressurization chamber was invented by Igor Gamow. Inside its cramped quarters, a climber can recover from AMS.

Most people think of technology as electronics. But technology can be a new tool or material, too. New technology allows people to create lighter, warmer, drier clothing for mountain climbers.

At such a high altitude, it is important to stay warm. The cold carries great dangers. These include severe frostbite. New materials, such as Gortex, are lightweight and warm. Facing bitter cold, climbers depend on a protective wind suit made of Gortex.

A Gamow Bag provides the pressure necessary to recover from AMS.

Science

Science

Physical Science

Sailing the Stars

by Anne Cambal

Genre	Comprehension Skill and Strategy	Text Features
Nonfiction	• Author's Purpose • Monitor Comprehension	• Diagram • Sidebar • Table of Contents

Scott Foresman Reading Street 5.5.3

PEARSON

Scott
Foresman

scottforesman.com

ISBN 0-328-13569-0

90000

9 780328 135691

Reader Response

1. What is the author's purpose for writing this book?

2. Reread pages 11 and 12. Then write a brief summary that explains why it took so long for American women to first become astronauts.

3. Read the following two sentences.

   *STS-9 crewmembers gather around television **monitors** in the Spacelab module.*

   *NASA researches, plans, constructs, and **monitors** the U.S. space program.*

   What does the word *monitors* mean in each sentence?

4. Read the caption for any of the photographs in this book. What information do they give you that the images do not?

Glossary

accomplishments *n.* successes; skills.

focus *v.* to concentrate on something.

gravity *n.* the force that pulls things toward Earth's surface.

monitors *v.* controls; watches over; observes.

role *n.* a purpose or use for someone or something.

specific *adj.* exact; definite.

Sailing the Stars

by Anne Cambal

PEARSON
Scott Foresman

Editorial Offices: Glenview, Illinois • Parsippany, New Jersey • New York, New York
Sales Offices: Needham, Massachusetts • Duluth, Georgia • Glenview, Illinois
Coppell, Texas • Ontario, California • Mesa, Arizona

On Space Shuttle mission STS-9, crewmembers gather around a television screen in the *Spacelab* module. This reusable laboratory allowed scientists to perform experiments in low gravity while orbiting Earth.

They work together to share knowledge and the costs of space exploration. Many of the Canadians and Europeans who participate in our space shuttle program come from the ESA.

In 2003, China joined an exclusive club when thirty-eight-year-old former fighter pilot Yang Liwei orbited Earth 14 times. China is now only the third country in history to have launched a person into space.

Space exploration is now a worldwide effort. Together, we can learn new and exciting things. And, if you really try, perhaps *you* will be one of the people who sail the stars!

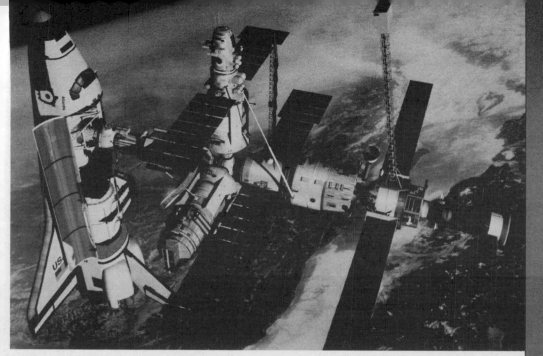

This technical image shows the Space Shuttle Atlantis docked to the *Kristall* module of the Russian *MIR* Space Station. The joint U.S.-Russian mission was completed in June 1995. This combination was the largest space platform ever put together in orbit.

Then, about thirty years ago, the USSR started hiring a few cosmonauts from other countries. Likewise, the United States teamed with Europeans on the *Spacelab* missions of the 1980s.

Other nations also wanted to develop their own space programs. In 1983, Canada was the first newcomer to have its own astronaut candidates. France chose its first candidates in 1985. Japan, the former West Germany, and Italy announced their own groups in the late 1980s.

The European Space Agency (ESA) was formed in 1973, but has roots as far back as the 1950s. Its member nations are the major European countries.

CONTENTS

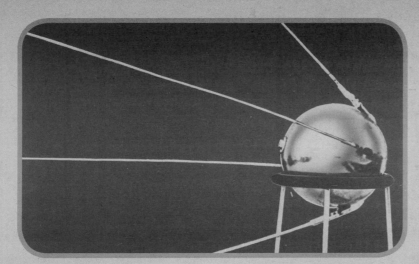

Sputnik I was the first satellite to be launched into space.

Chapter 1: Pioneers in Space

People have dreamed of space travel for many years, but it wasn't until the late 1950s that these dreams began to come true.

After World War II, the United States and the Union of Soviet Socialist Republics (USSR) were enemies in the Cold War. Instead of fighting each other face to face, the two nations tried to increase their influence all over the world. Each country wanted to be the first in space, in part to prove that its own society was the best.

The USSR struck first. On October 4, 1957, the USSR sent the first manufactured satellite, *Sputnik I*, into space. A satellite is something that orbits, or travels around, a larger body in space. For example, the Moon is a satellite of Earth.

Chapter 4: A Growing Space Family

Our study and knowledge of space has come a long way since the 1950s. We now have the *Hubble* Space Telescope and unmanned probes that show us never-before-seen pictures of our universe. Today, the space program is open to anyone who can make the grade. Instead of competing, now countries are working together to explore space.

In the beginning days of space travel, the United States and the USSR were the only countries powerful or rich enough to pursue space programs. This is why all of the space travelers in the first fifteen years were from these two countries.

Jet Propulsion Laboratory geologists Harrison Schmitt and Andrea Mosie study vesicles on a volcanic rock recovered from a lunar mission.

© Pearson Education, Inc.

The crew of the STS-61, the space shuttle mission to repair the Hubble Space Telescope, poses next to a pool used for simulating weightless conditions.

An Astronaut Candidate who completes the training program is not always chosen to be an astronaut. Sometimes, NASA may not have a mission for which that person's education and training are needed.

Even if a person is not selected for a mission, he or she may still be a part of NASA. Military people who have completed their training are assigned to NASA for all or part of their military careers. Civilian trainees are usually offered jobs at NASA. When NASA needs new astronauts, it is likely to choose first from its own staff.

One month later, the USSR launched *Sputnik II*. It carried the first live animal in space, a dog named Laika.

The United States hurried to catch up. Almost three months after the launch of *Sputnik II*, the United States launched *Explorer I*. Through this mission, scientists learned that Earth is surrounded by magnetic radiation belts.

On October 1, 1958, the National Aeronautics and Space Administration (NASA) was created. NASA researches, plans, constructs, and monitors the U. S. space program.

The United States launched its first satellite, Explorer I, on January 31, 1958.

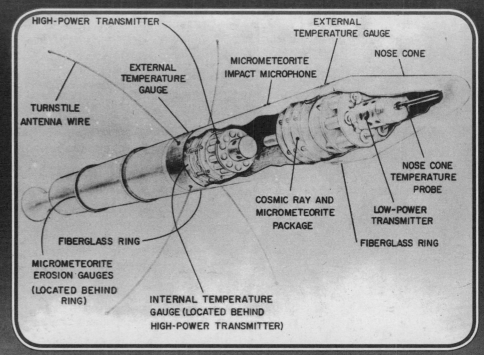

Cosmonaut Yuri Gagarin, 1961

Astronaut John Glenn, 1961

Astronaut Alan B. Shepard, Jr., 1961

What's in a Name?

astronaut: a person who travels beyond Earth's atmosphere; a trainee for space flight. This term is also used to specifically describe such a person in the U.S. space program, as opposed to other space programs.

cosmonaut: an astronaut of the USSR—now the Russian—space program

spationaut: an astronaut of France

taikonaut or **yuhangyuan:** an astronaut of China

Dressing for Space

There is no air to breathe in space, and temperatures are extreme. To survive, an astronaut must wear a spacesuit.

In the past, each astronaut had his own spacesuit designed especially for him. Today, spacesuits are made up of separate parts. Each part of the suit locks into another part. That way, each astronaut can use different parts according to his or her own body size. Now NASA can outfit all its male and female astronauts without having to make an individual suit for each one. As you can imagine, it takes some time to suit up. Some astronauts need several hours!

The spacesuit supplies air, food, and water. Suits are airtight, so the air inside can't leak out. They also have many layers of material to protect the astronaut from radiation, heat, cold, and flying particles in space. A spacesuit can keep an astronaut alive for up to eight hours.

The helmet is large enough for the astronaut's head to move around inside. A food bar and water bag are attached in a way that the astronaut can eat and drink inside the helmet without using his or her hands. A headphone and a microphone let the astronaut stay in touch with the onboard crew.

Spacesuits are white because white reflects heat. This helps to keep the astronaut safe—the temperature in space from direct sunlight can be over 275° Farenheit!

The United States and the USSR both wanted to be the first to put a man in space. Russian cosmonaut Yuri Gagarin won the title for the USSR. On April 12, 1961, he made one orbit around Earth in *Vostok I*.

The United States had its turn on May 5. Astronaut Alan B. Shepard, Jr., flew in space for about fifteen minutes in the *Mercury* capsule. During his flight, Shepard and his spacecraft escaped Earth's gravity. For about five minutes, he was weightless in space. Although his trip was short, Shepard proved that an astronaut could survive and work in space.

Unlike Gagarin, Shepard did not orbit Earth. His flight was also different in another way: The Vostok mission was conducted in secret. The world did not learn of the flight until after its successful completion. But 45 million Americans watched the *Mercury* mission live on television.

On February 20, 1962, John Glenn became the first American to orbit Earth. His flight lasted less than five hours, in which he orbited Earth three times.

When he returned, Glenn was hailed as a hero—in Washington, D.C., 250,000 people stood in the rain to cheer him. It was an exciting time in U.S. history.

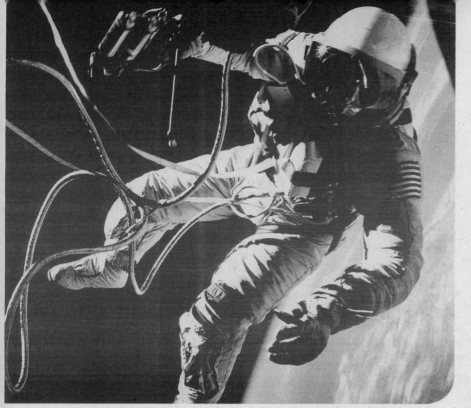

Edward White was the first American to walk in space. He holds the fueled "zip gun" in his right hand.

The 1960s saw many advances in space exploration. The first space walk was on March 18, 1965, during the USSR's *Voshkod II* mission. Co-pilot Alexei Leonov "walked" in space for about twenty minutes. His spacesuit had swelled a bit, however. He couldn't re-enter his ship until he let a little air out of the suit.

Edward White was the first American to walk in space during the *Gemini IV* mission. He used a three-jet "zip gun" to help him move around during the twenty-two-minute walk. On February 3, 1966, the USSR's *Luna IX* was the first spacecraft to land safely on the Moon and send information back to Earth.

Training and evaluation lasts from one to two years. Astronaut Candidates must learn to live, work, and survive in space and how to handle an emergency in space.

Training includes a lot of class work and study. Trainees take many classes in science, and they also get basic medical training. They study spacecraft systems and how to do everyday things while weightless. They spend many hours flying in training aircraft and working with ground control crews. They also get a lot of practice in simulators that are like the ships or space stations they will operate.

Early in their training, Astronaut Candidates must pass a swimming test. They have to do it while wearing a flight suit and tennis shoes! This test is part of their intense emergency training. Astronauts must be ready to land in water or on land. A trainee must also learn to escape the space vehicle, whether on land or sea or by parachute while in the air. They also receive survival training in case they land in a lonely area.

Trainees also learn what it's like to work in the zero gravity of space. They do this through scuba diving and by flying in special aircraft that can create brief periods of zero gravity. You probably think that weightless flying is nothing but fun. However, weightlessness can make you feel queasy and sick. Your body must get used to it.

Astronaut Guion S. Bluford and Aviation Safety Officer Charles F. Hayes, on a zero-gravity training flight, are in a KC-135 aircraft, also known as the "vomit comet." It creates 30 second periods of weightlessness.

Mission Specialist Ellen Ochoa practices an emergency escape from a space shuttle at the Johnson Space Center's Mockup and Integration Laboratory (MAIL).

These women scientists are scuba diving in the Neutral Buoyancy Simulator at the Marshall Space Flight Center in Huntsville, Alabama.

One of the greatest accomplishments in space travel took place on July 20, 1969. That's when the American astronaut Neil Armstrong became the first person ever to set foot on the Moon. This *Apollo 11* mission also included astronauts Edwin "Buzz" Aldrin, Jr., and Michael Collins.

Armstrong and Aldrin landed on the Moon's surface in the lunar module, or ship, while Collins stayed behind to operate the command module in orbit around the Moon.

The landing was one of the most-watched events in the history of the world. Armstrong's first step on the lunar surface was seen by about 1 billion people! When Armstrong stepped on the surface, he said "That's one small step for [a] man; one giant leap for mankind."

This is one of the first footprints made on the Moon.

Astronaut "Buzz" Aldrin looks back at the lunar module. To the left of the module is the American flag that was planted by Armstrong and Aldrin.

There weren't any women among the original astronauts (seated) selected by NASA in 1959, nor in the second group of astronauts (standing) selected in 1962.

Chapter 2: Women in Space

The word *astronaut* comes from the Greek and Latin words for *star* and *mariner,* or *sailor*. At first, the role of an astronaut was seen as a pilot in space.

Early spacecraft were often modeled after military planes, and all the early astronauts were military pilots. These pilots were believed to be among the very best, especially in dangerous flying situations. The U.S. Air Force chose the first astronaut trainees. Only military pilots could qualify, and all of the candidates had to be men.

In the 1950s and 1960s, space flight was just one of many fields that were not open to American women. Women often were barred from getting the same kinds of education and experience that men could get.

Every two years, NASA reviews thousands of applications for astronaut training. From these thousands, only about one-hundred men and women are chosen for interviews.

These one-hundred or so people are invited to the Johnson Space Center in Houston, Texas. After they are interviewed and receive medical exams, only about twenty will be accepted.

Making the final cut does not mean that you will be an astronaut. The new trainee, or Astronaut Candidate, still must pass the astronaut training and evaluation course given at several NASA centers. The training and evaluation will develop the specific skills needed for future space missions.

Chapter 3: Space Training

Here's what it takes to apply to be a NASA astronaut:
- You must be a U.S. citizen.
- To become a pilot, you must be between 5'4" and 6'4" tall. To become a mission specialist, you must be between 4'10 1/2" and 6'4" tall.
- You must be in good health, and your eyesight must be good.
- You must have a college degree. Candidates should have a degree in engineering, biological science, physical science, or mathematics.

Many types of careers were thought to be wrong for women. They were not expected to hold jobs that did not require motherly caring for others. Women at that time were expected to hold "women's" jobs, such as a teacher or a nurse, or low-paying jobs, such as a waitress or a maid.

Being an astronaut seemed definitely out of the question. Women were not allowed to attend pilot training in the U.S. military schools. Yet, while there were no women test pilots, things were beginning to change.

The *Columbia* space shuttle was commanded by Eileen Collins on the July 23–27, 1999, mission.

However, since the 1970s, beliefs about the proper roles for American women have changed a lot. There are women doctors, lawyers, and bankers. There are women police officers, carpenters, and truck drivers. And there are women astronauts.

In 1983, aboard the NASA space shuttle *Challenger*, Dr. Sally Ride became the first American woman to travel into space. (The first woman in space was Valentina Tereshkova on the USSR *Vostok 6* mission—twenty years before!) In 1995, Eileen M. Collins became the first woman to pilot a space shuttle. Then, in 1999, Collins set another record as the first female space shuttle commander.

© Pearson Education, Inc.

Dr. Sally Ride

Dr. Sally Ride began her astronaut training in 1978. The training included parachuting, gravity, and weightlessness training, water survival, radio communications, and navigation. During training, she served as one of the support crew for space shuttle flights. As a Mission Specialist she also was a member of mission control.

Dr. Ride has several degrees in physics and English. She is a physicist and a college professor. Her advice to anyone interested in becoming an astronaut is to focus on math and science, including physics, astronomy, and chemistry.

Dr. Mae Jamison

In 1992, Dr. Mae Jemison became the first African American woman in space, aboard the shuttle *Endeavor*. Like Sally Ride, she was a mission specialist.

When she was just 16, she got a scholarship to Stanford University. Like many astronauts, Dr. Jemison studied science, including chemical engineering and physics. Then she went on to medical school and became a doctor. Dr. Jemison's careers include physician, scientist, chemical engineer, astronaut, and college professor!

Today's astronauts come from a wider variety of backgrounds. Not all astronauts are pilots, and a military background is no longer required.

JOURNEY THROUGH THE EARTH

by Joe Adair

illustrated by Victor Kennedy

Genre	Comprehension Skill and Strategy
Fiction	• Cause and Effect • Summarize Text

Scott Foresman Reading Street 5.5.4

PEARSON

Scott Foresman

scottforesman.com

ISBN 0-328-13572-0

90000

9 780328 135721

Reader Response

1. The children had originally planned to take the Earth Exploration Craft directly home. They did not intend to go all the way through the Earth. What caused the original plan to change? Why did they go straight through the Earth?

2. Where did Toby, Kenny, and Maria begin and end their journey? What layers did they go through from beginning to end?

3. Fossils take millions of years to form. Many times the animals and plants they formed from cannot be found alive on the Earth today. Which of the following words means something that once lived and has since ceased to be?

   exist   *extinct*   *exit*

4. If you found Sir Edmond's machine and decided to journey through the Earth, where would you end up? Use a globe to locate your home and then look on the opposite side of it. Many times this may leave you in an ocean or near a small island.

Getting Inside Earth

We know little about Earth's interior. The biggest problem: how to get there. In all our attempts to drill into Earth, we've dug only 6.2 miles (10 kilometers). Earth's crust is at least 125 miles (200 kilometers) thick. Beyond that are the gooey mantle, liquid outer core, and then the inner core.

In 2003 David Stevenson, a geophysicist who studies Earth's physical processes, had an idea. Because Earth's inner layers are mostly made of iron, he decided to use iron to get through them.

The Stevenson's plan explodes a huge hole—900 feet (300 meters) deep and 30 feet (10 meters) wide into Earth's crust. Then, hot iron is poured down the hole, creating a crack through the crust. The force of flowing iron causes the crack to run all the way to Earth's core. Then, an electronic probe can be sent along the crack to the center of Earth.

Finally, the last thing to do is create a probe strong enough to survive the trip.

Earth's Interior

Crust

Mantle

Outer Core

Inner Core

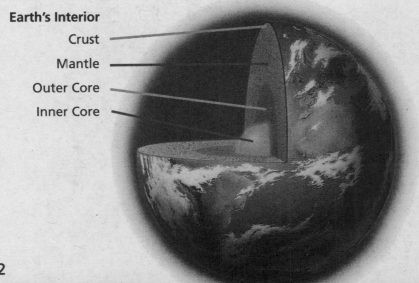

JOURNEY THROUGH THE EARTH

by Joe Adair

illustrated by Victor Kennedy

PEARSON

Scott Foresman

Editorial Offices: Glenview, Illinois • Parsippany, New Jersey • New York, New York
Sales Offices: Needham, Massachusetts • Duluth, Georgia • Glenview, Illinois
Coppell, Texas • Ontario, California • Mesa, Arizona

"Where on Earth do you think we are?" Marie asked. All they could hear from the barren landscape were birds and ocean waves. They began walking, hoping for some sign of human activity.

"Hey, there!" A man's voice called out, and behind them stood a man looking very shocked. "How did you children get here?"

Kenny asked, "Where are we?"

"This is Marion Island—just above Antarctica," the man said, "and this is a scientific research station. I can't imagine what brought you children here."

The children laughed when Toby said, "I don't think you would believe it if I told you." Then the man led them into the building where the children called their parents, ate dinner, and waited sleepily for their ride home.

31

The craft burrowed through the upper mantle and then the rocky crust of Earth. The children could hardly wait fill their lungs with fresh air again. They sat silently watching the computer. "Sir Edmond, you are now approaching the last ten feet of Earth's crust. Would you like to continue in this direction at the current speed?"

"Hey, this is the thinnest layer," Toby laughed, "so we should be back on the surface in no time." Boom! Moving at full speed, the craft cracked through the Earth's crust, ripping the ground and hovering ten feet over the ground.

"Hurray! Hurray! Hurray! We made it through Earth!" Kenny shut the drill off, and Toby used the rocket controls to bring the machine safely to the surface. Maria was the first to turn the wheel and climb free, with the boys right behind her.

Chapter One

A Special Day Starts

"Toby, Toby! Time to rise and shine," Toby's mother called loudly up the stairs. "Toby get out of bed, you have a big day today!" Toby, still groggy with sleep, could not remember anything special that was planned for the day.

Out the window he saw the leaves swirling around the ground over the grass below and felt a burst of energy. Way out in the distance he saw the shape of a mountain through the window. Suddenly, he remembered why it was a special day. Toby finished getting dressed and rushed downstairs with his unfinished homework in hand.

"Good morning, Mom," Toby said with a smile.

"Well, aren't we in a chipper mood this morning." She smiled and poured her son a glass of orange juice.

"Hey, Mom, you were right. Today is going to be a special day for me. I forgot that my science class is going to Mount Randall today!"

"Yes, and I am sure it is going to be very beautiful this time of year." His mother sets the juice before him and smiles again.

"Do you think they will let us go up to the volcano and go inside?"

"I certainly hope they don't. A volcano like Mount Randall is no place for a fifth grader," she replied.

"Oh man, I want to go and see the lava and monsters inside," Toby said.

4

Chapter Seven
Toby, Kenny, and Maria Complete the Journey

"Sir Edmond, you are now reaching the last 10 feet of the Earth's core. Would you like to continue in this direction at the current speed?" Toby breathed a huge sigh of relief. "Hey, we made it through the core!" Kenny, Maria, and Toby all jumped up and hugged each other. The worst was over. The machine had left the Earth's core. The lights went back on, and all the cooling vents began to blow again. Sir Edmond would have been very proud to know that his Earth exploration machine could make it through each of the Earth's layers, including the core.

The journey through the Earth was not over, though. The armor over the windows lowered to reveal the brilliant orange color that Maria so enjoyed. Kenny and Toby went back to their controls. The craft was once more on course.

Kenny went back to the laboratory to see the fossils of dinosaur teeth, bones, and leaves from what must have been gigantic trees. At the controls, Toby was notified that they had just passed through the outer core and were headed back through the mantle. Then he began to consider just what would happen when they did reach the other side of Earth. "Hey, Kenny, do you have any idea what is on the opposite side of the world from Seattle?"

"I have no idea." Kenny looked startled. "I suppose that is the next problem." Just then, the computer announced arrival at the upper mantle.

29

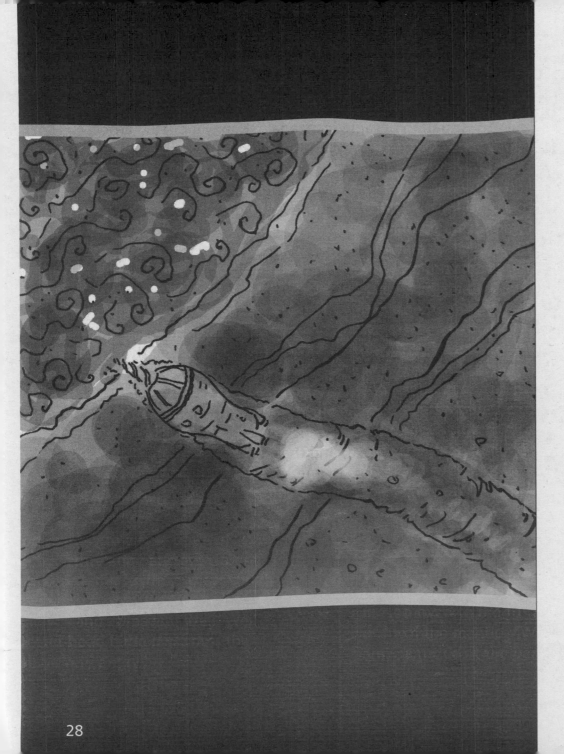

Toby sat next to his best friend, Kenny, and asked him if he remembered that they were going to Mount Randall that day. "Oh yeah, I am really excited about this field trip." Kenny lived only four houses down from Toby. They could both see Mount Randall from their bedroom windows when the weather was nice.

Mrs. Cieco gathered her class in the front of the classroom and made sure they were all there. She looked around, thinking all her students were present, and began to give instructions for the day. Just then a giggle came from behind the coats in the back of the classroom, and Maria jumped from behind the coats and ran to join the rest of her class. She ran to Mrs. Cieco's right side unnoticed and pretended she had been there the whole time. As usual, it worked, and Maria giggled again.

Chapter Two
The Field Trip to Mount Randall

"Everyone remember to stay together and listen to what the park ranger teaches us today," Mrs. Cieco said to the circled children. With that, Mrs. Cieco's whole fifth grade class boarded the bus and rode off toward Mount Randall. The mountain seemed to be growing larger as they drew closer.

When the bus stopped, a park ranger climbed up the steps and greeted the class with a friendly, "Good morning, I hope you are all ready for interesting day at Mount Randall! Let's get started and head to the visitor's center."

Once inside, all the students gathered in a circle around a big globe. The globe could be opened up because it had hinges, and the inside looked like it was painted. Toby asked why the globe could open and what the drawing inside was.

The exploration craft began to slow down. It could not drill through the inner core of the Earth and maintain the same speed. The inner core is very solid and required more energy to run the drill. The situation became scary again. Kenny looked worried. He feared the machine would not make it.

Marie felt his fear, too. "The drill sounds like it is going to break. We are going to be stuck in the middle of the Earth forever! Did I tell you guys I am really hungry, too?"

"Maria don't worry," Toby tried to sound confident. "Everything is going to be all right. This machine has not let us down yet."

The beautiful orange color outside the ship changed to a dull gray. The core of the Earth felt so hot. As the heat of the inner core pushed the machine to its limits, the craft automatically raised a thicker armor to cover the windows completely. The engine took all its power to run the drill and protect the children from the heat outside. The lights inside the craft shut off, and the cooling system switched from three vents to one. The exploration machine made the adjustments to get the power it needed. The little red light went on again, and this time Toby feared some very bad news.

Kenny still had more to say. "Fossils are really neat because they show us what life looked like long ago. A good example is the collection of dinosaur fossils in the natural history museum in Seattle. A couple of scientists took them from the Earth and put them all together." Kenny stopped talking for a moment and examined four of the fossils very closely. "My uncle would love to add these to his collection."

Toby glanced out of the little laboratory and noticed the red light on the control panel blinking again. The computer had another message. "Sir Edmond, you are now reaching the last ten feet of the outer core. Would you like to continue on this course at the present speed?" Toby let the computer know that it was their plan to continue straight through the Earth. The children had to reach the other side if they ever expected to get home. This time the computer said more. "Sir Edmond, are you sure you would like to attempt to drill through the core of the Earth. This is not advised. The risk is great." Toby did not read this second message to the others. He knew that it would only scare them. He commanded the exploration craft to continue through the center of the Earth.

"That's a great question" the ranger said. Toby's classmates were soon all seated on the carpet and began to listen. The ranger continued, "No one knows for sure, but some scientists think it may be several thousands of degrees Farenheidt. Maybe even as hot as the surface of the sun!"

Kenny, leaning over to Toby, said "Wow, the middle of the Earth could be as hot as the sun. Can you imagine what it would be like to go underground that far? It would be way too hot!" Toby just laughed and listened to the ranger. He was waiting to see the globe open and find out what the picture inside was.

As the ranger spoke, he unhooked a small latch on the big globe. "These five layers of the Earth are the crust, upper mantle, mantle, outer core, and the inner core." Kenny leaned in to say something, but Toby gently pushed him aside waiting to see the globe opened up. Inside each of the layers was labeled and further distinguished with warm colors. Toby sat up straight, eager to hear all the ranger had to say. Learning about Earth's layers is exciting—maybe even fun—Toby thought to himself.

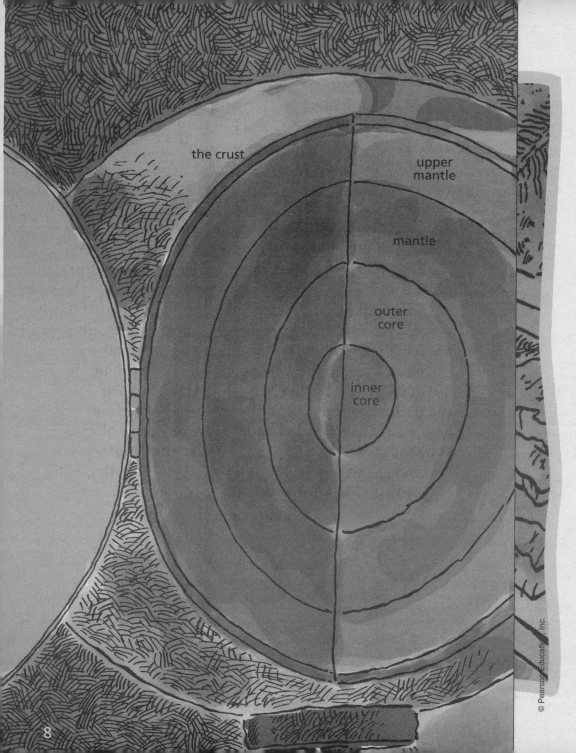

the crust

upper mantle

mantle

outer core

inner core

Chapter Six
Learning about Fossils

Expecting to find the kitchen, Maria was startled at the shelves of objects that Sir Edmond must have collected on his travels at various levels of the Earth. "Hey Toby, Kenny, check this out."

Leaving the controls, the boys joined Maria in her discovery of the hidden laboratory. "Wow, look at all these fossils," said Kenny. "My Uncle Pete has a fossil collection. I've learned a lot about them."

Kenny continued, "Fossils are the remains of plants and animals that lived thousands of years ago. Many animal fossils found are now extinct because they're from animals that have ceased to exist. The oldest one found is thought to be 600 million years old! The history museum in Seattle has dinosaur fossils that are about 65 million years old. People like my uncle have found fossils from teeth, bones, leaves, shells, and footprints."

Kenny liked talking about something he knew well. "It takes millions of years for something to become a fossil. For example, if mud or sand encases a seashell, as years go by, minerals sink in taking over the cells of the original seashell. When it is finally finished, the seashell fossil has become rock hard. Actually, it is a rock at this point."

Maria asked, "How did your uncle find fossils?"

"Well, some people dig them out of the ground," Kenny told her. "They may find one accidentally and dig up the area around it to look for more. Or, a rocky cliff may break away, revealing the fossils trapped inside.

"The crust of our planet is made up of all seven continents and each of the world's oceans. Oceans cover about seventy percent of the Earth's surface. This first layer, the crust, is thinner under the oceans than it is under the continents. The crust accounts for only one percent of the Earth's weight, or total mass. Where the crust meets the next layer, which is the upper mantle, are huge plates of rock under the continents and oceans. The upper mantle is stable for the most part. This portion of the mantle does show some plasticity though."

Maria's hand shot up. "What does plasticity mean?"

The ranger chuckled and understood that he was using too many scientific words. "Plasticity means this mostly solid part of the Earth is able to flow a little bit. Imagine a river of chocolate pudding. This part of the Earth would be like that. It does not flow as well as water, but it does flow." Maria was happy with this answer and liked the thought of a chocolate pudding river.

The ranger continued, "The next layer is made up of the rest of the mantle. Most of the heat underground comes from this part of the Earth. There are huge areas where this heat is shifted and moves around. The scientific name for these areas is convection cells. This heat can cause the huge rock plates, under the continents, to move very slowly. Below the mantle is the outer core. As you may have figured out, the core of the Earth is divided into two parts, like the mantle. This makes it easier to understand because these two parts are not the same and they affect the planet in different ways."

The ranger continued. "Many scientists have researched this part of the Earth, but this is difficult because it is too hot and far too deep a place for humans to visit." Toby stopped listening for a moment and imagined going through the outer core. He would be able to do what all the grown-ups have never been able to do. Then he snapped out of his daydream and kept listening. He wanted to learn more about this outer core. "So the outer core is made up of iron and some other metals. Scientists also believe that it is liquid and can flow a little faster than the chocolate pudding river." As the ranger continued, he glanced back to laugh with Maria again, but did not see her. "The inner core of the Earth is thought to be made of iron and another metal called nickel. It is very dense; this means that it is solid, unlike the outer core of the Earth. There is a great deal of pressure at this level of the Earth, and the metal's strength helps to keep the inner core solid. The weight of all the other layers above it creates the pressure needed to do this."

Kenny raised his hand and asked, "Do you think people will ever go to the core of the Earth and explore it?"

Toby kept an eye on the rocket controls and the main computer while Kenny ran the drill at top speed. Maria decided to have a closer look around the exploration craft. She found a little door near the floor that no one had noticed yet. She opened it and found a very small and dark room. The boys noticed she was out of sight and called her. She replied, "Hey I just found the bathroom." They all laughed. "I guess Sir Edmond thought of everything," Maria called out from inside. As she closed the door she noticed another one on the other side of the craft. "I wonder if this one is a kitchen. I sure am hungry."

Chapter Five

The Children's Journey through the Earth's Layers

The exploration craft continued burrowing deeper into the mantle. At times, the orange light inside became brighter and then died down again. Areas of greater heat seemed to cause the craft to slow down and then speed up again. The machine was encountering the convection cells that the ranger taught the children about back on the surface.

"I remember what the ranger said about the layers after the mantle," Maria offered. "After the mantle we will reach the outer core and then the inner core. The outer core is like melted iron, and he said the inner core is solid. I sure hope this machine is able drill us through each layer so we can reach the other side of the Earth," Maria said with a smile.

The red light went on again, and Toby read the message. "Sir Edmond we are now reaching the last ten feet of the mantle. Would you like to continue to the outer core at this speed?" Toby typed "yes" again, for there was no other way home.

The craft entered the outer core, and things became warm again. By now Toby knew how to ask the computer for things. As the world outside the machine became hotter, he asked for a cooler temperature. For the time being things were going as well as could be expected. The noise of the machine was not too bad, and the temperature was cool enough to stop them from sweating.

The ranger laughed a little. "No, I don't believe that would ever be possible. To take a trip through the Earth, and go through the layers we just learned about, can only be a dream. There are no machines made to take the heat that one would encounter along the way. And this is only one of the reasons such a journey would not be possible."

Kenny looked a little disappointed, and Toby had an unhappy look on his face at this news. They both had the same idea in their heads. They wanted to find a way to take the long journey through the Earth.

Mrs. Cieco said, "Let's get our jackets back on and get out to the bus. Next we are going back up the road to get as close to the mountain as we can. Oh, I mean, we are going to get as close to the volcano as we can." The ranger smiled to her and nodded his head. Mount Randall was a volcano, not a mountain.

At the volcano, everyone formed a line behind the ranger. Toby and Kenny decided to fall behind a bit and talk about their idea to go and see what was inside the mysterious volcano.

Chapter Three
The Plunge into Mount Randall

"Hey Toby," Kenny whispered, "do you want to see if we can get a little closer to the top so we can look inside?"

"I don't know. It's pretty cold. Maybe we should just forget about this plan."

"No way," Kenny replied. "This could be our only chance." Toby was not feeling too good about this, but went with Kenny's idea to wait until the class headed back to the bus to make a break for the top of the volcano. They heard the ranger stop talking and Mrs. Cieco loudly call for her fifth grade class to save questions for the bus ride back.

Soon their classmates were down the hill and out of sight. Toby and Kenny, both a bit nervous, decided to hike back up. There was snow on the ground, and their feet were getting cold. They both began to doubt the wisdom of this decision, but would not admit it each other.

Peering into the volcano, they saw only a great darkness, a huge black hole. The rocks leading into its mouth were broken into small pieces and looked slippery.

"Hey, Kenny," Toby said with a new sense of courage, "lets climb over this ledge and get closer." The two boys crawled up to the ledge so they would not slip. They were as close as they wanted to get as they peered at the volcano's amazing site. "Well, Kenny, I think we better head back. If we miss the bus, our parents will be very angry."

It became quieter inside the craft so Toby spoke up, "The globe in the visitor's center showed the outer mantle to be thinner than the rest of the mantle. I wonder how long it will take until we reach the rest of the mantle." None of the children really knew. They could only continue riding deeper and deeper toward the center of the Earth.

Maria began to complain about the heat again. Kenny moved closer to see the controls and had a good idea. "Hey, Toby, let's tell the computer that we are really hot and need to cool off."

Toby looked over to him. "I don't know if it will work, but it is certainly worth a try." Toby typed the message with his fingers crossed on one hand as he typed with the other. After about five minutes, the screen flashed: "Why didn't you tell me earlier, Sir Edmond? I would be happy to activate the onboard cooling unit to make the craft cooler." Three small vents along the top of the machine began to blow cool air over the children.

Maria jumped for joy and shouted, "Kenny, I have to hand it to you. The idea to simply ask the computer was fantastic. You are a simply brilliant!"

Toby leaned over to thank the computer and saw another message: "Sir Edmond, we are now approaching the last ten feet of the upper mantle. Would you like to continue at this speed and in this direction?" Toby typed yes as Maria and Kenny moved to the front to look at the rich orange glow of the mantle. "Wow, this is so neat." Maria was amazed at the beauty of the Earth's mantle.

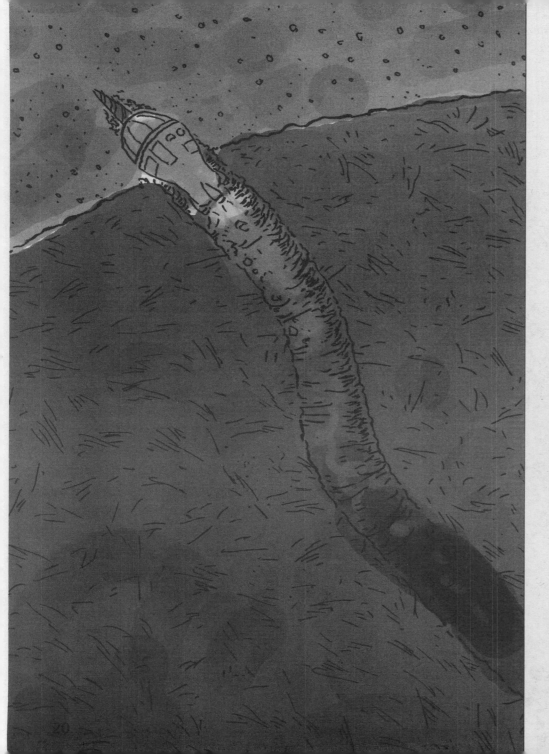

"Yeah, I think you're right," Kenny replied. They turned at the mouth of the volcano to head home. "Oh, my gosh!" Kenny screamed as he slipped and began to slide down the wrong way. He was headed into the volcano. Toby reached for him and grabbed his hand. Their hearts were beating wildly. Toby held on tight, but Kenny was too heavy to pull up.

Toby reached to grab a nearby rock. "Kenny, I'm slipping too!" The boys separated their hands and began to plunge head first into the great darkness below. With nothing to grab on the smooth walls of the volcano, they just fell deeper and deeper, wondering if they would ever reach bottom.

"Well, now what are we going to do? We broke the turning control, and we can only go straight." Maria glanced over to Kenny and added, "I guess we won't be back for dinner then."

Toby thought for a moment and said, "This means that we have to take this machine straight through the center of the Earth. If we stop, we will be stuck in this tunnel forever."

Kenny's and Maria's shocked faces revealed their memory of the ranger's words. "Toby, don't you remember that the ranger said it's not possible to go through the center of the Earth? It's so hot our craft could melt and boil us alive."

"We have no choice in the matter," replied Toby calmly. It began getting warm in the craft as a small light on the control panel glowed with the message: "Sir Edmond, we are now approaching the last ten feet of the Earth's crust. Would you like to continue into the upper mantle?" Toby read these words and typed in yes. The computer responded, "We are now entering the upper mantle of Earth."

"It's getting really hot in here," Maria said, "Do you think the upper mantle will be a little cooler?"

"No," Toby said. "Don't you remember? The upper mantle is just the beginning of the Earth's heat. It is going to get much hotter as we continue going deeper and deeper." The craft kept its course for the other side of the world. Sir Edmond was able to make a tunnel and steer the craft during his exploration from England. The children became worried that the ship would not be able to handle the extreme heat of the Earth's outer core and inner core.

Chapter Four

Sir Edmond's Earth Exploration Craft

Thud! The boys hit the bottom. "Are you all right?" They both asked at the same time. The boys could only see shadows. Kenny looked at Toby and said, "There has got to be some way out of here." They looked around for a ladder, a rope, anything that would help them get home again. There was nothing. Both boys were stunned with fear.

Toby explored a dark corner hoping to find something. Suddenly, he bumped into something made of metal. He could see that it was a huge machine of some sort. It had one tiny door on the side and four windows near the top. It was shaped like a pear. On top was a huge drill that pointed up toward the top of the volcano. Toby called out, "Kenny, what is this thing?"

Kenny spotted a note tied to the door and tore it off and read it aloud. "Hello there, you must have had a bumpy ride down. My name is Sir Edmond, and you have found my Earth Exploration Craft. I came to this volcano from England. Please do not take this craft; I will be back in two days to drive it home." Kenny looked sad, "Toby, this note was written March 3, 1903."

This was not good news. Toby tried to open the door, but it was rusted shut. Just then, Kenny screamed, "Toby, Toby, look!" There was a huge serpent coming toward them. Both pulled until the door finally opened. The snake pounded the windows, releasing hideous sounds before it stole away into the dark corner.

"Toby, what was that thing?"

Toby looked at Kenny and said, "That giant serpent would have eaten us alive if we hadn't found this machine." The boys decided not to go back out, as the serpent was still hiding in the darkness. Toby pulled a red lever and a bunch of lights went on. The machine still worked! Toby and Kenny began reading the labels on the different levers, switches, and buttons. Kenny figured out how to run the big drill on top, and Toby was able to start the rockets on the bottom of the machine. The machine was not made to fly, though. Sir Edmond designed it to burrow into the ground and make tunnels. Toby excitedly said, "Sir Edmond tunneled his way here from England! Wow, this is so neat! Maybe we can use this craft to get home."

Just then, there was a knock at the door. Feeling tormented, they jumped and feared the serpent had returned. "Help me, I'm really scared!" The boys looked at each other in amazement as they recognized Maria's face. "Let me in! That hideous serpent is still here," she screamed as the boys opened the door for her. "I heard you talking about the volcano and thought it sounded like a good idea, so I followed you to the top and slipped on the rocks," Maria explained.

Toby replied, "Well, you can stay with us. We figured out how to drive this machine, and we plan on being back home in time for dinner."

The boys started the engine. It sputtered at first and then hummed nicely. Kenny started the drill, and Toby turned the rockets on. The machine rose about 10 feet from the ground and then turned upside down. Toby, Kenny, and Maria were belted in place, so they did not fall out. Toby steered the machine closer to the ground, Kenny ran the drill at full speed, and in they plunged!

Kenny was worried because there was no map. "I only know that we are going straight down," he told the others. "Now turn right, Toby!" shouted Kenny. Toby tried, but the lever snapped off.

Social Studies

Social Studies

The United States Goes West

by
Adam McClellan

Genre	Comprehension Skill and Strategy	Text Features
Nonfiction	• Generalizing • Graphic Organizers	• Captions • Graphic Organizer • Maps • Sidebar

Scott Foresman Reading Street 5.5.5

PEARSON

Scott
Foresman

scottforesman.com

Reader Response

1. Based on Lewis and Clark's travels, what do you think early trips to the west were like?

2. Describe three ways the Louisiana Purchase changed the United States and Native Americans. Use the graphic organizer below to organize your ideas and then make one statement from your information.

United States	Native Americans

3. On page 20, how can the prefix co- help you figure out the meaning of the word coexist?

4. What does the map on page 13 show you about Lewis and Clark's journey?

Glossary

economic *adj.* related to money, business, and trade

freight *n.* transported goods

independence *n.* not ruled by another country

overrun *v.* to spread through quickly

recalled *v.* remembered

scrawled *v.* wrote quickly

vacant *adj.* empty

ventured *n.* did something risky

The United States Goes West

by
Adam McClellan

Editorial Offices: Glenview, Illinois • Parsippany, New Jersey • New York, New York
Sales Offices: Needham, Massachusetts • Duluth, Georgia • Glenview, Illinois
Coppell, Texas • Ontario, California • Mesa, Arizona

A pioneer family moves all of their belongings into the wagon going west.

Settlers would move into an area and fight with local tribes. To resolve the conflict, the government and the tribes signed treaties setting aside certain lands for the settlers and other lands for the Native American tribes.

The treaties promised that the tribes would have their lands forever. This didn't happen. Instead, more settlers arrived to **overrun** the tribal lands, causing more conflict.

Within a hundred years of Lewis and Clark's expedition, the Native American tribes these men had met were all forced onto reservations. This land made up only a small part of the lands on which they once lived. Jefferson's hopes for peace had died. Lewis and Clark unknowingly opened up the west for one group of people and closed it for another.

The choices Thomas Jefferson made in his first years as president forever changed the United States' shape, size, and history.

It's a Small World

Imagine if the United States still had only 13 colonies. America just wouldn't be the same without sunny California or the big state of Texas.

In 1776, the United States only had thirteen colonies. At the time they were controlled by Great Britain. These colonies spread up and down the Atlantic coast.

The colonies gained their independence with the American Revolution. Other countries controlled the rest of North America. Britain kept control over colonies in Canada. Spain controlled the territory west and south of the United States. France's territory was called Louisana.

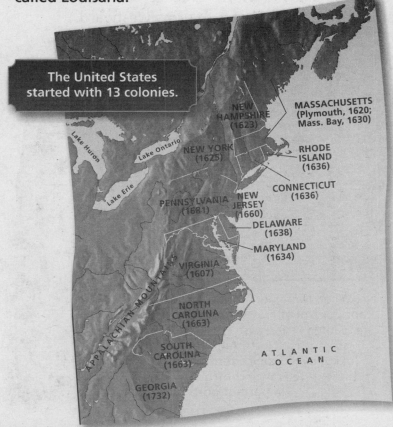

The United States started with 13 colonies.

When President Jefferson took office in 1801, he had a great interest in exploring lands to the west. He knew that the future of his country depended on control of this territory.

As long as Spain controlled the west, Jefferson was not worried. By the early 1800s, Spain's hold on its colonies seemed to be slowly slipping. Jefferson was sure that the United States could make a deal with Spain to gain Louisiana.

In 1802, Jefferson got shocking news. The Spanish had handed Louisiana over to the French! This changed everything. At the time, France was becoming the strongest country in Europe. If the French had plans for North America, it would be very hard for the United States to grow westward.

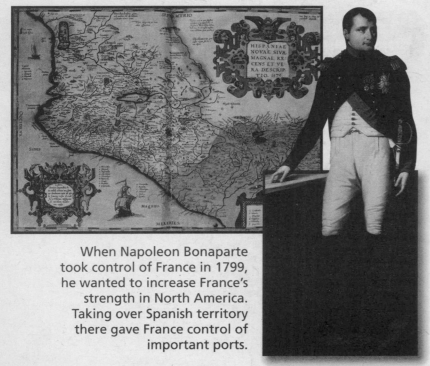

When Napoleon Bonaparte took control of France in 1799, he wanted to increase France's strength in North America. Taking over Spanish territory there gave France control of important ports.

Soon, Native Americans, forced to leave their settlements, made their long and difficult journey to the Indian Territory in Oklahoma.

© Pearson Education

Many hoped that Native American tribes and settlers would coexist peacefully. Unfortunately, by the late 1820s, the government started a policy of keeping Native American tribes separated from settlers. They did this by using land gained in the Louisiana Purchase.

Beginning in 1830, many tribes were forced off their homelands in the south. They were marched westward to a new "Indian Territory" west of the Mississippi River, in what is now Oklahoma. These areas are called reservations.

This also affected the Native Americans already living in the territory. Settlers began moving into the area. As new settlements grew, the **vacant** land left for the Native American tribes grew smaller and smaller.

The Native Americans packed up their homes.

Thomas Jefferson was greatly concerned when Spain handed Louisiana to the French. Suddenly, expanding westward became more difficult.

In 1803, James Monroe went to Paris to try and buy Louisiana from the French. Jefferson told him, ". . . all hopes are fixed upon you . . ."

The U.S. government promised land to Native Americans.

Settlers traveled up and down rivers on flatboats loaded with freight.

The port of New Orleans in the early nineteenth century was an important trading and shipping center.

Native Americans and the West

It didn't take long for people in the East to begin moving west. On their return trip down the Missouri River, Lewis and Clark met traders with boats loaded with **freight**, hoping to trade with Native American tribes in the new territory.

As it turned out, however, Native Americans had an uneasy relationship with the settlers.

The Louisiana Purchase

French control of Louisiana gave Jefferson another worry: the Mississippi River. The United States and Spain agreed that settlers could sell their goods in New Orleans because it was run by the Spanish.

No one knew what the French would do now that they controlled Louisiana. Jefferson feared that they would block American boats from using the port of New Orleans. This would cause damaging economic results.

With that in mind, Jefferson sent James Monroe to Paris to make a deal with the French. Monroe was to offer to buy New Orleans. The U.S. government would offer to pay almost nine and a half million dollars for the city.

When Monroe got to Paris on April 12, 1803, he was in for a surprise. Facing a possible war from England and other concerns, France was losing interest in controlling Louisiana. The day before he arrived, the French government had made an offer to the U.S. agent in Paris. They said the United States could have all of Louisiana for the right price. Monroe and the agent signed a treaty agreeing to buy the entire Louisiana territory. The territory cost the United States only 15 million dollars.

As the western territories opened, many people moved west to make a new home.

In the summer of 1805, the explorers ran into a huge barrier, the Rocky Mountains. It took two months to cross the mountains and find another river to follow to the Pacific.

In November, they finally reached the Pacific Ocean. The team spent a cold, rainy winter in what is now Oregon. On March 23, 1806, they turned east and headed home.

The Louisiana Purchase was a big step toward making this country what it is today. It opened up new lands and erased a foreign power from the map of North America. The Lewis and Clark expedition inspired Americans to look west for their future. These key events in our history also came with problems.

Native Americans and settlers depended on each to trade.

In 1793, Sir Alexander Mackenzie left his mark on a rock in Bella Coda, British Columbia, on the Canadian coast.

Exploring the New Lands

Jefferson had already made plans to explore the west. He wanted to find an easy route to the Pacific Ocean. He was inspired by the explorations of Sir Alexander Mackenzie. In 1793, the Scottish fur trader discovered a route through western Canada to the Pacific. Mackenzie's route was traveled almost all the way by boat. Jefferson hoped to keep British traders from gaining control of the fur trade near the Pacific Coast. He also was curious about the plants and animals in the lands west of the Mississippi.

Sir Alexander Mackenzie

Jefferson put together a small group named the Corps of Discovery. The group had about thirty men. The journey was to be led by two men who were already known for their skills in the wilderness: Meriwether Lewis and William Clark.

Jefferson planned for the trip to take place no matter who owned the territory. Now, the Louisiana Purchase gave the explorers a new purpose. They would map out the country's new lands and make contact with Native American tribes who made their homes there. These tribes had never heard of the United States.

Explorers and Native Americans trading. Members of Corps of Discovery included skilled frontiersman, hunters, woodcutters, and interpreters.

a bitter December day. The Mandan gave the explorers a warm place to spend the winter.

The explorers made friendly contact with many tribes in the west, including the Shoshone, the Nez Perce, and the Walla Walla. They traded horses, food, and other supplies with these Native American tribes.

Near the end of October, the explorers came to a group of villages that belonged to the Mandan tribe. The villages were on the Great Bend of the Missouri River in what is now North Dakota. Here, they suffered the long winter. In his diary, Clark **scrawled** that the temperature was 45 degrees below zero on

Meriwether Lewis was also a U.S. army captain. He worked closely with President Jefferson to plan a westward expedition.

William Clark was a Virginia-born U.S. army captain. He was recruited by Lewis to help lead the expedition.

Native American tribes settled around the Missouri river.

Lewis and Clark led the journey west.

The explorers planned to follow the Missouri River as far west as they could and then find a way to the Pacific Ocean. In the fall of 1803, the Corps of Discovery arrived at the village of St. Louis, on the Mississippi River. They spent the winter there, waiting for Louisiana to become official property of the United States. While they waited they collected and sorted supplies, and worked at becoming fit for the tough journey ahead. A treaty was signed the following spring and the explorers ventured out.

In early August, the explorers came across members of the Oto tribe of Native Americans. Lewis gave a speech explaining that the French and Spanish no longer ruled their land. They would now be part of the United States. The Oto chief thanked Lewis for his speech and Lewis gave him gifts. The speech was repeated each time the explorers met a new tribe.

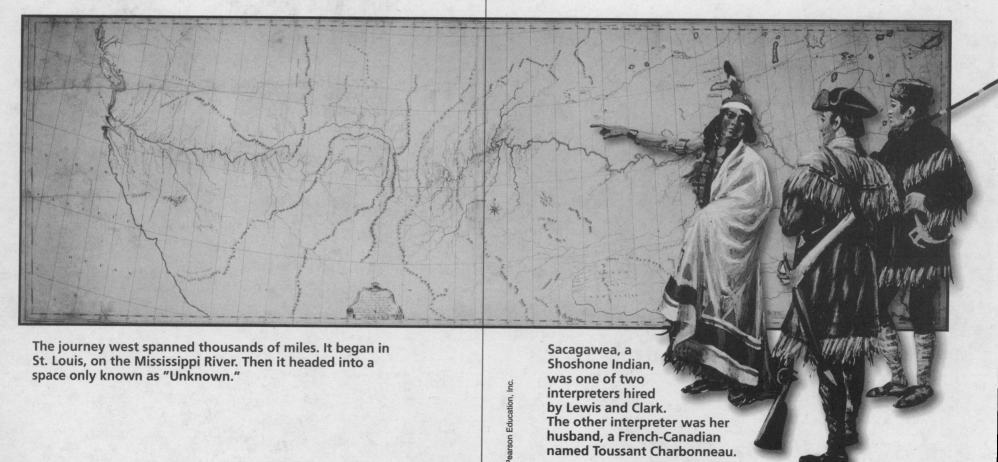

The journey west spanned thousands of miles. It began in St. Louis, on the Mississippi River. Then it headed into a space only known as "Unknown."

© Pearson Education, Inc.

Sacagawea, a Shoshone Indian, was one of two interpreters hired by Lewis and Clark. The other interpreter was her husband, a French-Canadian named Toussant Charbonneau.

Science

Science

Life Science

Life in the Sea

by Lara Bove

Genre	Comprehension Skill and Strategy	Text Features
Nonfiction	• Draw Conclusions • Visualize	• Captions • Headlines • Photographs

Scott Foresman Reading Street 5.6.1

PEARSON

Scott
Foresman

ISBN 0-328-13578-X

90000

9 780328 135783

scottforesman.com

Reader Response

1. Reread the second paragraph on page 5. How much water do you think black periwinkles need? Explain your reasoning.

2. Look back at the description of a riftia on page 21. Draw a picture of it.

3. Look up *hydrothermal* in a dictionary. Describe the definition that is used in this selection.

4. The author organized this selection by area of the ocean. How else could the author have organized it?

Glossary

algae *n.* a one-celled plant that grows in the ocean

concealed *v.* hidden

driftwood *n.* wood floating in the water

hammocks *n.* swinging beds made of fabric

lamented *v.* regretted or wished that something had not happened

sea urchins *n.* soft-bodied sea creatures

sternly *adv.* in a very strict or serious way

tweezers *n.* tools used to pick up small items

Life in the Sea

by Lara Bove

PEARSON
Scott Foresman

Editorial Offices: Glenview, Illinois • Parsippany, New Jersey • New York, New York
Sales Offices: Needham, Massachusetts • Duluth, Georgia • Glenview, Illinois
Coppell, Texas • Ontario, California • Mesa, Arizona

Research Continues

Though scientists have lamented not making more progress, they have learned much about the oceans' regions and sea life. Already they have learned that there is much more life in the sea than there is on land. Perhaps you can become an oceanographer and continue their important research.

Research in the Deep Sea

Scientists first discovered hydrothermal vents about 30 years ago. Because these vents are so far below the surface, researchers have a difficult time conducting research. Using a mini-submarine, two or three people can descend about 8,000 feet. (A scuba diver can usually descend only about 100 feet.) They collect water from the vents in special titanium containers, which won't melt from the extremely hot water.

You and your family may have spent a summer day resting in hammocks by the sea, but have you wondered about life below the ocean's surface?

The oceans have several different regions. Each region has a unique variety of animals, fishes, and plants that have adapted to the area.

Tidal pools, for example, are found along the ocean's shores and have two totally different kinds of animals. One kind needs to be covered with water all the time, and the other can survive with just a little bit of ocean spray each day.

Read on to learn more about these and other ocean habitats.

Waves break against the sandstone cliffs of Cape Kiwanda.

Special Sea Creatures

It is difficult for animals to live in a place where the temperature varies so much. Still, scientists have been amazed to learn that there are many creatures who are well suited for this environment. Most of these creatures eat the bacteria found inside the hot water.

One special sea animal found near these vents is the giant tube worm, or riftia. They use tentacles to eat bacteria from the hot water. Riftia grow to around six feet long. Clams also live near the vents. Some are as large as the tube worms. They eat the bacteria, too.

A tubeworm with spines enclosed

Hydrothermal Vents

In very deep parts of the sea there are hydrothermal vents. *Hydro* means *water*. *Thermal* means *heat*. So these are places where very hot water rises to the surface of the sea floor.

Ocean water flows through cracks in the sea floor, down below the earth's surface. It is very hot below the sea floor. In this area the water gets as hot as 750° F. The pressure under the earth is too strong for the water to boil. Instead, the water blasts back up through the sea floor cracks. The ocean water is much colder than the water coming up. This cools the hot water very quickly. All of the minerals in the hot water separate and form chimneys. The largest chimney is 165 feet tall. It is known as Godzilla.

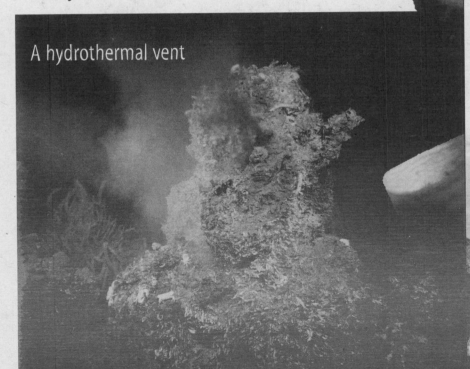

A hydrothermal vent

Intertidal Region

The intertidal region is located on the ocean's rocky shores. In this region, the shores get wet during high tide and dry out during low tide. This is why it is called the intertidal region. It is between the tides. This region is divided into four zones: splash, high tide, mid tide, and low tide. Different creatures live in each zone.

The Splash Zone

Animals and plants that live in the splash zone only get wet from water splashing on them during high tide. Most of the time this area is dry. Only a few sea creatures live here. Black lichens live on rocks in the splash zone. Other splash zone creatures are black periwinkles, isopods, and limpets.

High Tide Zone

The high tide zone is wetter than the splash zone. It gets fully soaked twice a day during high tide, but it still dries up. Sea life in the high tide zone must be able to live in dry air for much of the day.

Crabs can live on dry land for hours. They use their strong claws to hang onto slippery rocks. They also use their claws like tweezers to pull food from cracks in the rocks.

Mid Tide Zone

The mid tide zone stays wet much longer than the high tide zone. It dries out only during low tide and has much more sea life.

One creature that lives in this area is the sea anemone. Sea anemones use poisonous tentacles to paralyze their prey. Once an animal has been paralyzed, the anemone pulls it in and eats it. Anemones eat small fish and shrimp. Larger anemones also eat crabs, sea stars, mussels, and limpets. To stay wet during low tide, anemones cover themselves with rocks. Unfortunately, people sometimes step on them because they blend in so well with the rocks.

Sea stars and mussels are found in both the high tide zone and the mid tide zone. Sea stars are flexible and can wrap themselves tightly around rocks using suction. This is especially helpful in the crashing waves of rising and falling tides. Sea stars also use suction to help them eat. A sea star will wrap itself sternly around a mussel and use suction to force the mussel open.

Sea anemones and
sea stars in a tidepool >

Mud, Sand, or Rock

The sea floor is made of areas of mud, sand, and rock. In each area, creatures adapt to that type of sea floor. Sea creatures with long legs, such as the crab, do well in the muddy areas, since they can keep from sinking in the mud.

In areas with rocky soil, you will find animals such as worms, mussels, and sea lilies. Sea lilies have feathery arms to pick up food from the sea floor. Some sea lilies have deep roots in the sea floor. Other sea lilies can use their arms to move around, dragging their roots behind them. In this way the sea lily is not really a plant.

The octopus is another creature that likes the rocky sea floor. It uses the different colors and textures of the rocks to hide during the day. At night, octopuses come out and hunt for food, such as crabs and lobsters.

< A red crinoid on
coral polyps

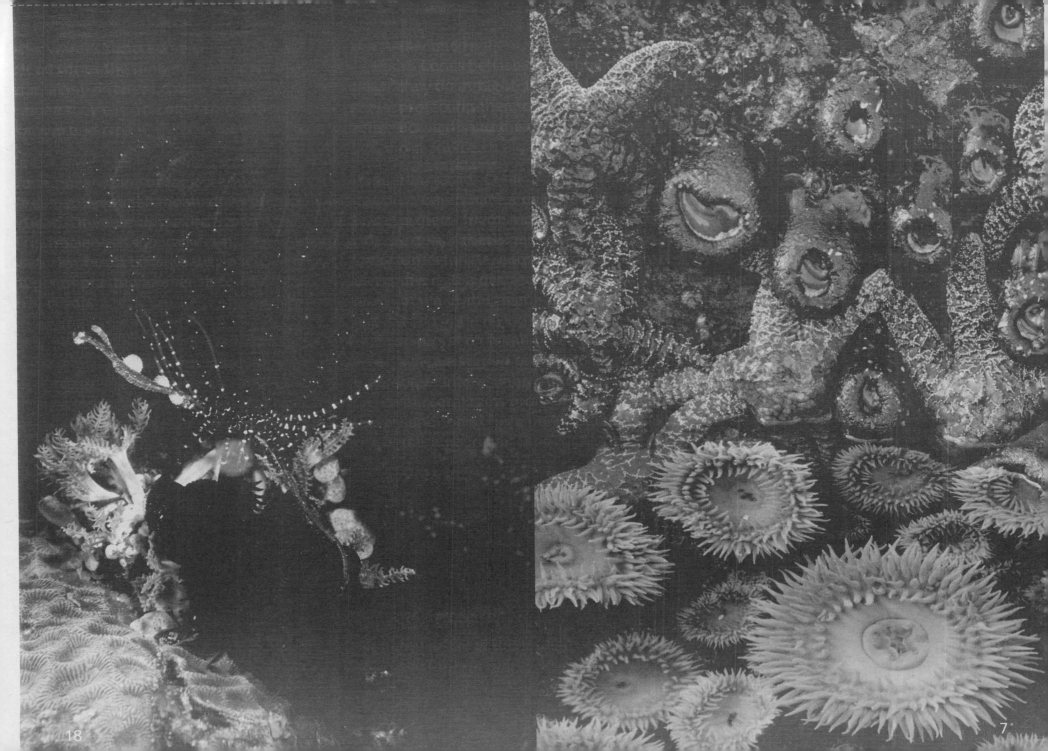

18

7

Low Tide Zone

The low tide zone is the wettest in the intertidal region. It never completely dries out.

Many sea creatures make their home in the low tide zone. Sea urchins eat seaweed from tide pools that form during high tide. During low tide, they hide in the holes in rocks to keep from drying out. The holes also protect them from the force of the pounding waves.

Another low tide creature is the nudibranch. Nudibranches look sort of like slugs but are actually anemone fish. They have the same poison in their bodies as the sea anemone and are not harmed by a sea anemone's sting. They eat many things, including sponges.

A nudibranch

The Sea Floor

Another region of the ocean is the sea floor. As there is so little sunlight, creatures on the sea floor cannot rely on algae for food. Other types of fish and animals live here.

The most common type of creatures in the deep sea are scavengers. A scavenger is an animal that does not hunt living prey. It eats whatever floats down to it or whatever it finds on the sea floor. The deeper in the ocean you go, the less food you find. After all, other fish above this level already ate most of the food. This means that food is scarce for scavengers of the very deep sea floor. It also means that these creatures are small and grow slowly.

< A blue spotted stingray on the ocean floor, covered in sand

Coral Reefs

Another ocean region is the coral reef. Reefs lie farther out in the ocean, beyond the intertidal area. Reefs are home to the ocean's greatest diversity of sea life.

The most prevalent sea creatures in reefs are called polyps. Coral is a very tiny kind of polyp. Millions of coral polyps live together on a coral reef. A coral reef has living coral on the outside. It also has dead coral bones on the inside. The dead coral bones consist of a very hard rock, called limestone.

Soft coral with open polyps

< Clusters of Grape Algae on coral reef

Corals live near the water's surface and eat very small algae, which feed off of the sunlight.

Corals are found in many different colors. Corals get color from the algae they eat. The most common colors of coral are brown and cream.

The Ocean's Rain Forest

Coral reefs are found near many of the oceans' shores. In shallow areas, you may see the shadows of the reefs from overhead. Or you may see driftwood floating above the reef. Scientists sometimes call coral reefs the ocean's rain forest because they have so many different types of plants and animals for the amount of space they cover.

Driftwood can come from miles away and end up on a beach.

Day and Night

Corals behave differently during the day than they do at night. During the day corals retract, protecting themselves from predator fish, which are active during the day. Then, at night, corals stretch out and catch algae.

Danger for Coral

Corals have a delicate layer of mucous that protects them. Mucous gives the coral a slippery exterior that algae have trouble attaching to. Unfortunately, this mucous is easily destroyed by divers. If a diver touches it, the mucous layer breaks down. If the layer is damaged, algae can grow on it and kill the living coral.

Coral reefs can break apart naturally. Reefs break when a section grows too large for the limestone base. Interestingly, nature uses these breaks to help the coral reefs grow. Some of the broken pieces survive and form new coral reefs, allowing reefs to get bigger over time.

< The Great Barrier Reef in Australia is the largest reef in the world.

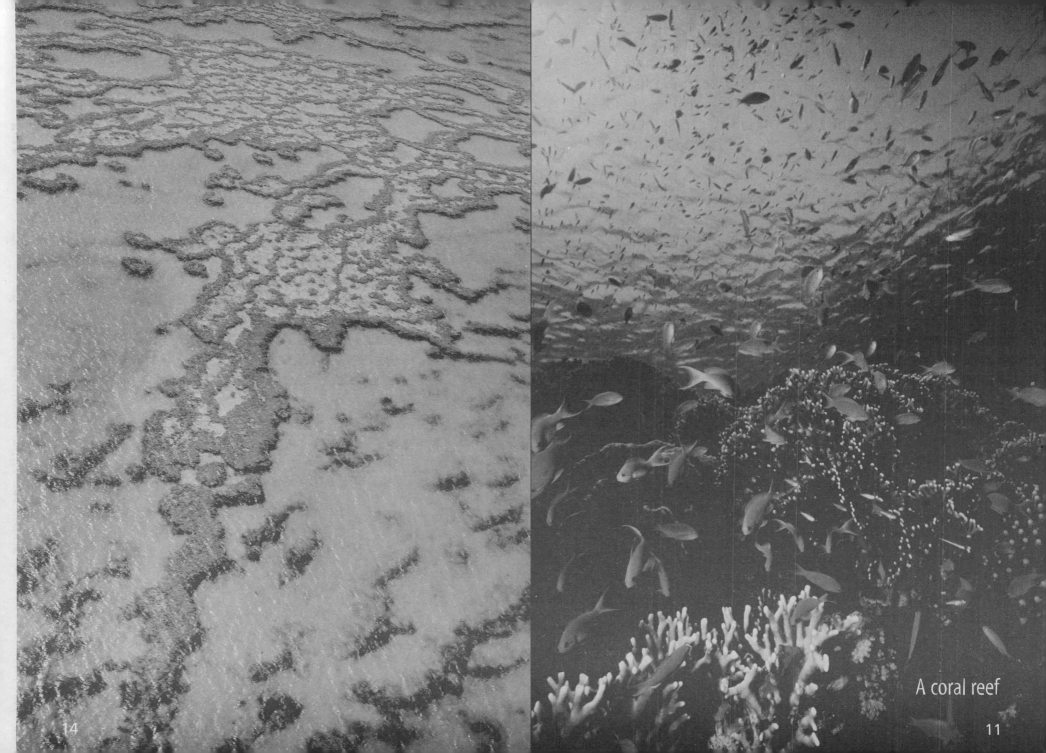

A coral reef

14

11

Some of the creatures found in coral reefs are blenny fish, scorpion fish, stonefish, lionfish, and barracudas. Camouflage helps keep scorpion fish and stonefish concealed in the corals. Their colors blend with the color of the sand. These fish can lie in the sand to wait for prey. They use their large mouths to quickly swallow other fish.

Parrot fish also live near coral reefs. They help the coral survive by eating the algae, that grow on the dead coral. New coral could not grow on the reef if the algae were there. By providing food in the form of algae, the coral, in turn, help parrot fish.

Coral reefs are home to more than just plants and fish. There are mollusks, too. A mollusk is a sea animal without bones. Mollusks include nudibranches, octopuses, and cuttlefish.

Can you see the octopus in this section of corals? >

Social Studies

The Kudzu Invasion

by Lillian Forman

Genre	Comprehension Skill and Strategy	Text Features
Nonfiction	• Main ideas and Details • Text Structure	• Captions • Diagrams • Glossary • Quotes

Scott Foresman Reading Street 5.6.2

PEARSON

Scott
Foresman

scottforesman.com

ISBN 0-328-13581-X

90000

9 780328 135813

Reader Response

1. Look at the diagram on page 23. Which animals in the food chain control the increase of plant-eating insects?

2. Suppose you wanted to get rid of some kudzu on your property. What are three questions you might ask yourself in order to choose the best method?

3. Look at the glossary word *investigate*. What ending would make this verb past tense? What ending or endings would turn the verb into a noun?

4. Using the dictionary, find the root of the word *habitat*. Define the root. Make two other words using that root.

Glossary

bleached *adj.* having become paler or whiter than before.

carcasses *n.* dead bodies.

decay *n.* rotting.

starvation *n.* death from lack of food.

scrawny *adj.* very thin; bony.

parasites *n.* things that feed off of other things.

suspicions *n.* doubts.

tundra *n.* frozen earth.

The Kudzu Invasion

by Lillian Forman

Editorial Offices: Glenview, Illinois • Parsippany, New Jersey • New York, New York
Sales Offices: Needham, Massachusetts • Duluth, Georgia • Glenview, Illinois
Coppell, Texas • Ontario, California • Mesa, Arizona

It is important to stop kudzu and other invasive plants from coming into our country. We cannot survive without a healthy environment. A healthy environment depends on a good mixture of plants and animals. Sadly, many exotic plants and animals are taking over large areas of the United States. They are harmful to the ecosystem. They add little or no benefits to the ecosystem and use up all of its resources.

Asian people also use kudzu as a medicine. They make starch cakes and brew tea from its roots. They claim that these products can cure headaches, muscle stiffness, stuffy noses, and other sickness.

The kudzu's vine stem is also useful. The core of the stem has fibers that can be woven into colorful paper, wallpaper, and fishnets. The elastic young vines can also be made into baskets. The whole plant is ground up to make pulp for cardboard and other paper products. People who want to protect the environment approve of this practice because it lessens the need to cut down trees.

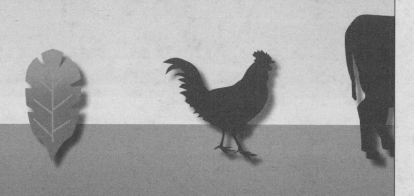

You might not think that a plant can take over part of a country, but one did. It's called the kudzu. In 1876, kudzu was brought to the United States for the Centennial Exposition in Philadelphia. This event celebrated the United States' 100th birthday. Many people from other countries came to celebrate and share things from their own countries The Japanese created a garden with some of their native plants. One was a vine called kudzu. It was very pretty with big green leaves and sweet-smelling flowers.

The kudzu is native to Japan.

The kudzu plant grows and spreads quickly.

Kudzu's strong fibers have many uses.

© Pearson Education, Inc.

The fight against invasive plants is a long and hard one. Until the fight is won we should try to imitate the Southerners' attitude toward kudzu. We might try to tame the pests by finding creative ways to put them to work.

Kudzu is also a healthy food for animals. It can be used for human food too. Chinese and Japanese cooks have ground up its roots to make a thickener for sauces and soups. They have also steamed its leaves for vegetable dishes, or dried and powdered them to make dough. In the United States, health food stores sell a variety of kudzu food products. Southern cooks make jelly and tea from its flowers.

Travelers had been transporting plants and animals from one country to another for centuries. Christopher Columbus and his followers brought plants and animals from the Americas to Europe and from Europe to the Americas. Most of these transplants improved their new home by adding variety to its plant and animal life. They also added to its way of life. For example, Italian cooks could never have created marinara sauce for spaghetti without tomatoes from the Americas.

American gardeners loved kudzu and began to grow it. Southerners liked its thick leaves. They saw it as a way to shade their porches during long, hot days. The plant could take root in soil where nothing else could grow. It did well in warm, humid weather. It soon became common in the South.

Bringing plants from one country to another is not always a good thing. The exotic plant may grow so fast that it crowds out local plant life. The kudzu has been doing this in the South. It has found a habitat without insects or frost to kill it. During the summer, kudzu can grow as much as a foot a day.

In the early 1900s, Charles and Lillie Pleas of Florida discovered some of kudzu's benefits. They saw that it could prevent erosion. Its long roots could grip and hold soil that might otherwise be worn away by wind or flood. They also found that it contained protein and vitamins A and D. This made it good food for cattle. Eager to spread kudzu's benefits, the Pleases opened a nursery to sell the plant.

During the late 1930s, a farmer named Channing Cope became a supporter of kudzu. Cope had seven-hundred acres of eroded soil. After planting kudzu, Cope's once worthless acres were soon providing nourishing feed for his livestock. Cope wrote newspaper articles about this "miracle vine," praised it over the radio, and set up the Kudzu Club of America. He announced to the public, "Cotton isn't king in the south anymore. Kudzu is king."

Most methods of destroying kudzu are gradual. Southerners know they will have to put up with the nuisance for a long time. Therefore, many of them have found creative ways of coping with the weed.

Some people take advantage of its thick, rapid growth. They make fences and other barriers out of it. It is also a good place to hide things. A U.S. soldier in the South Pacific during World War II had to find a quick way to hide some antiaircraft guns from enemy planes. Recognizing some kudzu plants growing nearby, he remembered how quickly the plant grew and how thoroughly it could hide large objects. So he dug them up and replanted them around the guns. In a few days, the guns had completely disappeared from view.

People use kudzu as a barrier.

Kudzu plants can prevent erosion.

Grazing is the safest way to destroy the kudzu plant.

Poisons are the fastest way to destroy kudzu. They are very risky though. Before using any poison, a farmer has to make sure that the kudzu is not covering a drinking water well or spring. The poisons can also harm wildlife and prevent new crops from growing.

Conservationists prefer the grazing method for destroying kudzu. It's safer for the environment. If farmers let their livestock graze on kudzu, the starch in its roots will be used up in its efforts to repair itself. The kudzu will then die of starvation.

Probably the only place kudzu couldn't grow was the Alaskan tundra. Cope and the Pleases did a lot to make the kudzu popular but no one did more to promote kudzu than the U.S. government.

During the 1930s, floods and droughts were ruining U.S. farmers. The topsoil they needed was being washed and/or blown away. President Franklin D. Roosevelt started a government service to protect farmland from damage by flood and drought. This service hired young men to build levees, or embankments, to prevent rivers and dams from flooding and to plant kudzu on riverbanks to help keep them in place during heavy rainfalls. The government also advertised the benefits of kudzu and gave farmers eight dollars an acre to plant it on their property.

In the early 1900s, a biologist named David Fairchild had suspicions about the kudzu. He warned people that it might invade and damage farms. The idea that a single plant could overrun the environment was a new idea. Few scientists supported his warnings.

Many farms have been destroyed by kudzu plants.

By the mid-1990s, kudzu had taken over almost 11,000 square miles of the southern United States. A scrawny kudzu plant can quickly develop into many hardy plants. Every year it takes over another 120,000 acres. Its vines take over tree branches and smother them like parasites. The trees become lifeless carcasses. The kudzu has left over seven million acres of forest in a state of decay.

The plants and animals that live in these forests lose their food and shelter. Without sunlight, the plants growing on the forest floor fade to a bleached green and die.

Other serious losses occur as well. The people in damaged wilderness areas often lose their means of making a living. When commercial forests are destroyed, forest workers' jobs vanish. Products made from these forests become scarcer and more expensive. If storeowners must import these products then the U.S. factories that once made them must close, thus putting many more people out of work.

Mowing is one way to destroy the kudzu plant.

Southerners have found many ways to destroy this harmful plant. These include mowing it, burning it, poisoning it, and letting animals eat it.

Mowing can rid the land of kudzu. Before mowing, a farmer should investigate to make sure that the kudzu is not hiding ditches, logs, or wells. Otherwise the tractor driver might crash into these obstacles. Also, kudzu is so tough that the mowers have to have strong, specially made blades.

Fire can also be an effective weapon against kudzu. Even if it does not kill the kudzu, it clears away the vines and leaves. It is true that fire causes kudzu seeds to sprout, but this can be an advantage, The seedlings, no longer hidden by the full-grown plants, can then either be poisoned or burned again.

The kudzu has taken over forests.

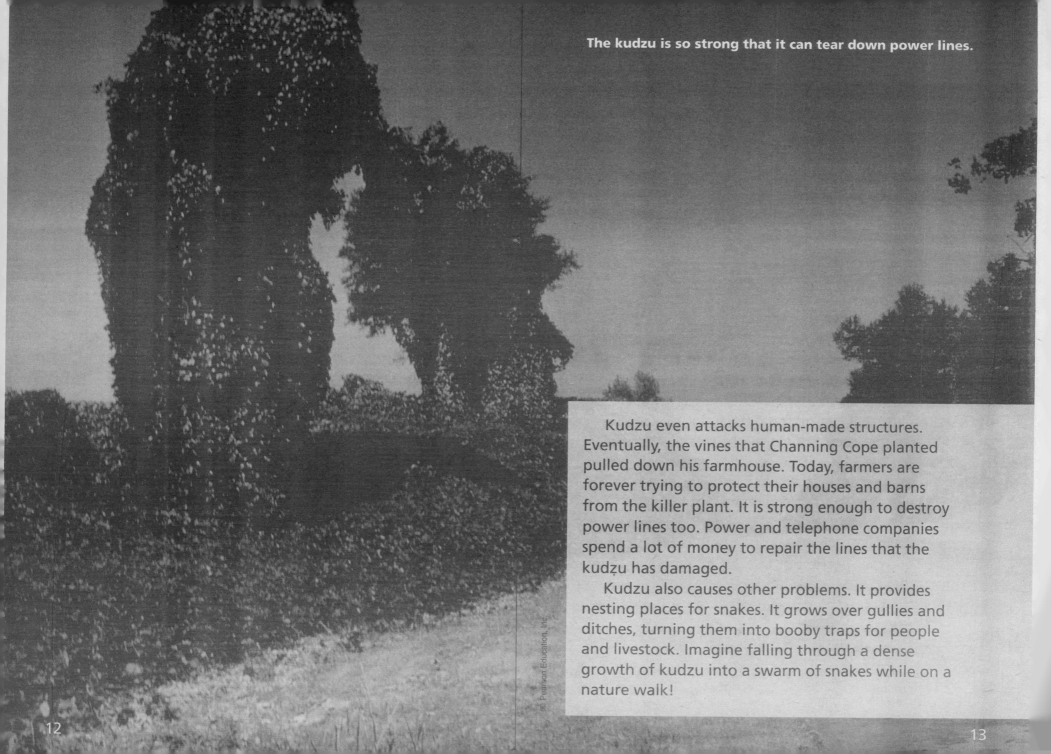

The kudzu is so strong that it can tear down power lines.

Kudzu even attacks human-made structures. Eventually, the vines that Channing Cope planted pulled down his farmhouse. Today, farmers are forever trying to protect their houses and barns from the killer plant. It is strong enough to destroy power lines too. Power and telephone companies spend a lot of money to repair the lines that the kudzu has damaged.

Kudzu also causes other problems. It provides nesting places for snakes. It grows over gullies and ditches, turning them into booby traps for people and livestock. Imagine falling through a dense growth of kudzu into a swarm of snakes while on a nature walk!

Social Studies

Social Studies

THE GOLDEN YEAR

Genre	Comprehension Skill and Strategy
Fiction	• Compare & Contrast • Answer Questions

Scott Foresman Reading 5.6.3

PEARSON

Scott
Foresman

scottforesman.com

ISBN 0-328-13584-4

90000

9 780328 135844

BY RENA KORB

ILLUSTRATED BY ERIC REECE

Reader Response

1. How was Joshua's life at the mining camp different from his life in San Francisco? How was his life similar?

2. Why do you think Joshua wanted to give the gold he found to his family?

3. Use the following vocabulary words in sentences that deal with the Gold Rush: *spoonful; precious; cleanse*

4. What kind of people were likely to have gone to California in search of gold?

From Beginning To End

James Marshall started the California Gold Rush. In 1848, Marshall found pea-sized lumps of gold in the American River. Word spread quickly. By the winter of 1848, the news reached the east coast of the United States and even countries around the world.

Thousands of Americans and people from other countries flocked to this land of gold. They were willing to suffer the long, dangerous journey to strike it rich. Most people traveled along the California Trail. Other people sailed around the tip of South America and then north to San Francisco. By 1853, about 330,000 people had traveled to California. Few of these people found their fortune, but most stayed and started new lives.

Today, people can still visit the California Trail through the many books and Web sites that explore this journey. Many families have even joined a wagon train along the trail. They re-create the journey by dressing like the early pioneers. They cook over open campfires and use only pioneer's tools.

THE GOLDEN YEAR

BY RENA KORB
ILLUSTRATED BY ERIC REECE

PEARSON
Scott
Foresman

Editorial Offices: Glenview, Illinois • Parsippany, New Jersey • New York, New York
Sales Offices: Needham, Massachusetts • Duluth, Georgia • Glenview, Illinois
Coppell, Texas • Ontario, California • Mesa, Arizona

February 1, 1850: We've moved again. Pa gave looking for gold. We're back in San Francisco. Ma says we have moved more in the past year than she ever did in her whole life.

A year after they moved to San Francisco, Pa came home holding up a newspaper. The headline read, "Gold found in Australia!"

"What do you think?" Pa asked. "Should we go to Australia? We could make our fortune in gold!"

Joshua, Ma, and Susannah looked at Pa with alarm. But then a smile broke across his face, and the whole family burst into laughter.

CHAPTER 3:
SETTLING IN SAN FRANCISO

Pa started a construction business. "More and more people are moving to the city," he said. He started his new work with the good spirit he had put into gold mining. He did so well, that soon he hired several workers to help him.

That fall, Joshua's family gathered with the rest of San Francisco for a happy event. California became part of the United States. They walked through the streets, cheering and tooting horns.

CONTENTS:

CHAPTER 1
GETTING READY TO GO

January 16, 1849: Pa came home with news today. He said we are going to move to California. He said gold is everywhere, even in the streets! Ten-year-old boys like me can dig for gold. I think it sounds like a grand adventure, but Ma and Susannah looked a little scared. This means we are probably leaving Macon, Missouri forever.

Ma and Pa found a place to stay on the second floor of a wooden house.

The family settled into their new home. Joshua and Susannah started going to school. Ma was making plans for the garden she would plant in the spring. Pa went out to the American River each day to pan for gold. Nothing could dampen their excitement. Not even December, when the rain poured down and turned the streets into mud.

In January, a heavy storm hit. Joshua went outside to watch rain pour down in sheets. He was relieved to see Pa come home.

"The rivers are overflowing.," Pa said. "They collected so much water last month from the rains. Then snow melting in the Sierras ran down the mountain into the river too. Now the river water has nowhere to go. But we do. Let's get inside. Your ma will be worried."

When the rains finally ended and the water ebbed back into the riverbeds, most of Sacramento had been washed away. Ma and Pa decided to return to San Francisco. They used the last of their money to buy a little house. "Good," Ma sighed. "This means we're here to stay."

Since Pa's big announcement, the whole family had been hard at work. Ma and Pa sold the farm and just about everything they owned. Ma shed more than a few tears as she gathered her pewter bowls and plates to sell. They wouldn't fit in the wagon. Susannah joined in the tears as she had to decide which of her dolls to leave behind.

Joshua didn't feel bad about leaving most of his possessions behind. His favorite things were small enough to fit in his pocket—a marble and a slingshot Pa had carved out of wood.

It was now time to leave. From the back of the wagon, Joshua watched as the only home he had ever known fell farther and farther away into the distance.

First, Joshua and his family had to make their way to Independence, Missouri, before setting out on the California Trail and the unknown realm of the Great Plains. Joshua helped Pa prepare for their journey. At the store, they bought warm clothes, sturdy boots, and needles and thread. They picked out barrels for storing water, an iron cookstove, tin plates and cups, tools, a canvas tent, and even a spare wagon wheel. They bought bacon, ham, and bags of rice, dried fruit, tea, coffee, and flour.

"I can't wait to get started, Pa," Josh said one afternoon. "This is going to be the best trip ever."

"I hope so," said Pa. "You know, Joshua," he said slowly, "at times, this journey is going to be very hard." That night, the family sat around the fire long after dinner was done.

"Pa, will you tell us about the Great Plains?" asked Susannah.

So, Pa told stories about the buffalo stampeding across the landscape. Susannah and Joshua listened excitedly. "The Great Plains lie before us for miles, empty except for buffalo, jackrabbits, Indians, and our little wagon train. Now off to sleep, you two."

restaurants lined the street. Sacramento even had its own theater! Off the smaller streets that led away from Front Street, Joshua could see new wooden houses. Only here and there were people still living in tents.

"Pa, can we get down and walk around?" asked Susannah.

Pa considered it for a moment. "I don't see why not. Let's go explore our new home." He pulled the wagon over and the whole family stepped down into the streets of Sacramento.

It seemed that their new home had something for everyone. Susannah got a tea set and held a party for her dolls. Pa eyed some shiny new tools at the dry goods stores, and Ma couldn't stop looking at a bonnet with bright blue ribbon adorning it. Joshua was sure he would soon find friends.

CHAPTER 5:
MOVING TO SACRAMENTO

Pa decided that their next stop would be Sacramento. One day in late November, the family set out once again for a new home. That afternoon they arrived in Sacramento. "Oh, my!" cried Ma. "I forgot how nice a town could be." The town was bustling with activity. Wagons carried lumber, shovels, and large sacks of grain. Couples walked arm in arm along the wooden sidewalks.

Being in Sacramento was quite a change from Weaverville. Bakeries, blacksmiths, hotels, and

November 18, 1849: Pa and Ma have decided it's time to move from Weaverville. Susannah and I miss having friends. Ma says she's tired of living in such a dirty town. Last week, a lot of people were sick with fever. Pa hasn't found much gold here.

At Independence, Pa joined several other gold seekers who were traveling across the Plains. Ten or so wagons had decided to make the journey together. "It will be easier that way," Pa said. But Joshua knew that Pa also thought that traveling with more people would make the trip safer.

Whatever the reason for the wagon train, Joshua was happy with the plan. He had just met the Krupps, a family from Germany, who were part of the group. Their son Hermann was about his age. At first, Joshua found it difficult to communicate with Hermann. The German boy had recently arrived in America and spoke little English. But when the boys weren't helping their fathers, and when Joshua wasn't minding Susannah, the two boys explored the town of Independence. Even if they didn't have long talks, Joshua liked having a friend again.

Joshua spent most of his time helping Pa. One of the most important jobs was packing their covered wagon. It stretched nine feet long and five feet wide. When Joshua had first looked inside the empty wagon, it had seemed huge. Now that everything the family owned had to fit inside the wagon, Joshua wasn't so sure.

CHAPTER 2:
LIFE ON THE TRAIL

May 12, 1849. Tomorrow is the big day. We're all packed up and ready. We have to get up really early and take the wagons out on the trail. I just know this is going to be the best adventure of my whole life.

Finally, the day had come. The wagon train was ready to go. The sun had hardly risen in the sky when the line of wagons slowly moved away from the town of Independence. Susannah sat up on the wagon's seat with Ma, who was holding the reins. Joshua walked with Pa next to the oxen that hauled the wagon. "If I'm not in the wagon, the oxen won't get as tired," Josh explained to Ma.

As he walked, Joshua looked all around. He could see the long line of wagons tramping slowly before him. The prairie seemed to stretch endlessly in every direction. It looked like a **realm** of **enchantment**. The tall grass waved in the breeze and rustled as a rabbit or a prairie chicken ran through it. Wildflowers poked their heads above the grass. Above them, not a cloud dotted the bright, blue sky.

Joshua ran to get his shovel, bucket, and pan. At the claim, Pa told Joshua to dig up a square of land next to the river. That's how Joshua learned that gold was not just in the riverbed, but in the land all through the hills. Joshua carefully dug up the dirt. Then he put the dirt in a pan and poured water from his bucket to **cleanse** it. This was long, slow work. By the end of the day, Joshua didn't find anything but a **spoonful** of yellow specks.

Joshua often went with his father to the claim. Day after day, he worked digging up the dirt in hopes of finding gold. The day finally came when he found a nugget! It wasn't very large, just the size of the head of a pin, but Joshua was happy.

"What are you going to do with it?" Pa asked.

Joshua thought for a moment and then reached out his hand. "It's for the family," he said.

"That is awfully grown-up of you, Joshua, but you keep the gold," said Pa.

That night, Joshua put the gold in his box of most precious treasures.

When the wagon stopped, Ma and Pa could switch off handling the reins, Susannah jumped down. "I want to pick some flowers for you, Ma," she said. She and Joshua ran across the prairie, picking flowers and feeling the warmth of the sun on their faces. When Susannah gave the flowers to Ma, she smiled and then tucked them into her bonnet. "Thank you, Susannah," she said.

"Pa, we must have gone ten miles," said Joshua as the sun sank lower in the sky.

"More than that, Joshua" Pa said. "I'd say we'll go at least fifteen before we make camp."

Just before the sun set, the wagon train came to a halt. The wagons formed a tight circle with the travelers in the middle. Next to their wagon, Pa and Joshua pitched the tent while Ma and Susannah made dinner. Then they gathered around and had their first meal on the prairie.

As they walked out of town, Joshua tugged on Pa's sleeve. "Where do we find gold?" asked Joshua. It seemed that everywhere he looked, miners were already at work. Dusty-looking men, most with long beards and floppy hats, knelt by the river.

"What are they doing?" asked Joshua.

"They're washing off the dirt to find the gold," Pa explained.

Joshua watched as they used a shovel to dig up a big pile of sand and gravel from the bottom of a riverbed. They put the dirt in a large, shallow pan. Then they filled it with just a little water. The miners then shook the pan, letting the dirt wash away. All the while, they watched with the eyes of a hawk for a flash of gold. Only lucky miners found gold nuggets on the bottom of their pan.

At first, they had a lot to do. Pa rented a little cabin and Ma did her best to make it seem like home. The men staked a claim by setting their picks and shovels into an empty spot by the river.

Joshua was unhappy. "There aren't any kids to play with," he grumbled. There were only a few children in the camp and no boys Joshua's age.

"If you promise not to get underfoot, you can come with me and work on the claim," Pa said.

Josh's family stayed in San Francisco for only a few days. It was too expensive. Their room in the boarding house cost ten times as much as it would have back home. "My word!" Ma said when she found out that one apple cost ten cents. After buying supplies, the family packed up their wagon and headed for the land called Gold Mountain.

At the foot of the hills, they passed new arrivals buying supplies. These gold seekers looked tired and dusty. For a while, their wagon rattled through empty, grass-covered land. "This is beautiful," Ma said softly.

Then they rode into the Pleasant Valley Gold Mines that Pa had read about in the guide book. "Looks like a lot of other people read the same book," Ma said, as they saw the main street lined with tents.

When Pa returned, he had a smile on his face. "Pleasant Valley has been mined out. I've learned there is gold just a ways from here at Weaverville," Pa said.

The next morning, Ma fried up a few slabs of bacon and served biscuits sweetened with sugar because it was a special day. Then Pa took Joshua with him on his search for a spot.

Before turning in that night, many of the pioneers gathered around the campfire. Together, they sang about the promised land ahead.

*We've formed our band and we're all
    well-manned
To journey afore to the promised land,
Where the golden ore is rich in store,
On the banks of Sacramento shore.
Then, ho! Boys ho! To California go.
There's plenty of gold in the world we're told
On the banks of the Sacramento!*

That night, Joshua barely got any sleep. When he closed his eyes, he saw a buffalo stampede and then some coyotes and bears.

Joshua and Hermann spent long afternoons making up games so the time would pass more quickly. They scampered next to the wagon train, pretending to be different animals. Hermann, slithering along on his belly through the tall grass, was a snake. Joshua put his hands to his forehead, made horns with his fingers, and charged toward Hermann like a buffalo.

Poor Susannah didn't have anyone her age to play with. She sat in the wagon, a doll in each hand. One day, Susannah didn't even want to play with her dolls. "I'm tired of this," she announced.

"Hop on down and explore with your brother," Ma suggested. "Don't wander too far from the wagons."

Joshua clasped Susannah's hand. At first, they trailed along behind the wagons, but then Susannah saw a small critter in the grass. "Let's follow it," she pleaded. "Oh, please, Joshua, please." So they bounded after it. Soon the wagon train was so far behind them that they couldn't see it.

Joshua and Susannah didn't notice how far they had wandered off. They had stumbled into a clearing with a stream. As the stream moved, it got bigger and faster. They kept following the stream, until it plunged off a high cliff. Joshua and Susannah ran to the edge of the rock and looked over. The water from the stream struck the rocks below with such a force!

October 10, 1849: Finally we have arrived in California. After making our way down the Sierra, we crossed the Sacramento Valley and arrived in San Francisco. Ma said if she couldn't have a hot bath and a new dress, we might as well just leave her in the Sierra. Pa said going to San Francisco was a good idea anyway. We could pick up supplies and trade our oxen for horses before heading out to pan for gold and make our fortune. Hermann and his family headed straight out to the diggings. I hope we'll see them again.

Joshua walked around the buzzing city of San Francisco in a daze. To his surprise, the streets were not paved with gold. Still, it was thrilling to see tall buildings lining the streets, stores and theaters, and signs in many different languages. "Look! Look!" Joshua and Susannah called out, tugging at each other's arms to point out another tall building.

If the sights of San Francisco did not overwhelm Joshua, the steady noise did. Newsboys cried out the headlines at every corner, and storekeepers stood in front of their shops and called out their goods. Music tumbled out of the doors of a cafe.

CHAPTER 4:
WELCOME TO CALIFORNIA

Their adventure came to a quick end as Pa and Mr. Krupps charged up. "Where have you been? We had to ask other travelers to help us search for you! Your ma was afraid you'd be eaten by wolves."

"I'm sorry, Pa," Joshua said, hanging his head. "I'll be more careful in the future, I promise."

CHAPTER 3:
PROBLEMS IN THE PLAINS

July 3, 1849: The grown-ups seem to be getting more nervous the farther we travel from Missouri. They miss their homes, is what they say. The land is changing too. The prairie looks empty. There aren't any trees and the grass is low and dry. It's hard to believe that anyone, even the Indians, can live out here.

A few days later, the mountain got steeper. The oxen could not go any further. The men unhitched them and roped them together in one long chain. Then they hitched the oxen to Mr. Krupp's wagon. The animals struggled to pull the wagon up the mountain. Once they reached the top, the men unhitched the team and led them back down for the next wagon. All the wagons were finally pulled to the top.

© Pearson Education, Inc.

On their second day in the desert, Joshua heard water bubbling softly. Before them was a hot spring with water boiling to the surface. The water looked good, but smelled bad. A few of the travelers rushed forward. "Wait!" cried Mr. Krupps. "Don't drink it! This water will make you sick." Most people listened; the few who didn't got stomachaches.

A few days later, the travelers walked down a gently sloping ridge. To their delight, they saw a grove of trees ahead. They had made it!

After leaving the desert, the travelers rested for a day. They knew that ahead of them loomed the hardest part of all. They had to cross the dreaded Sierra Nevada mountains before snow started to fall. As they climbed higher into the mountains, it got much colder. The campfires burned only dimly, barely able to chase away the cold air. Susannah shivered while she slept. The next night, Ma pulled Pa aside. In an instant, Pa chopped up Ma's favorite chair and threw it on the fire. The blaze shot up and Susannah and Joshua inched closer to the flame. Joshua looked at his mother as she watched a piece of her family history go up in smoke. She didn't look sad, just determined.

Soon, problems started. First, a terrible hailstorm hit the plains. To Joshua, the hailstones looked as big as fists. The wagons had to stop and the travelers lost **precious** time. Pa looked nervous. He knew it was important to reach California before winter came and the snow fell on the Sierra Nevada mountains.

When the wagons were able to move again, the rain and melting hail left the Plains covered in mud. Every step from the team of oxen was a struggle. Then the wagons reached one of the rivers, criss-crossing the Plains. Flowing calmly, the rivers would have provided much-needed drinking water for people and animals. Only this river was swollen and raging.

Several of the men gathered on the bank to see how fast and how deep the water was.

The men decided the group needed to go forward. One by one, the wagons slowly picked their way across the river, the women and children in the back of the wagon, and the men sitting up front and guiding the oxen. One by one, the families gathered on the opposite shore and watched the people still to come. Finally, the last wagon, with a hog tied to its back, was making the crossing. When a gush of water came down the river, the hog disappeared. When the wagon finally made it to solid land, the woman looked like she was about to cry. Her husband put his arm around her shoulders. "At least it was only the pig," he said.

Within a week after the scary river crossing, the Plains had totally changed. All the water and mud had dried up. The lifeless surface of the Plains had baked into hard clay.

The group marched along for days. Joshua and Hermann even stopped chasing each other, which they did almost every day. Then something happened which perked up everyone's spirits, if only for a short time.

It started with a slight tremble. Then the ground began shaking. Within a few minutes, Joshua could feel his whole body vibrate and hear a steady thumping sound. "What is it, Pa?" he called. Pa held up a hand. He jumped down from the wagon, and placed his ear against the hard surface. Then he called for the wagons to stop.

As the noise grew louder, a herd of buffalo charged past them. Joshua felt like a dream had come true. Though the animals moved swiftly, Joshua saw their dark brown fur, their horns, and some young calves. Joshua was spellbound by these amazing animals.

The families now prepared to face the desert that stood between them and the Sierra Nevada mountains. At a clear stream, they filled up their water barrels.

The travelers reached the desert early in the morning. Nothing seemed to be alive except for a few buzzards.

Social Studies   Social Studies

Train Wreck!

by Edie Kast

Genre	Comprehension Skill and Strategy	Text Features
Nonfiction	• Fact & Opinion • Ask Questions	• Captions • Heads • Maps • Sidebars

Scott Foresman Reading Street 5.6.4

PEARSON

Scott
Foresman

scottforesman.com

ISBN 0-328-13587-9

9 780328 135875

90000

Reader Response

1. Carefully reread page 10. Find one fact and one opinion.

2. One way to make sure you understand what you read is to ask questions. First, look at the pictures and heading on pages 10-11. What are some questions you could ask about this topic? Write them down. Then, read the page to try to answer your questions.

3. Look again at page 17. What does *collapsed* mean? What other things can you think of that might collapse?

4. Study the map on pages 8-9. Tell how you figure out which company laid the longest track.

Glossary

criticizing *v.* saying someone did something wrong

cruised *v.* traveled

drenching *v.* getting something soaking wet

era *n.* a period of time

explosion *n.* the process of something bursting open

hydrogen *n.* the lightest of all the gases

Train Wreck!

by Edie Kast

PEARSON

Scott Foresman

Editorial Offices: Glenview, Illinois • Parsippany, New Jersey • New York, New York
Sales Offices: Needham, Massachusetts • Duluth, Georgia • Glenview, Illinois
Coppell, Texas • Ontario, California • Mesa, Arizona

Casey Jones is the most famous engineer to die in a train wreck.

Casey Jones

Train wrecks have always been headline news. On the night of April 30, 1900, Casey Jones was the engineer on a train going from Memphis, Tennessee to Canton, Mississippi.

When the train pulled out two hours late, Jones wanted to make up for lost time. His fireman, Sim Webb, loaded the engine with coal. Soon, the train cruised at 70 miles per hour.

Just then, Jones saw a freight train dead ahead. He yelled for Webb to jump. Jones died in a heroic effort to stop his train. A nearby worker, Wallace Saunders, saw the event and wrote a famous song about Casey Jones.

Trains Today

Today, people ride buses, cars, and planes more than the rails to get to their destination. Trains are still being developed, however, such as one that uses a hydrogen fueling system.

Trains will always be an important part of our history—and the stories of the brave people who died building and driving them will continue to inspire us.

In 1820, the United States had been an independent nation for just over 40 years. Back then, daily life was different from what it is now. Most Americans lived in rural areas. There was no electricity. There were no phones. This was a time before planes or cars.

Texas, Oregon, and California didn't belong to the United States yet. Native Americans hunting and living on their ancestral lands, still controlled vast areas of the West. This was the era when railroads were developed, which soon changed the face of America.

The Railroad Era Begins

In 1830, there were only 23 miles of railroad tracks in the whole United States. By 1930, there were more than 400,000 miles of rails! To lay those tracks, and to build safe trains to ride them, took a lot of hard work. It also took the lives of many workers and passengers.

The railroad era began in the 1820s. The steam engine was invented in 1825. A year later, the locomotive was invented. During this time, people

The United States adopted official time zones in 1884. That year 27 nations met in Washington, D.C. They created time zones for the entire globe. There are 24 time zones. The prime meridian is the first time zone. It runs through Greenwich, England. The first time zone to the east is one hour earlier than England. The next time zone to the east is two hours earlier than England. The time zones to the west are later than England. You can see this on the map on page 21.

The time in England is called Greenwich mean time. This is because England's time is in the middle of all the other times.

Time Zones

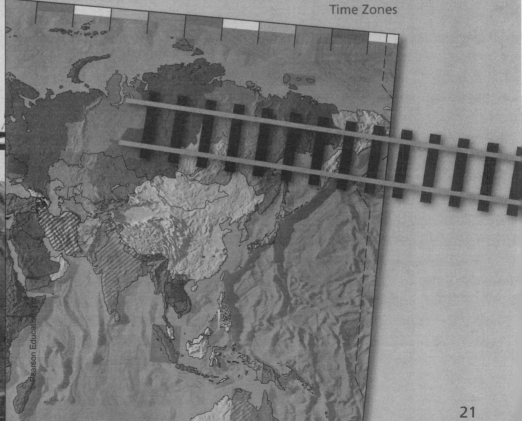

Time Zones

Train travel created a new need. People needed standard time. The railroads solved this problem in 1883. They created time zones in the United States. This did not mean that people in each town used that time. It did mean that the railroads used it. It also meant that people could travel around the country more easily. They could figure out when they would arrive in each city.

traveled by horse and buggy. If you didn't have a horse or mule, you walked. There was no other form of transportation.

You'd imagine that everyone would want to ride the new trains. That wasn't true. Some people thought trains were a bad idea. Most people, however, were very excited about this new way of getting from place to place!

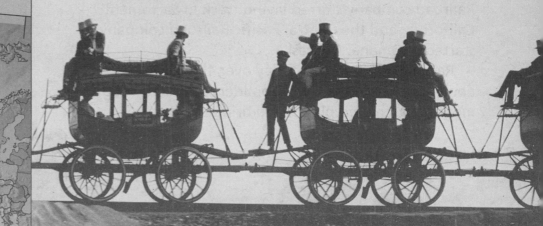

Go West!

By 1840, there were already over 2,800 miles of railway stretching across nine states. Naturally, early trains were different from today's trains. At one time, you risked death to ride a train! It took the effort of many inventors to design trains that worked safely.

As Texas, Oregon, and California became states, easterners began dreaming of a transcontinental railroad. They were thrilled at the idea of a railroad that covered the entire country.

In 1853, The U.S. government funded the building of a transcontinental railroad. The Union Pacific Railroad company started laying track in Sacramento, California, and the Central Pacific Railroad company started in Omaha, Nebraska.

Railroad workers had to lay over 1,700 miles of new rails. To join the tracks, builders blasted through mountains, crossed plains, and bridged rivers.

By the 1860s, railroad companies each had their own standard times. This meant that the railroad had a set time for each town or state.

Different railroad companies could have different times, which made things hard for a person traveling by train. The traveler might have to change trains. The railroads printed a timetable, like the one pictured here. These timetables helped people figure out the time in other cities.

Time Trouble

In the mid-1800s there were no standard time zones. This meant that local towns and counties decided on their own time. They usually went by the sunrise and sunset of the area. Many towns had standard clocks. The standard clock might be a city clock tower. It could also be the time at the General Store.

These time differences did not cause any problems—for awhile. People did not travel long distances to work. They did not have telephones to talk with people far away. They did not have radios.

Most of the workers on the Union Pacific were Chinese immigrants. The railroad company even advertised in China for more workers to come to the United States, for they needed lots of men. In 1868, more than 12,000 Chinese men were working on the Union Pacific line.

Unfortunately, there was much prejudice against the Chinese. They were paid $30 a month, while other workers received $35 a month and room and board.

Most of the workers on the Central Pacific line were Irish immigrants or Civil War veterans. Sometimes they were attacked by people who didn't want the railroad running through their land.

Race to the Finish

Tunneling through the Rocky Mountains, between California and Nebraska, was difficult and scary work. It involved many difficult steps.

Workers lowered a man on ropes down the mountain, where he drilled holes in the cliff. He put explosives into those holes and lit the explosives. When he jerked the rope, the workers at the top pulled him up. This process created tunnels quickly.

The rails on top of the bridge had held together. Unfortunately, they had nothing supporting them. As soon as the train rolled onto the bridge, it collapsed. Most of the train cars fell into the channel. The parts of the train above water burst into a fiery explosion. Nine people died.

Bridge Collapse!

Even if trains were running on schedule, there were other hazards to watch out for. One such wreck happened on a weak bridge in Rhode Island.

In the middle of the night, in April 1873, a large train traveled toward Providence. It had three cars of freight and five coach cars carrying about 100 passengers.

As the train headed for a bridge, disaster struck. Just days before, heavy rains had fallen, drenching the area and causing floods. A dam gave way, sending water to the bridge's base.

Many train wrecks were caused by weak bridges.

The railroad companies were racing to the finish, because the government was offering them lots of money for every mile of track laid. Each company wanted to lay the longest track possible, so that they could earn the most money. Finally, on May 10, 1869, the railroads met in Promontory Point, Utah. The coast-to-coast railroad was finished at last.

UNION & CENTRAL PACIFIC RAILROADS

WYOMING

NEBRASKA

Omaha

Union Pacific Railroad

COLORADO

N W E S

500   1000 Miles

Stop That Train!

During this time, trains continued to run on rails all over the country. Yet they weren't very safe. For one thing, they didn't have good brakes.

To stop a train, the engineer pulled a lever from inside the train. The lever pushed a block onto the wheels. A brakeman had to be on each train car. The engineer whistled for all the brakemen. Most of the time the brakemen did not pull the lever at the exact same time. This could cause a train to derail.

To stop a train another way, the driver could put the train into reverse, but this action ruined the wheels. An inventor named George Westinghouse found a better way to stop trains. He invented the air brake in 1868.

All the brakemen had to pull their brake levers at the same time. If they didn't, the train would derail.

Train Traffic Jam

To keep trains on schedule, the railroad companies used a timed system. As one train started out, the next train waited at least 10 minutes before leaving, and so on.

This system did not always work. Trains could break down. If the first train broke down, the next would have to try to stop as soon as it saw the stopped train.

The railroads also decided that the 10-minute wait hurt their business. They could not add more trains unless they made it a shorter wait time. With less time, however, there were more accidents.

Clearly, the railroads needed a better way. Again, George Westinghouse had the answer. He invented the first automatic train signals in 1881. Train signals are lights that give directions to the engineer and tell him how fast he can drive. They also tell the engineer if he needs to stop ahead.

You might wonder how you can stop a train with air. Here's how. An air compressor is placed in the locomotive, the first car of the train. The compressor is attached to a valve that the engineer controls. When the engineer releases the air, it goes through pipes connected to the rest of the cars on the train. In between each car, the air goes through rubber pipes that can bend with the curves. Inside each car, another valve is sensitive to the flow of air. If the air stops, a brake pad drops onto the wheels of the car. This way, with one touch of a lever, an engineer can stop a whole train.

This invention changed trains forever. The U.S. Congress passed a law in 1893 saying that trains had to use air brakes. Today, air brakes are used in trains, buses, streetcars, and even planes in flight.

Air brakes allowed one engineer to control the braking system of an entire train.

The Baltimore and Ohio Railway Disaster, January 15, 1887, took place near Republic, Ohio.

© Pearson Education, Inc.

Train Crash!

Even with air brakes, it was still hard to stop a train. This train wreck in Ohio shows just how dangerous it was.

The crash happened on a very cold night in January of 1887. One freight train was heading east when it broke down.

The conductor waited for the train to stop completely. Then he ran forward with the lantern, but he did not get very far. A passenger train, coming toward him, did not have enough time to stop. It ran into the freight train, sending the two engines off the tracks. The train cars burst into flames as the hot coals that fueled the engines scattered across the cars. By morning, all of the cars had been burned to a crisp. Hardly any of the passengers survived.

Because the conductor made a bad decision, the railroads ended up criticizing him and he lost his job.

Suggested levels for Guided Reading, DRA,™
Lexile,® and Reading Recovery™ are provided
in the Pearson Scott Foresman Leveling Guide.

Genre	Comprehension Skill and Strategy
Fiction	• Sequence • Prior Knowledge

Scott Foresman Reading Street 5.6.5

PEARSON

Scott
Foresman

scottforesman.com

ISBN 0-328-13590-9

90000

9 780328 135905

Grandma Betty's Banjo

by Camilla Calamandrei

illustrated by Diana Kizlauskas

Reader Response

1. What are some of the different ways that people are affected by music? Give examples from the story.

2. Do you play a musical instrument, or have you ever tried? What are some of the qualities one needs to have in order to improve?

3. A homograph is a set of words that appear to be the same because they are spelled the same but they actually mean two different things and are often pronounced differently too. For example, the word *wind* can be "The wind is blowing hard." Or "I forgot to wind my watch." *Beat* (p.3), *racket* (p.5), *jammed* (p.21), *break* (p.22) *strap* (p.26) are all homographs. Give two definitions for each word and use each variation in a sentence.

4. How is the text of the story organized? Part of the story is in the recent past and part in the distant past. How are these two strands presented?

© Pearson Education, Inc.

A Whole New Sound

Many types of music and musicians have been considered controversial, especially when they first came on the scene. This was true of Elvis and it was true of the jazz musicians of the Harlem Renaissance.

Langston Hughes, a poet of the Harlem Renaissance period.

The Harlem Renaissance was born after World War ended in 1918. At the time of the Great Migration, many African Americans migrated from the rural South to large cities in the North. Many came to New York City and settled in the section called Harlem. Beginning with the Negro spirituals, African-American musicians of that time started "playing" with these sounds. Eventually playing with and having fun with music turned into jazz.

Jazz was started as a rebellion against all the restraints African Americans had had to endure in the United States. This rebellion was a way to improvise, or have fun, with chord progression. Jazz musicians were able to create rhythms and repeat chord progressions in a way that often imitates the human voice.

Since the early 1920s, jazz has branched out and influenced many styles of swing and other popular music. The Harlem Renaissance is remembered as the first time that mainstream musicians began to take seriously the contributions of African-American music.

32

Grandma Betty's Banjo

by
Camilla Calamandrei

illustrated by
by **Diana Kizlauskas**

PEARSON

Scott Foresman

Editorial Offices: Glenview, Illinois • Parsippany, New Jersey • New York, New York
Sales Offices: Needham, Massachusetts • Duluth, Georgia • Glenview, Illinois
Ccppell, Texas • Ontario, California • Mesa, Arizona

She looked out at the audience and saw her parents and her brother. Most importantly, she saw her grandmother, who was looking quite shocked indeed. After just a few minutes Grandma Betty jumped out of her chair and shouted. "Oh just stop, stop. Wait a minute! You better wait for me!" Then she ran out of the lounge and down the hall to her room. She came back with that old banjo in her hand and announced that the song could start again.

Mr. Mike and Susan looked at each other and laughed. Grandma Betty was a lot more competitive than she was sentimental. She hated to be left out. If her twelve-year-old granddaughter was going to be playing music with her friends, she wasn't about to sit on the sidelines and let them have all the fun. Grandma Betty never put that banjo away again.

Susan played again. And Mr. Mike was right, it was easier this time. They practiced together a little and then they focused on parts of the music. He would play. Then she would play. It was really terrific. They did this for two whole hours that first Saturday and agreed to meet the next Saturday. By the third time they met for a lesson, Mr. Mike announced that he had an idea.

"Susan, your song sounds really great. It's going to be a huge hit at the party, but it occurred to me that you could also have fun playing with other people too."

"Sure," Susan said, shaking her head in agreement. "Elvis always played with a guitar player, a drummer...He had a whole band, even though you hardly ever see them in the movies. I would love to play with someone else. I just don't know anyone who would play with me."

Mr. Mike laughed. "Well this is what I was thinking..." Mr. Mike explained that it would be nice to organize a few songs for Grandma Betty's party. His band could play along with Susan on some of them. Susan loved this idea.

The day of the party, Susan was very nervous. The big lounge at the retirement home was completely full. Grandma Betty sure had a lot of friends!

Grandma Betty still didn't know about the big surprise. The band assembled in a corner. Then they turned the overhead lights down. Susan began strumming her guitar. The band joined in after a moment. It sounded great. The lights came back up and Susan's nervousness passed.

Chapter 1: Susan Falls in Love with Elvis

It was a rainy Friday afternoon when Susan Tribula fell in love with Elvis Presley. She was home after school watching TV when she saw Elvis singing in an old movie.

Susan was so excited by Elvis's beautiful voice and the beat of the music that she began to dance around the room imitating Elvis's moves. He belted out the words as he played the guitar, and Susan danced. As the song went on and on, Susan got happier and happier.

Susan sat down, took out her guitar, and began to play the piece of music Mr. Mike had given her. She did not need to warm up, she had been playing so much all week. Mr. Mike listened and was impressed. Susan kept on playing as though Mr. Mike were not even there. She was making some mistakes, but she got all the way through the song. When she was done she looked eagerly at Mr. Mike to see what he thought.

"Susan, your grandma is going to be very proud. You are a natural," Mr. Mike said as he set the coffee cup down.

Susan was very pleased. "Don't you think it's a bit slow though, Mr. Mike?" Susan asked.

"Now, Susan, everything in good time. Just play that song one more time and really let it roll. Don't worry about any mistakes. Making a few mistakes is just fine."

When she was tired of practicing the chords, Susan would dance around singing to the CD, as if she had already learned how to play the guitar. In its own way, this actually helped her learn the song.

The next Saturday arrived very quickly. Susan found herself on the bus headed for her grandmother's retirement home. Grandma Betty knew that Susan was taking lessons with Mr. Mike, but she did not know about the birthday plan. Susan stopped in to say hello to her grandma and to show off her guitar. Then she told her she needed to rush off to her first guitar lesson.

Susan found Mr. Mike standing just outside the little lounge drinking a cup of coffee.

"Good morning, Susan," Mr. Mike called out as she raced down the hall. "I see you have a guitar."

"Good morning, Mr. Mike, I hope you weren't waiting too long," Susan said a little breathlessly.

While Susan was rock 'n' rolling in the living room, her mother was in the kitchen cooking dinner. Mrs. Tribula heard the racket and snuck a peek to see what Susan was up to.

Mrs. Tribula was struck with how much Susan looked like her Grandma Betty when she was playing her imaginary guitar. Grandma Betty had been an enthusiastic musician when she was younger. She was a neighborhood celebrity in her day, playing the banjo at all kinds of street fairs and parties. For many years, Grandma Betty was never without her banjo. Then, as she got older, she slowly stopped playing so much.

Mrs. Tribula had learned to play the banjo from her mother. She thought reading music was too hard and the music never sounded as good as she wanted it to. She admired her mother for how much she contributed to people's lives with her simple, cheerful tunes.

Smelling something on the stove cooking away without her, Mrs. Tribula shook herself out of her reminiscence and tiptoed out of the living room.

That night at dinner, Susan went on and on about the Elvis movie she had seen. Susan's father was a huge fan of old movies so he was more than happy to talk about all the details of Elvis's amazing performance.

Susan asked her mother if she could call her Grandma Betty to tell her about the movie too.

While Susan bubbled over excitedly about Elvis Presley to her grandmother on the phone, Mrs. Tribula thought about her own mother and the banjo some more. Mrs. Tribula remembered being about Susan's age when a neighbor and friend of the family became quite ill. He had to stay in bed and be taken care of by a nurse. Grandma Betty would go over every weekend with her banjo. Sometimes Mrs. Tribula would go with her mother.

She remembered seeing the neighbor's face light up when he would see Betty and her banjo walk in the door. After an hour of listening to her play and sing, the man looked more relaxed and a little healthier. That neighbor was never one hundred percent better, but he lived for a number of years more. Grandma Betty played the banjo for him every Sunday for all those years. Before he died he told Mrs. Tribula that her mother had made a big difference in his life. "She's an angel," he said.

6

Chapter 5 Grandma Betty's Birthday Party

That entire week, Susan went to school as usual. She raced home to do her homework each day. In the nighttime, when her homework was done, she would pull out her new (but old) guitar. By studying the book her father got her she was able to learn some basic fingering. It was hard work, but fortunately, Mr. Mike had chosen a song that only needed a few chords. So once she learned those, she could start working on getting through the song.

27

"Okay" Mrs. Tribula said. "That's a good idea."

When they got home, Susan tossed her jacket on the couch and went right to the CD player to listen to the CD Mr. Mike had loaned her. That night, Mr. Tribula surprised Susan. He showed up with four Elvis movies he had rented and a used guitar that he had bought at a music store downtown. He also bought her a book on basic guitar playing and a shoulder strap, which he thought would be important if she wanted to dance around.

Mrs. Tribula and Susan both gave Mr. Tribula a big kiss for being such a good father. Susan was thrilled. The guitar was beautiful and the perfect size for her. She even liked the print on the shoulder strap.

Suddenly a new idea swept over Mrs. Tribula, maybe Susan could be as good on the guitar as Grandma Betty always was on the banjo!

Perhaps they had made a mistake by having Susan take piano lessons for all these years. She never seemed overly happy about it, yet, here she was after one afternoon singing all the songs from the movie by heart and copying Elvis moves with the guitar.

Mrs. Tribula turned to her husband who had been washing dishes. "Honey, do you think we should..." Without turning around, Mr. Tribula interrupted her and finished her sentence.

"Let Susan take guitar lessons? Sure, honey."
They both smiled.

"Oh I hate to wait a whole entire week. Is there something I can do before we meet?"

Mr. Mike told Susan to wait a minute. He dug up some sheets of music and a few CDs for her to borrow. "Can you read music?"

Susan reached for the music saying, "Sure." Which was true. She just wasn't so good at it, just like her own mother had not been good at it. Now she was really inspired to get better at it.

"This one is one of Elvis's early songs. I think you can learn it in time for the party."

"Thanks, Mr. Mike! You're the best."
Mr. Mike chuckled.

On the ride home, Susan explained all the details of the arrangement she had worked out with Mr. Mike, and her plan to play the guitar for Grandma Betty's 80th birthday.

Mrs. Tribula suggested that if Susan would give Mr. Mike a little money out of her allowance each week as a payment for his lessons, then she and Mr. Tribula would get her a guitar.

"It can be a secondhand one," Susan volunteered.

Mrs. Tribula laughed. Susan had always wanted everything new. Now that she heard that her grandmother's beautiful and famous banjo was secondhand, she seemed to understand that new things weren't necessarily better than old things. No one had more positive influence over this child than her grandmother!

"When do you want to start this little adventure? And how much time do we have until this party?" asked Mr. Mike.

"The party is in five weeks so we better start right away!" Susan said.

"Well, first things first, missy. Do you have a guitar?" Mr. Mike asked, in a nice way.

"Oh, that." Susan suddenly realized that she had overlooked a big piece of the puzzle.

Mr. Mike reassured her, "Well, you can work that out and we can start next Saturday morning."

Chapter 2 A Visit to See Grandma Betty

Mr. and Mrs. Tribula decided that they would talk to Susan about switching from piano to guitar in a few days. The next morning Susan brought it up herself.

"You know, I just don't seem to be doing too well at the piano. I think I could be really good at the guitar," explained Susan to her mother.

"I have no idea what we would say to Mrs. Jones," said Mrs. Tribula, teasing Susan about letting the piano teacher know she would be quitting. "I don't have any idea where we will find a decent guitar teacher."

Now they were both smiling. Susan knew her mother was just goofing around. Everything was going to work out just great.

The next day was Saturday. Susan got out of bed and went downstairs to find something to eat. After some toast and orange juice, she told her mother she was ready to go. Susan and her mother were going to see Grandma Betty.

"Slam!" She heard the sound of the door swing shut behind them. She noticed that her own feet were making tap, tap, tap sounds as they walked to the bus stop. Her mother's feet were bigger and were making a louder noise. It was a beautiful day.

The bus ride to Grandma Betty's would take half an hour, but Susan didn't mind. Beep, beep, beep— people hit their car horns in the distance. Tap, tap, tap—the person sitting next to her was fidgety and tapping his fingers on the seat. Ring, ring, ring— someone wanted to hop off at the corner. In the middle of all this, a baby cried and an old man with a big belly, laughed.

"You sure do!" said Susan enthusiastically. "I think you sound great. Do you know who Elvis is?"

"Of course. I am a big fan. Why do you ask?"

"Well, Mr. Mike" Susan asked a bit fearfully, "could you teach me how to play the guitar, like Elvis?"

He laughed and then sat quietly for a moment and looked at her. After about a minute he replied, "Well, I have not taught the guitar in quite a few years. I used to teach young people just like you, but that was so long ago. And of course, I am no Elvis Presley."

"Oh, that's no big deal," she said. "You teach me to play and I'll learn the Elvis stuff. Please, Mr. Mike. I really want to learn how to play the guitar so I can play for Grandma Betty at her 80th birthday party next month."

Mr. Mike looked around the room for a bit and then back at Susan. He could see that she was sincere, and that she really would love to do this. He finally spoke. "It would be a crying shame to let your Grandma Betty down. Especially with you so excited to do this." Susan's eyes lit up. She jumped over to Mr. Mike and gave him a big hug, "Hurray!"

Susan could see how much her grandmother enjoyed listening to the music. Just like when she was talking about her banjo earlier, she seemed energized just sitting there. Susan decided that she would like to learn to play the guitar in time for her grandmother's birthday. She was sure this was a great idea and she knew just who she needed to help her.

The band finished their tune and decided to take a break. Mr. Mike stayed in his chair. He wiped his brow with a handkerchief and then kept strumming his guitar a little.

"So what do you think of our little group, Susan?" he asked. "It would be better if we could get your Grandma Betty to play with us, but, I guess we do OK."

The whole thing was like one big musical number. Susan imagined herself dancing and singing to the people on the bus, just like Elvis in a movie. She smiled to herself as this chain of events became a Hollywood fantasy in her mind.

When they got to the retirement home, they found Grandma Betty in the lounge. Grandma Betty was very popular and cheerful, but she wasn't moving around as much as she used to. She would just sit in one place for a long time. Today she was looking at an album of old photographs. Some of the pictures were of her playing the banjo.

Susan thought to herself, "It was more fun when Grandma Betty was younger. She would always tickle me and want to dance." Of course, they would all sing to Grandma's crazy banjo.

"Grandma Betty," Susan started. "Why don't you play your banjo anymore?" Mrs. Tribula was a bit startled to hear her daughter ask this question so directly, but she was curious about what Grandma Betty would say.

"Oh Susan," Grandma Betty said. "I'm old and can't remember the tunes anymore. No one wants to hear an old forgetful grandmother play her secondhand banjo."

Susan looked at her puzzled. She didn't really believe that her grandmother couldn't remember the tunes, but she didn't know what to say about that. So instead she said, "But Grandma, you've always had that banjo. How could it be secondhand?"

"Well, you're right, this is the only banjo I have ever had," Grandma Betty explained pointing to a photo of herself holding a banjo. "Someone did own it before me. In fact, that is an important part of the story of how I learned to play the banjo."

"Tell her the story, Mom," encouraged Mrs. Tribula.

At the other end of the building, near the fire exit, there was a smaller lounge with the door closed. When Grandma Betty opened the door, Susan and her mother were surprised to see three old men and two women playing rock 'n' roll. One woman was playing the bass guitar, and a man was playing the guitar. Another guy was playing the drums. And the last two people were singing and playing the tambourine.

Grandma Betty's friends had jammed together many times. They were able to listen to each other as they played, and come in and out in cool ways. Susan thought it was kind of funny to see such old people playing rock 'n' roll, but she recognized the songs, and they played them pretty well.

When they got to the end of the song they were playing, they stopped to say hello to Grandma Betty. They were all really happy to see her. "Got your banjo, Betty?" asked the plump man with gray hair who was playing the guitar.

"No, Mr. Mike, but I want to introduce you to my daughter Helen and my granddaughter Susan.

"Glad to know you Helen, Susan." Mr. Mike introduced the rest of the band, and they played another song.

Chapter 4 Susan Gets a Guitar Teacher

"Grandma, the banjo seems a lot like the guitar. Don't you think you could teach me to play the guitar? Mom and Dad said that I could switch from piano to guitar but I need to find a teacher."

"I have a much better idea, sweetie. I am going to introduce you to some friends of mine who can probably help."

Mrs. Tribula and Susan were both a little sorry that Grandma Betty didn't seem to want to play the banjo, especially since it was to teach Susan. Even so, they followed her down the hall without saying anything more.

Chapter 3 How Grandma Betty Got Her Banjo

"Well, my parents really wanted me to play the clarinet. I did that for a few years, but I wanted to learn the banjo. Eventually, I found a friend whose father had a banjo and convinced her to get her father to loan it to her. In reality, she was then loaning it to me. I was very careful with it, but neither of us ever did get up the nerve to tell her father that I was using it.

"Anyway, I got a book on how to play the banjo out of the library and secretly taught myself to play. The only problem was that I loved playing that banjo so much that I just stopped practicing the clarinet altogether."

"Did you get in trouble?" Susan asked, looking a little worried. Mother smiled in the background.

"Actually, my parents weren't too happy about me accepting an outright gift. So we made an agreement. I would play for my friend's family at all their holidays. In that way we kind of shared that banjo for a number of years. In the end, my parents did let me keep it." Grandma Betty looked at Susan peacefully and sincerely. Just talking about that old instrument brought more color to Grandma Betty's face.

"Wow. That all worked out great," Susan thought out loud.

"Yes, I was very lucky," agreed Grandma Betty.

"And your friend's father was lucky that someone finally appreciated that banjo as much as his father did," said Mrs. Tribula.

"I guess that's true." Grandma Betty let out a happy kind of sigh.

"Well, I told my parents that I had been using my friend's father's banjo for all those months without him knowing about it. They felt bad about that so they went to him and offered to buy it from him. He said it had been in his family for a long time. He couldn't sell it but he would like to hear me play it. So the next Sunday I went to their house with my parents."

"You must have been very nervous," said Susan.

"Of course I was! First I felt bad that I had been using it without him knowing and then I was nervous that I wouldn't play well."

Mrs. Tribula jumped in here. "I know what happens next."

"Okay. You tell the rest, Helen," said Grandma Betty.

"Well, of course, your grandmother played very well. Her friend's father was so impressed that he wanted to give the banjo to Grandma Betty as a gift. He said that his own father had been very disappointed that none of his children had wanted to play the banjo, and that he would have been very happy to see it being so well loved and used."

"I couldn't believe it. I was shocked," added Susan's grandmother.

"Sort of. No one knew why I was so bad at the clarinet but it was just obvious that I wasn't going to get any better. So my parents just gave up."

"Oh, so they let you play the banjo!" Susan was relieved.

"Well, not quite," said Grandma. Susan was confused.

"My mother had been raised to think that only poor people played the banjo," Grandma Betty explained. "So she felt like somehow it would be a bad thing for her daughter to play a poor person's instrument."

"So what happened?" This was getting more and more interesting.

"Well, I kept playing on my own and the next year I entered a local music contest at the 4H fair. We would go to this fair every year. Of course, my parents didn't know that I was going to play in the contest. They thought I was off buying popcorn, so when they saw me get up on stage, they were pretty shocked."

"My sister told me later that my mother was furious, but my father made her stay in her seat and listen. Well, sure enough, it went very well. I played a song my mother had taught me when I was a young child and the crowd really liked it. They sang along and cheered a little at the end."

"By the time I got back to my parents, my mother had dried her eyes, but I could tell she had been crying. She was so happy that I had found a way to make music; she realized that it didn't matter what instrument I was playing. She changed her mind right then, and decided that there was nothing embarrassing about having a daughter who was really good at the banjo."

"That's a good story, Grandma. But when did you get your very own banjo?" Susan asked.